Parenting with Grace

Catholic Parent's®
Guide to Raising Perfect Kids
^
almost

Gregory K. Popcak, MSW, LCSW
and Lisa Popcak

Our Sunday Visitor Publishing Division
Our Sunday Visitor, Inc.
Huntington, Indiana 46750

Cover design by Monica Haneline

PRINTED IN THE UNITED STATES OF AMERICA

Contents

Acknowledgments

First, we wish to express our gratitude to Eric and Donna Franco and their children, whose loving example first opened our hearts to the style of parenting we present in this book.

We also wish to thank Fr. Mark Gruber, O.S.B., for granting his permission to reprint parts of his writing on allowing children at Mass, Dr. Brian Donnelly for his kind permission that allowed us to reprint Dr. Herbert Ratner's work on "The Natural Institution of the Family," and Fr. Val Peter for the supportive words that grace the opening of this book.

A debt of gratitude is likewise owed to the good folks of Our Sunday Visitor; especially Greg Erlandson and Jackie Lindsey, for their support of our project, as well as Cathy Dee, Woodeene Koenig-Bricker, David Scott, and Michael Aquilina for their editorial assistance with articles (our own and others) that eventually found their way into this book.

Likewise, we wish to thank God the Father, both for His generous and merciful love and for the gift of our children, with whom we are well pleased. We also extend heartfelt thanks to our Mother the Church and the Holy Family for their example and intercession.

And finally, we offer thanks to you, dear reader, for waking up every morning to do the hardest, most blessed work there is, the work of parenting. May you find this effort of use to you on your journey.

Preface

A few short months ago, I celebrated my fortieth anniversary as a priest. One of the things the Lord promised me four decades ago was that if I left my mother, father, brothers, and sister and followed the Lord, I would have hundreds of children. I trusted He would be ever faithful to His promises. How could I ever have dreamed that so many years later I would be the father to so many kids at Boys Town? I feel like our father Abraham.

One of the joys of parenting is that you get to raise your children the way that you want to. You get to bring them up without some outsider like the government telling you how. What a joy to pass on our Catholic Faith to our children.

This book is all about what a joy it is to pass on our Catholic Faith and way of life to our children. Greg and Lisa Popcak, the authors of this volume, do a great job in providing you assistance in this marvelous task.

This book is based on the premise that Catholics really do see the world in a way that is different from so many other wonderful Christians of other denominations. We really do see the world as a sacrament. We see the good creation. We see salvation coming to us through the community. Some say that "if all is right between me and Jesus," church is unnecessary. Catholic people don't believe that. Church is necessary. The Gospels speak powerfully to us of salvation, which comes from God's Son made of flesh, born of the Virgin Mary, who suffered, died, rose from the dead, and poured out His Spirit upon the apostles. Those witnesses to the resurrection went out and preached the Good News and joined together in the breaking of the bread.

The Cross is not just horizontal, it is not something just between me and God. It is vertical. Salvation comes through the community, through the family. That is where you come in as Catholic parents.

I received my faith from mom and dad and from grandparents and brothers and sister and all the family. The kids at Boys Town receive their faith through the Boys Town family.

You and I as parents are at center stage only for a few, brief moments. Birth, infancy, childhood, and adolescence go by all too fast. What a glorious vocation it is to stand center stage. What a moment of marvelous glory.

The most characteristic thing we Christians do is not private prayer, but public prayer — the Eucharist, the breaking of the bread, the sacrifice of the Mass. St. Paul tells us that by our offering the Eucharist, that is, by our eating the body of the Lord and drinking His blood, we become His mystical body: mom, dad, and all the kids.

Some days family life is easy, but many days family life is hard. On all days, God is good to us. Praised be the name of the Lord.

I wish you the very best as you read this book and profit from it. There is hardly a page from which you cannot take one or two ideas and put them into practice in your own lives.

I write this little preface on September 8, the birthday of the Blessed Virgin Mary. May she who brought Christ into our world, show you her Son, now and every day of your family life.

Fr. Val J. Peter, J.C.D., S.T.D.
Executive Diretor, Boys Town

Part One

Catholic Parenting: Building a Community of Love

Introduction

What's So Special About Catholic Parents?

Exactly what is a "Catholic parent"? Are we really any different from other Christian or even non-Christian parents, except perhaps in the prayers we teach our children? Could it be that there is no such thing as a Catholic parent, and this book is merely a cynical niche-marketing ploy?

The truth is even more shocking. We believe that even beyond the obvious essentials of prayers and parish life, Catholic parents really are a different breed of animal. This book will introduce you to some of those differences and demonstrate how you can make use of them to help your family become a truly exceptional, Catholic family.

A People Set Apart

Scripture tells us that we, as Catholic Christians, are called to be a "a chosen race, a royal priesthood, a holy nation, a people of his own" (1 Pt 2:9 NAB). So, what sets us apart from all other parents, Christian and non-Christian? For starters, we Catholics have several resources available to us that our Protestant and non-Christian brothers and sisters simply choose not to take advantage of. Let's take a look at some now.

A Close Encounter of the Jesus Kind

It is true that God works with all parents who call upon him. After all, our children are really His children: we all "belong to God." But we Catholic parents are empowered to experience Christ "up-close-and-personal" in the Eucharist. More than simply acknowledging Jesus

11

as our "personal Lord and Savior" as our Protestant brothers and sisters do, we receive the Blessed Sacrament and His Flesh becomes our flesh, His Blood courses through our veins. Time and again, Scripture demonstrates the transformative power of an encounter with Christ, and so, we Catholics rely on the innate and independent power of Christ in the sacraments to lead our children on "the pathway of righteousness." No, Jesus doesn't parent for us (we don't get off that easily), but if we let Him, He will parent through us and, when our children receive Him, He will become their best friend. With peer pressure like that, faithful, conscientious Catholic parents can't lose.

We Get By with a Little Help from "Mom"

Catholics think of the Church as our Mother, and we are called to parent our children like she parents us. This is one of the things the Holy Father means when he calls the family the "domestic church" (*Familiaris Consortio*, "On the Family"). So, what parenting tips can "Mom" offer us? First, through the family meal she prepares for us (Eucharist) we learn that God is a hands-on parent. Any time we call upon Him, He takes time out of the busiest schedule in the universe to be there, Body, Soul and Divinity. Definitely a strong argument for quantity-time parenting.

The second most obvious lesson can be found in the Sacrament of Reconciliation. On the one hand Mom (the Church) has very high expectations for our behavior; on the other hand, when we fail, she is an extremely gentle disciplinarian. In fact, she never wastes time coming up with creative punishments. Taking her cue from the parable of the prodigal son, her entire discipline strategy consists of strengthening our relationship with the Father so that we will never want to leave home again. Remember, the whole point of those "five Hail Marys" penances is not to punish us (it would be a pretty stupid punishment if it was). Rather, it is an invitation to spend some time seated in the lap of our Mother, before our Heavenly Father, who showers us with a love so profound that we cannot help but be made better by it. Catholic parents are called to do no less for our own children.

We Love Two Holy Books

It is a common lament, "Why don't kids come with an instruction manual?" Well, they do. But they're written in "Catholic." Allow us to explain.

Protestants distinguish themselves for their reliance on *sola scriptura*, "the Bible alone," to tell them how to live life in general and parent in particular (curiously, though, the doctrine of *sola scriptura* is found nowhere in Scripture). This can lead some non-Catholic Christians (though certainly not all) to express a kind of self-righteous disregard for what science has to tell us about human nature, saying, "If it's not in the Bible, then it just isn't so." By way of illustration, allow me to quote from a review of fundamentalist author Dr. Ed Bulkey's book *Why Christians Can't Trust Psychology*.

> We [Christians] are a Body with deep hurts.... But where do we go to heal those hurts? If our sufficiency is not in Christ, and we do not believe God's Word provides answers for today's problems, then what's the point of being a Christian — other than for eternal fire insurance? Any time we say we need the Bible plus psychology (even Christian psychology) to deal with the modern "dysfunctions" that face our families, we are questioning the adequacy and sufficiency of the Scriptures.
> — Review of *Why Christians Can't Trust Psychology* in *The Book Peddler*

Contrast this with John Paul II's assertion in the "Gospel of Life" (*Evangelium Vitae*) that "marriage and family counseling agencies by their specific work of guidance and prevention ... *offer valuable help in rediscovering the meaning of love and life*, and in supporting every family in its mission as the 'sanctuary of life' [italics mine]." Clearly there is a noticeable distinction of which we Catholics need to take note.

Of course, Catholics must also ground our lives in Sacred Scripture, but we — the Church that actually compiled the Bible as we know it (you're welcome) — recognize that there is another source of Divine Revelation that is at least as important as Scripture — Creation itself — which the Church has referred to as the "Book of Nature." As the Catholic physician and philosopher Dr. Herbert Ratner was fond of saying:

> ... There are two revelations: one found in the Book of Scriptures and the other in the Book of Nature; one communicated through the Words of the Son, the other through nature from a lexicon written by the Father. However, the Father, the Author of nature, does not go about teaching one truth while the Son teaches another.

Good science and good theology are completely compatible with one another because both are derived from the same source: God who is Father, Son, and Holy Spirit, the Author of all Truth, whether created or revealed, and who does not contradict Himself! Of course, this exact line of reasoning was promoted by Pope John Paul II in his encyclical *Fides et Ratio* ("Faith and Reason").

In a sense, the Catholic attitude toward the sciences could be summarized by the witness of the Three Wise Men. For thousands of years, man's study of the stars led them to worship the stars. But the Three Wise Men's study of the stars led them to worship the Lord. Perhaps more than any other group of Christians, Catholics are able to access the fullness of Divine Revelation — not because we're such hot stuff — but because we are among the few groups of Christians willing to read both "books."

Likewise, while secular parents may also rely on the Book of Nature for parenting hints, they don't have access to Divine Revelation in Scripture or Sacred Tradition, which tell them how to use the information they gain from science. The result is that while the secular world seeks to bend creation to its will, Catholics seek to use the knowledge we gain from science to learn how to cooperate with creation and use it in the manner God intended. Practically speaking, this is the difference between the Catholic use of Natural Family Planning versus the secular world's preference for chemical abortifacients (i.e., the pill). Or the Catholic "Brother Sun and Sister Moon" versus the secular "Uncle Global Warming and Auntie Dioxin." Or, for that matter, the Catholic assertion that the technology exists to keep a community safe while protecting the dignity of even the worst criminal's life versus the secular world's cries for the blood "justice" of capital punishment.

Learning about God's creation and using it in the manner God intended is one aspect of what Catholics call "natural law." In applying natural law to parenting, Catholics are able to use science and Scripture to raise the kind of children God would have us raise for Him. Remember, our children are not ours to raise as we choose. Scripture teaches that "both in life and death we belong to God" (see Rom 14:8). As such, we are obliged to follow the instructions He gives us in the Book of His Word *and* the Book of Nature to bring them up according to His will and purpose. While some parents talk about "parental rights," Catholic parents can speak only of their duty to serve justice; that is, the obligation to give God's children all the good gifts He wants them to have — the way He wants His children to have them. (Moral theologians traditionally define "justice" as the act of giving a person all that is rightfully due him or her.)

We Know What You Get When You Cross God and Human Beings

When God united Himself with man in the person of Jesus, He redeemed all of humanity. To paraphrase the Eastern Fathers of the Church, when you cross God and humanity, humanity gets a "divinized nature." This teaching goes back to the earliest days of Christianity, which explains why Catholicism offers a stunningly optimistic view of human nature. Consider the following quote from the *Catechism of the Catholic Church* (460):

> The Word became flesh to make us *"partakers of divine nature"* (2 Pet 1:4): "For this is why the Word became man, and the Son of God became the Son of man: so that man, by entering into communion with the Word and thus receiving divine sonship, might become a son of God" (St. Irenaeus, *Adv. haeres.* 3, 19, 1:PG 7/1, 939). "For the Son of God became man so that we might become God" (St. Athanasius, *De inc.*, 54, 3:PG 25, 192B). "The only-begotten Son of God, wanting to make us sharers in his divinity, assumed our nature, so that he, made man, might make men gods" (St. Thomas Aquinas, *Opusc.* 57: 1-4).

In light of such remarkable statements, Catholics have no choice but to believe that God is the author of our children's will, reason, emotions, needs, and personhood; each of which is deeply respected by the Catholic Church.

However, some non-Catholic and non-Christian groups have a very different idea about human nature and will. Martin Luther once compared humanity to dung, saying that God's grace covers us like the snow, but inside we're still dung. This attitude is reflected in much evangelical Protestant literature on child-rearing in which children's wills are often said to be easily influenced, or "oppressed," by the Evil One and so must be "broken," or "subverted." For example, in the December 1998 issue of *Focus on the Family* magazine, Dr. James Dobson argues that even though they are cute and lovable, "infants are inherently evil." It is exactly this negative view that breeds a curiously strong devotion to corporal punishment as a means of "beating the devil out" of children. (For a more thorough examination of this issue, please see *Beating the Devil Out of Them: A History of Corporal Punishment in America*, by sociologist Dr. Murray Strauss.)

But the Church's optimism regarding human nature compels us to take seriously psychotherapists like John Grinder and Richard Bandler, who assert that "every behavior is the attempt to meet a need or a positive intention." It is true that our needs and intentions can be perverted almost beyond recognition by our obnoxious and self-destructive behaviors, but even so, at the core, a godly need remains and we must be sensitive to it. Thus, the child who throws horrible tantrums may at heart lack appropriate ways to express frustration and anger (emotions given to him by God). It is up to the compassionate parent not to punish the child for being ignorant or "willful" (as if that was a bad thing) but to teach their child those skills which comprise emotional control. As Fr. Flanagan was fond of saying, "There are no bad boys [or girls]. There is only bad environment, bad training, bad example, and bad thinking." For the Catholic, the will must be taught, disciplined, and channeled, but never disparaged or broken. Catholic parents must be careful to use their authority in a manner that is "in conformity to the dignity of the human person."

We must choose those parenting methods which contribute to "a respect for others, a sense of justice, cordial openness, dialogue, generous service, solidarity, and all the other values which help people live life as a gift" ("Gospel of Life").

"Obey." It's Not Just Another Four-Letter-Word.

Few words raise our hackles more than the word "obey" and yet, obedience plays an important role in all Christian relationships, especially in the relationship between us and God.

Perhaps the reason so many people think "obey" is a dirty word is that they don't understand the Catholic meaning of the term. Everyone thinks of obedience as implying an authoritarian, fear-based relationship between two unequal parties, but the Catholic context is quite different. Fr. Richard Hogan and Fr. John LeVoir, summarizing the Holy Father's teaching on marriage and family in *Covenant of Love*, note that obedience is a relationship between persons of equal dignity. How can this be? Perhaps an illustration from St. Ambrose, one of the Fathers of the Church, will help.

St. Ambrose was contemplating the Scripture "You are my friends if you keep my commands" (Jn 15:14), but he observed that friends don't command other friends; if they did, it would no longer be a friendship but a relationship between a superior and inferior person (the commander and the commanded). What could Jesus mean by tying our friendship with Him to obedience to Him? Ambrose realized that Jesus was talking about a new kind of obedience based on friendship rather than fear, an "obedience" that meant anticipating and fulfilling the needs of another. Seen in this light, obedience is really another form of intimacy, where one person attentively seeks out the needs of the other and lovingly fulfills them, often without being asked, certainly without being asked twice. This is the essence of true Christian obedience.

Understanding obedience in this way presents a challenge to all of us. Obviously Christian obedience is a good and desirable thing, and yet we cannot demand obedience from another (nor can we nag, whine, threaten, beat, or manipulate it out of someone) if it is to remain true Christian obedience. In fact, there is only one way Christian parents can "command" obedience of their children — the same way Jesus commands it of us: through an example of loving service.

St. Thérèse the Little Flower wrote in her *Story of a Soul* that she never wanted to do anything to offend her parents because the love and service they showered upon her compelled her to offer nothing less than her best behavior. Her obedience was a logical and spontaneous response to the generous, loving service of her parents. Thérèse's parents took their cue from the parenting model of their Savior. Jesus Christ "commands" our obedience by virtue of His total self-gift. If we obey Him, our obedience comes only as a logical and spontaneous response to His complete gift of self. As the children's Sunday school song says, "O, how I love Jesus, because He first loved me." This is the heart of the obedience Christ invites us to offer Him — our loving response to His having loved us first.

Christian parents must "command" obedience from our children the same way Christ commands it of us, the same way St. Thérèse's parents commanded it from their "Little Flower" — by being selfless servants to our children, meeting their needs, responding to their cries, giving generously of our time, our bodies, our energy, and our love. The objection that we will "spoil" our children by loving them in such a demonstrative and all-encompassing way is as absurd as saying Jesus "spoiled" us by His passion, death, and resurrection. Of course He did! And, He commands us by His example to go and do the same. For the Christian, parental authority does not come from God placing us over our children. It comes from God having given us the responsibility to serve His children whom He, for a time, has entrusted to our care.

The psalm says, "How can I repay the LORD for all the good done for me?" (Ps 116:12). This Scripture can be taken to be the model of obedience in family life. When parents love their children as God loves them, anticipating and meeting their children's needs freely and gladly, their children are compelled to offer obedience in return as if to say, "What can I give back to you, Mother and Father, for all the goodness you have shown to me?"

This is not some pie-in-the-sky ideal. It is an observable reality which Lisa and I have had the privilege of witnessing many times in both our professional and personal lives. It is a phenomenon which is also borne out in psychological research on parent-child relationships. Psychologically speaking, generously loving, anticipatory parental service to a child builds both attachment and rapport with that child. Because a child values the intense relationship that is built by a caring, generously loving parent, the child — like St. Thérèse — is loathe to do anything that offends the parent. Likewise, such a child quickly corrects his own behavior when his parents note an offense.

Unfortunately, our world offers many obstacles to parent-child attachment and rapport, and frustrates the Christian obedience which logically flows from this relationship. Every day, what Pope John Paul II calls our "culture of death" seduces parents into undermining the attachment and rapport we have with our children, beginning with making our babies "cry it out" and "training" them to live by "more convenient" adult schedules, and continuing by our placing work and social commitments over our God-given responsibility to love and build secure families. But as the Holy Father observed, the Book of Genesis teaches that the responsibility to love was given to us before the necessity of work was created. Parents can only receive true Christian obedience from their child when that child has been physically, emotionally, psychologically, and spiritually convinced on a continuing basis that his parent loves him. (Of course, the same is true of our slow, ongoing conversion to greater obedience to God.) How do Christian parents convince a child of this love? By putting in what can seem to be an immense amount of one-on-one time, by respecting the needs a child says he has — especially when they seem silly to us, by teaching a child to express himself and his emotions respectfully instead of merely punishing inappropriate displays, and by showing our children their worth to us through our willingness to make career and social sacrifices for the greater good of our family. The amount of true Christian obedience we can expect from our children is directly proportional to how good we are at serving our children in the ways we have mentioned, and then some. To do less is to take a relationship that is meant to be based on intimate obedience and turn it into a constant power struggle over the child's life and behavior.

We Aren't Too Proud to Listen to Our Older Brothers And Sisters.

Catholic parents are called to be our children's most important teachers. Fortunately, we have the example of several charitable and effective Catholic educators to follow. Read the lives and educational thoughts of St. John Bosco, St. Maria Dominic Mazzarello, St. John Baptiste de la Salle, St. Benildus, or St. Elizabeth Ann Seton (who herself had a "strong-willed" child). Of course, just as important as being able to follow the example of these heroic individuals, we Catholics can also avail ourselves of their intercession.

And as if the example of these great men and women weren't enough, take a look at the educational philosophies of Catholic educators like Dr. Maria Montessori, Boys Town's Fr. Flanagan, the Catholic apologist and child psychologist Fr. Leo Trese, or even the extraordinarily influential views of Catholic physician and philosopher Dr. Herbert Ratner, who was a valued consultant to the Vatican and several national governments, and was a major force behind the La Leche League, as well as the Catholic Family Movement. In the third millennium, this school of thought continues to be developed by moral theologian Fr. William Virtue. You can read his fascinating thoughts in *Mother and Infant: The Moral Theology of Embodied Self-Giving in Motherhood* (Pontifica Studiorum Universitas, 1995). Let these individuals guide you in choosing those parenting methods which "respect the dignity of the human person. " You will be impressed and inspired by the compassion and heroic love that all of these luminaries exhibited for children.

I Did It Whose Way?

Now that you have an idea of what sets Catholic parents apart from others, let's take a brief look at how the popular parenting theories already on the market fit into our quest to develop a uniquely Catholic style of parenting.

We have always found it to be irritatingly amusing how different parenting books each claim to be the "one right way" to parent — and then go on to contradict each other. Why is that? The surprising answer is that at their core, each parenting program implicitly (and sometimes unintentionally) promotes a different set of values (for example: Americanism, evangelical Protestantism, etc.). And the methods described in those books are in fact a kind of catechetics program designed by the author to promote the values that are most important to him or her. Since each author gets to decide what set of values are "most important" and what methods are most likely to encourage those values, each author can claim to have "the one right way to parent" to their particular value system. Without the wise counsel of an institution like the Catholic Church, who through the Sacrament of Baptism shares and clarifies the values most important for walking the Christian walk, anybody could write anything about parenting and claim that theirs is the "one right way." But as far as the Church is concerned, it would seem that some ways — like some value systems — are better than others.

In order to devise a parenting style that faithfully supports the values, ideals, and goals promoted by the Catholic Church, we need to turn to the science of ethnopediatrics: the study of how different parenting styles work to support a particular culture's values. For example, in her groundbreaking book *Our Babies, Ourselves*, ethnopediatrician Dr. Meredith Small notes that the Japanese, who as a group value both community and strong family units, encourage parents to practice co-sleeping (a.k.a. "the family bed") with their children for many years. Likewise, the !Kung San [sic] people of Botswana — known as some of the most peaceable people on Earth (readers may recall them as the people featured in the movie *The Gods Must Be Crazy*) — seek to increase the chances that their children will exhibit the generosity and cohesion their culture values by engaging in parenting practices such as extended breast-feeding up to about age four or five, "wearing" their babies close to the breast in a sling until they are old enough to walk on their own, and co-sleeping. And the list goes on. Through trial and error over centuries, a particular culture will identify the parenting practices which increase the odds of a child developing a certain set of values and traits. Then, that culture will assert those parenting methods as the "right way" to parent, to the point of looking down its nose at any parent or group of parents who rear their children differently.

Of course, once one begins making connections between the parenting styles encouraged by a culture and that culture's strengths, one also begins to wonder about the influence parenting styles wield over a culture's well-known vices. For example, British parents are well known for their reliance on non-parental caregivers (i.e. nannies), their traditional use of boarding schools, and their historical affection for corporal punishment. As comedian Mike Meyers's "Saturday Night Live" character, Simon, used to sardonically say, "Nobody does childhood like the English!" In light of this uniquely detached parenting style, one cannot help but wonder how much of an influence these parenting methods have in producing a culture which, besides having accomplished many positive things, is also the undisputed sadomasochistic sex capital of Europe. (For a closer look at this issue, see Ian Gibson's book *The English Vice* [a play on words since sadomasochism is often euphemistically referred to as "the English vice"]; or Christopher Middleton's article in the Sunday London *Times* [April 27, 1997] entitled "Oh, the Cheek of It!".)

Likewise, studies have shown that Dutch parents as a whole are proud of the fact that they cuddle their infants less than any other parents in the world. Though the intention of this is to promote "independence" from the earliest age, one cannot help but wonder what contribution this hands-off parenting style makes to a culture where prostitutes ply their wares in shop windows, drug use is largely legal, and even active euthanasia is garnering the overwhelming support of the populace.

Similarly, in the United States, where family life has been significantly devalued since the 1960s when opportunities for greater social success increased for both women and men, did something change in American parenting styles that contributed to the three-hundred-percent increase in the adolescent suicide rate in the years between 1960 and 1990? Could it be that parents spend — according to government statistics — forty percent less time with their children than they did in 1960?

Regardless, the one thing all these Western parenting styles have in common is their ever-increasing reliance on detachment-oriented parenting strategies (e.g., letting babies "cry it out," substituting "transitional objects" and technology for parental contact and attention, day care for children as young as six weeks, corporal punishment, etc.) as methods intended to inspire "individualism" and "self-reliance" in their children. Granted, these goals certainly sound desirable, but the irony is that research shows that the detachment-oriented parenting strategies practiced in the West have exactly the opposite effect on children. Detachment parenting has led Western parents to create what we call a "Dilbert Culture" made up of people who have learned to sit in their cubicles and shut up, expecting little emotional and relational satisfaction from life, and instead pacifying themselves with materialism. As a surprised Dr. Small states in *Our Babies, Ourselves*:

> Perhaps the most startling finding of ethnopediatrics so far is the fact that parenting styles in Western culture — those rules we hold so dear — are not necessarily best for our babies. The parental practices we follow in the West are merely cultural constructions that have little to do with what is "natural" for babies.

Quite the contrary, it is solid attachment that leads to good self-esteem, healthy sexual attitudes, the willingness to take appropriate risks, demonstration of an appropriate balance of independence and reliance on others, and the valuing of persons over things. In fact, as Dr. Ken Magid has observed in his book *High Risk,* the more detached a child is, the more that child is likely to exhibit depression, acting out, promiscuity, estrangement, depression, and criminal behavior. Of course, the Catholic take on all of this is that in spite of all the material blessings Western culture has to offer, Pope John Paul II has branded it as a "culture of death" due to the disposable attitude we have toward others, especially the youngest, oldest, and weakest members of our society. It is our considered opinion that nothing short of the ever-increasing trend toward detachment parenting lies at the heart of this "culture of death." You've heard the saying "the hand that rocks the cradle is the hand that rules the world." Once upon a time this may have been true, but perhaps the more apropos sentiment for contemporary civilization is that the world is being rocked because no one has time for who's in the cradle.

Raising Your Child — The Nazi Way

"Vee Have Vays ov Making You Parhrent!"
The work of Drs. Samuel and Pearl Oliner provides a chilling look at the power that parenting styles have to bring out the worst in a

culture. In their book *The Altruistic Personality* they report the findings of their fascinating study, commissioned by the State of Israel, to answer the question, "Why did some gentiles heroically risk their lives to rescue Jews from the Nazis while most others either collaborated in the atrocities or simply stood by while the evil happened around them?" Their findings inadvertently give Catholics a lesson plan for raising a child who is capable of true Christian heroism.

Among the surprising results, the Oliners reported that of all the possible factors, parenting styles had the greatest influence on determining whether a person would in adulthood choose to be a Nazi collaborator, a bystander, or a rescuer. Specifically, the study noted the high priority nonrescuers' parents placed on extracting "blind obedience" from their children (as opposed to the Christian obedience we described earlier), as well as unswerving respect for parental authority. These findings support the results of previous studies like those conducted by Dr. Alice Miller, who has asserted that "parental emphasis on [blind] obedience was critically important in preparing Germans for the success of the Nazi regime, paving the way for the necessary submission it required."

Likewise, the Oliners found that in addition to their authoritarian style, nonrescuer's parents tended to view misbehavior as evidence of their children's innate badness or manipulativeness. Because of this, they believed strongly in the value of corporal punishment. It was a statistically significant finding that nonrescuers experienced more corporal punishment — though not necessarily abusive forms of corporal punishment — than rescuers.

By contrast, rescuers' parents were often considered "permissive" by their stricter neighbors. Rescuers' parents tended to view childish misbehavior as resulting from ignorance rather than badness. As such, rescuers' parents tended to forgo corporal punishment, instead placing a strong emphasis on explaining why certain behaviors were wrong, demonstrating how inappropriate behaviors affected another's feelings, and teaching their children more acceptable ways of behaving, instead of merely punishing bad behavior. Over and over again, words like "explaining" and "reasoning" were used by rescuers to describe their parent's discipline strategies. Those few rescuers who did experience corporal punishment reported being spanked "once or twice" in their lives, and only for the most serious infractions.

Finally, rescuers were taught to have a faith that formed the core values of their everyday lives and affected their everyday choices. This is in contrast to the faith of nonrescuers, which tended to be viewed as a cultural inheritance, an upstanding way to spend Sunday mornings, or a way to bring glory to themselves. Interestingly, rescuers recalled learning the lessons of respect, compassion, and care for others at their father's knee, both by his example and by the active lessons he taught his children. Statistically speaking, significantly fewer fathers of nonrescuers had an active role in their children's values education. In nonrescuers homes, it was most often the mother alone who was religious. (For a closer examination of these factors, I refer you to Dr. James Fowler's review of the Oliner's study in the June/ July 1990 issue of *First Things*.)

In 1998, the Church released *We Remember: Reflections on the Shoah*. In it, she attempted to examine what more she could have done to respond to the unspeakable evil of the Third Reich, and what she could do to make certain that such evil would never again place an indelible stain on the collective soul of humankind. As members of this Church, Catholic parents would do well to also reflect on their part in saying "Never forget. Never again." In essence, if studies like the Oliner's are correct, the ability of Catholic parents to raise Christian heroes — by practicing loving guidance in our homes, exhibiting a firm but understanding attitude toward misbehavior, transmitting a deep and personally meaningful value system to our children, and having solid Christian fathers take the lead in modeling and teaching the Faith — has everything to do making the world safe from the unspeakable.

Such studies expose in a very dramatic way the powerful effect parents have not only on their children, but on society as a whole. Those who say that it is parent's job to change the world one diaper at a time are not exaggerating. The fact is, the ethnopediatric idea of parenting models as the basis of culture and vice-versa is a very Catholic idea, because it gives empirical support to John Paul II's assertion that the family is the basic unit of society (see *Familiaris Consortio* ["On the Family"]) and must be given the respect it is due for the influence it wields both for good and evil.

"Beep! Greg, Mother Nature's on Line One."

In our continuing mission to devise a parenting model that supports Catholic virtues, we have to take a minute to consider nature. Specifically, how does a child's temperament figure into all this?

It is true that the genetic factors affecting personality (commonly referred to as "temperament") cannot allow any one method of parenting to guarantee that every child will exhibit a certain characteristic (say, independence, or generosity) in spades. But current research strongly suggests that a particular parenting style can ensure that even a child whose temperament is completely opposed to a certain characteristic will still be able to exhibit that quality or virtue to a socially acceptable degree. So, to use a previous example, even a Japanese child with an extremely strong, independent temperament — if parented in the traditional Japanese way — will still be more likely to exhibit a greater sense of community and solidarity than the average Dutch child parented in the traditional Dutch manner. Even though genetic temperament wields an undeniable influence over personality, the most respected studies show that it can only account for thirty to sixty percent of the mix, leaving the lion's share of influence over a child's personality to — what else? nurture. And the cultural values that dictate a particular style of nurture. As Dr. Small writes in *Our Babies, Ourselves*:

> With reports in the paper every day about the discovery of the gene for this or that disease or mental disorder ... the public has been bombarded with the idea that genes are primarily responsible for who or what someone is. What the news reports fail to explain is that when researchers suggest that some behavior or personality tic is heritable, they really mean that genes can account for thirty to sixty percent of the variation you see in that trait. In other words, personality — even those parts of it that might be highly tied to genes — is still a complex mixture of biology and life experience.

I Did It Whose Way? Part Two

So, to return to our original question, when you consider the view of ethnopediatrics, it becomes easier to see how different parenting books can offer different advice and all claim to be "the best way" to parent. Dr. Spock and his heir apparent, T. Barry Brazelton, M.D., offer the "best ways" to raise a child who exhibits the values espoused by "Americanism." Dr. James Dobson, on the other hand, can offer "the best ways" to raise a child according to the morality and values promoted by evangelical Protestantism, and so on. Moreover, each child raised in each particular parenting model can be said to be "OKAY" in a grow-up, get- a-job, basically-decent-person, daily-functioning-sense, but even so, each of these children will exhibit a decidedly unique perspective on life and demonstrate a decidedly different value-set as they grow up.

"I'll Tumble 4 Ya" — Parenting and the Catholic Culture Club

Which brings us to the one-hundred-bazillion-dollar question: Is there a Catholic way to parent? And if so, what parenting style is dictated by Catholic culture? It might strike some readers — especially those readers who have been raised entirely in the post-Vatican II Church — as rather odd to talk about parenting in a way that is consistent with Catholic culture. After all, practically speaking, Catholicism no longer has a common language (Latin) that unites its followers. Likewise, both worship styles and issues that define "social justice" vary greatly from region to region. In light of such diversity, it can be tempting to think that Catholic culture plays second fiddle to the various national cultures in which it can be found. But while the superficial aspects of Catholicism — its linguistic, political, and liturgical fashions — are greatly influenced by national cultures, the substance of Catholicism remains a distinct thing. Regardless of our nationality or ethnic heritage, Catholic people must first and foremost be a "a chosen race, a royal priesthood, a holy nation, a people of his own." While it may not be so obvious at first glance, Catholics do share a common language. It is a language written by the God we serve and communicated through the universal values and virtues all Catholics everywhere are committed to exemplifying in their everyday lives. More than anything else, it is this common "language of virtue" that causes us to suggest that there is a parenting style which — though it may or may not be different than what our neighbors are doing — is decidedly more "Catholic" than others.

Now, we admittedly have to be careful about this because the Church, herself, has not officially endorsed any one parenting style over another. But the Church does have a tradition of strongly supporting certain parenting practices (like breast-feeding, for example), and she does endorse particular values as being uniquely important to her — values which can be understood to be the essence of Catholic culture. While we cannot claim to present the one, right, Catholic way to parent (we have neither the authority nor the desire to do such a thing) we can enumerate some of the values which stand at the heart of Catholicism and, using an ethnopediatric approach, introduce you to the parenting methods which research suggests will increase the odds of your children exemplifying those values in their own lives.

Faithful Catholic parents who are sincerely concerned with the proper catechesis of their children, who are anxious for their children to learn the prayers, rituals, customs, and doctrine of our Church, should take note. The real training-up of a child in the Faith is done in the daily life of the family. Especially considered in the light of ethnopediatrics, it would be safe to say that the parenting style you choose is the single most important catechetical program your child will ever experience. Education in the facts of the Faith must be founded on an ongoing education in the heart of the Faith, and this can best be accomplished by choosing to parent to the values and attitudes most closely identified with the heart of Catholicism. As John Paul II has told us, parents are the "primary educators" of their children. What lessons are being taught by your parenting style? And are they consistent with the values and life-lessons our Church asks us to teach?

... And the Greatest of These Is Love

Obviously there are many virtues which lie close to the heart of Catholicism; the three theological virtues of faith, hope, and love, and the twelve fruits of the Holy Spirit, are among them. But if there is a "Catholic" parenting style, then it would have to have as its goal the quality that most defines Catholicism at the dawn of the new millennium, a quality known as "self-donation." Self-donation figures prominently in John Paul II's writings on family life, and since, as Archbishop Charles Chaput has observed, Pope John Paul II has personally penned about two-thirds of everything the Church has ever written on family life, it seems that this quality might be the best place to start.

In a sense, self-donation is another word for love, but it is a specific kind of love. Self-donation is a supremely responsible love, empowering those who practice it to use their bodies, minds, and spirits to respond with justice and compassion to the deepest God-given needs of others. Self-donation is the kind of love that mirrors the self-gift Jesus Christ gave us, through His incarnation and through His passion, death, and resurrection. Further, it is the love that lies at the heart of both Catholic social justice and Catholic family life. Because self-donation requires us to be willing to make personal sacrifices — sometimes significant ones — for the good of another, it can understandably make us squeamish at times. But self-donation is about so much more than making sacrifices. Ultimately it is about "finding ourselves" by doing the work God created human beings to do — the work of responsible, active love. As John Paul II has written, "Love is the fundamental and innate call of every human being" ("On the Family"). While it is tempting to try to discover our true worth in the work we do, the possessions we have, and the clubs to which we belong, both good theology and the sound research of psychologists like Abraham Maslow (developer of *Maslow's Hierarchy of Needs*) show that those people who achieve the highest levels of personal fulfillment do so by practicing love. As Boys Town's Fr. Flanagan once said:

> No man or woman can deem himself or herself a success in life, no matter how far up the ladder they have climbed, either socially, mentally or materially, if they cannot say that they have the confidence, comradeship, and love of their children.

Be a Saint! Be a Saint! All the World … Loves a Saint!

Even though self-donative love is the secret to fulfilling the purpose of our lives and the activity in which we have the greatest chance of "finding ourselves," it does not come easily. In my Catholic marriage book *For Better … FOREVER!* I observe that, in my own life, knowing that I have a responsibility to be loving is not often enough to motivate me to actually be loving. Sometimes, I need a more "selfish" reason for doing what my soul needs me to do. In a similar way, the choice to parent in a self-donative manner and to raise children who are capable of self-donative love is certainly in keeping with the Catholic call to pursue sainthood, but like it or not, sainthood is often a poor motivator for most of us. It just seems to high a goal to strive for, and we often need more "selfish" reasons to keep us going.

Emotional Intelligence: Our Earthly Reward for Love

Fortunately for us, God is merciful. Beyond the spiritual benefits of pursuing self-donation as a way of life and goal of parenting, there are many psychological and social benefits as well. Dr. Daniel Goleman's work on emotional intelligence (EQ) bears this out. Emotional intelligence is the psychological term that most closely resembles the quality Catholics refer to as self-donative love. Like self-donative love, emotional intelligence refers to one's ability to be generous with one's resources, to empathize with others, to display compassion and sensitivity, and delay personal gratification. In his book *Emotional Intelligence*, Dr. Goleman effectively demonstrates that social success depends less upon a person's IQ (basic intelligence) than it does upon their ability to demonstrate the qualities represented by EQ (emotional intelligence). Children who demonstrate high EQ are more well-adjusted, better socialized, more well-liked by peers, and — due to their ability to delay gratification — more able to set and meet long-range goals. Incidentally, that last factor, the ability to set and meet long-range goals, is essential for developing healthy self-esteem.

There are those individuals who would suggest that the Church is an outdated institution and parenting to the Church's values would simply create a backward, guilt-ridden, warped child. But these individuals are simply showing their ignorance. The child raised in an atmosphere of self-donative love, where the discipline strategies and parenting styles reflect "a respect for others, a sense of justice, cordial openness, dialogue, generous service, solidarity, and all the other values which help people live life as a gift" ("Gospel of Life") is a child who is well-balanced and capable of compassion, healthy socialization, and even — as the Oliner's study of rescuers in Nazi Germany showed — Christian heroism. Who wouldn't want a child like that? At the very least, we believe that every Catholic parent does.

In our attempt to clarify a uniquely Catholic parenting style for the new millennium, we apply what we believe are three essential questions to the various parenting methods and models from which we must choose. Specifically, they are:

1. Which parenting methods and models present the greatest opportunity for parents and children to practice self-donative love?
2. Which provide the greatest opportunity for families to exemplify "a respect for others, a sense of justice, cordial openness, dialogue, generous service, solidarity, and all the other values which help people live life as a gift"?
3. Which are most consistent with both the Book of God's Word and the Book of Nature, and are likewise supportable in the writings of prominent Catholic educators and in the traditions of the Church, herself?

As you consider your own response to the information presented in this book, we ask you to keep these questions in mind as well, because they will help clarify for you the powerful ministry that parenting really is, and the wonderful opportunities for personal and spiritual growth that parenting provides.

Mall Rats

As this chapter draws to a close, I'd like to share something that happened to us the other day. Lisa and I were shopping at the mall with our children. As we were paying for our purchases, the cashier, a woman in her late fifties, said to my wife and me, "You have such wonderful children. Enjoy them while you've still got them. My boys are grown. And looking back, I didn't appreciate them as much as I should have."

Her comments both saddened us and gave us a greater sense of urgency for this book, because if nothing else, we believe that any parenting method that wants to call itself "Catholic" must be one which invites parents to suck the marrow out of every stage of family life. Only then will we be able to experience the joy that longs to fill the place in our hearts formerly occupied by the desire for mere comfort or self-importance. We believe that the most "Catholic" parenting methods invite the parent and the child to find joy — indeed, to find God — in the little things of everyday life: in sharing a meal, solving a problem, cuddling together, completing a project, crying over an injury, celebrating a victory, learning a new skill, or just being in each other's presence. Choosing — or having chosen — not to use the parenting attitudes and techniques we present in this book does not make you a "bad parent." As we have shown, there are many ways to raise a basically well-adjusted "good kid." But speaking with the authority I have as a Catholic counselor to "… offer valuable help in rediscovering the meaning of love and life," and support "every family in its mission as the 'sanctuary of life' " ("Gospel of Life"), I believe that the parenting methods we present in the following chapters have the greatest potential for teaching your children — on an experiential level — the heart of the Faith, and allowing you and your child to make the most of what is always too short a time together.

By personally practicing the methods and mindset Lisa and I will outline in this book, we hope to one day find ourselves a doddering old couple, sitting on a bench at the mall, saying to a young couple with a babe-in-arms, "What a wonderful child. Enjoy her. We sure enjoyed raising ours, and when we look at them now — all grown — we're grateful to God for every drop of energy we spent. What a gift!"

Better still, we would like nothing more than to find you sitting next to us, nodding and smiling at that couple because you have experienced the very same thing in your own life.

Chapter One

Perfecting Your Kids in Love:
Twelve Ways to Raise a P. K.*

(*Perfect Kid)

Every parent wants a perfect kid. Virtually every parent dreams of having children whom everyone likes, who are on their way to making their first billion before age twenty-one, who rise at four o'clock in the morning so that they can serve breakfast to homeless people on their way to morning Mass, after which they will go to school, where they will eagerly work to maintain yet another 4.0 average, all while chairing several school committees and sorting through all those lucrative scholarship offers.

And then we wake up.

The fact is, when most of us view our home lives, what comes to mind isn't so much the Holy Family as "Holy cow!" But it is our belief that as Catholics, it is not our primary mission to raise children who are perfectly well-behaved, or who make our lives perfectly easy, or who grow up to be perfectly successful, or even perfectly popular. Our mission is to raise children who will grow up to be "perfect as their Heavenly Father is perfect"; that is, perfect in love. After all, what would it profit any of our children — or any of us for that matter — to gain the world and lose our souls? No, we believe the primary mission of every Catholic parent is to raise children who will grow up perfectly, in the sense that they know how to love and be loved, both by others and by the God who made them. As stated in *The Truth and Meaning of Human Sexuality* from the Pontifical Council for the Family, "Children, adolescents, and young people, should be taught how to enter into healthy relationships with God, with their parents, their brothers and sisters, with their companions of the same and opposite sex, and with adults" (#53). With these words, the Council outlines your mission as Catholic parents — should you choose to accept it....

The Affection Connection

"And how exactly am I supposed to complete this mission?" you ask. Well, the Church tells us that the secret to parenting success is building deeply intimate, character-affirming, godly relationships with our children, what the Holy Father calls a "civilization of love," that will ultimately transform the world by its powerful example.

Put simply, everything in parenting depends upon your kids knowing you love them and teaching them how to love you in return. Without that, all of the best discipline strategies in the world will fail.

Studies have shown that marriages which do not maintain a "positivity-to-negativity ratio" of five-to-one are in danger of divorcing within five years. In other words, unless a couple is five times more complimentary, affectionate, supportive, and encouraging as they are critical, nagging, and confrontational, their rapport will deteriorate until it ceases to exist. Additionally, we have found that unless parents and children maintain a similar five-to-one positivity-to-negativity ratio in their relationships with each other, yelling and defensiveness increases, discipline breaks down, and all hell breaks loose. Considering the importance of parent-child rapport as a foundation for effective discipline, we are going to spend the rest of this chapter examining some of the most powerful tools available to parents to build strong relationships with their kids. But first, take the "Affection Connection Rapport" quiz on the next page to assess the strength of your own relationship with your children. (In order to best assess the level of rapport you have with each child in your family, take the quiz once for each child you have).

The Eleven Basic Rapport-Builders

Regardless of your score, we could all use a periodic refresher course in maintaining a good relationship in our families one in a while. Here are twelve ways (eleven basic rapport-builders, and one advanced strategy) to make sure that your relationship is always as close and effective as it can be.

The Affection Connection Rapport Quiz

_____ My child acts disgusted even when I ask him/her to do the simplest things.

_____ My child DOESN'T act as if (s)he's missed me when I come home from work (or come home after being away from him/her).

_____ My child constantly speaks disrespectfully to me.

_____ My child only listens to me if I yell at him/her.

_____ My child complains that (s)he feels as if (s)he can do nothing right as far as I am concerned.

_____ My child is secretive around me.

_____ My child tells my mate (s)he can't talk to me.

_____ I DON'T enjoy my child's company.

_____ I feel burned out as a parent.

_____ My child accuses me of not listening to him/her.

Scoring

Give yourself one point for each "true" answer. The lower the score, the better.

0-1 True

Congratulations! You probably have good rapport with your child. But be careful not to rest on your laurels. Use the "Eleven Basic Rapport-Builders" in order to keep a solid parent-child rapport.

2-4 True

Your rapport could use some shoring up. Pay close attention to the "Rapport-Builders" or you run the risk of your children losing heart, and of you losing control of your house.

5+ True

You need to take emergency measures. Follow the "Rapport-Builders." If you need support or additional suggestions for repairing the relationship with your children, contact the Pastoral Solutions Institute at (740) 266-6461.

1. Say The Love Words

Don't be shy about saying, "I love you" to your kids (and your mate, for that matter). Say, "I love you" and "I'm proud of you" at least one hundred times a day. Say it until they are sick of hearing you say it and then say it one more time just to be sure. Tell them how proud you are of them. Often say, "You are my greatest treasures. There is nothing I have that is more important than you." Take your cue from the Heavenly Father, who publicly announced at Christ's baptism, "This is my beloved Son, in whom I am well pleased."

Moreover, we encourage you to seek out opportunities to comment on your children's successes and strengths. Praise them. Don't offer insincere or too-general praise, but instead be specific: "I love the colors in your picture." "I admire how hard you worked on your project." "Thank you for being so generous to your brother." Don't complain about them publicly — ever. Especially not in front of their friends. If you have to criticize your children, do it privately and respectfully. But by all means do compliment them publicly, as long as you do it to make your kids look good, not yourself. (Your kids know the difference.)

2. Show Them

People thrive on touch. Be generous with physical displays of affection for your kids, because — as the Church teaches — such displays respect the self-donative meaning of the body. Our bodies were created by God to give and share love — first and foremost. Don't be shy about using yours to this end.

Hug, kiss, cuddle your kids. Fathers, you especially need to do this. After all, God the Father is unquestionably demonstrative of His love for us. First, when fathers are affectionate, it shows your daughters what to look for in a man, and second, it shows your sons what a man should look like. Of course, mothers must be affectionate as well, but affection often comes more easily to many mothers — if not all.

Beyond being physically demonstrative of affection, both parents should ask themselves, "What is one small thing I can do today to give a little bit more of myself to my children?" (Of course, children should be taught to ask this same question of themselves — real love is reciprocal.)

Remember, for your child five extra minutes of playing with you or sitting and talking with you is worth a million times more than all the toys and trinkets you could ever buy. Your loving example will teach your children to turn to people, not things, when they need help or comfort. And your affection will help them be better equipped to experience the power of God's own love for them.

3. Keep Your Promises

It is one thing to say, "I love you." It is another thing to exemplify the motto "You can count on me." If you say you are going to be there, be there. If you set a limit, stick to it. If you promise a surprise, deliver on it. If you say you will do it, do it.

If some cataclysm prevents you from making good on your promise, make a specific time to make good on that promise and then fulfill your commitment. Let nothing stand between you and this make-up date. As Jesus said, "Let your 'Yes' mean 'Yes,' and your 'No' mean 'No' " (Mt 5:37 NAB). Be a person of your word and your children will respect you for it.

4. Play Together

Make time to have fun together. The importance of play for both the adults and children in a family cannot be overstated. As Fr. Flanagan wrote, "Some of the finest people in the world go through life under a handicap because they never learned how to play when they were children." Expand your capacity for silliness. Learn to patiently play your children's games. Teach your children your games. Tell jokes at dinner. Tickle each other. Reserve at least one day a week for having fun as a family.

We also recommend that, once a month, you and your mate each take turns getting some one-on-one time with your children. Treat each son or daughter to some special time with just you. Use these opportunities to really listen to your child. Learn about their thoughts, joys, and struggles. Taking this time to listen and play together is one of the best ways we know to build a solid relationship with each of your children.

5. Work Together

Of course, activities don't have to be dripping with sentiment and bursting with fun in order to exhibit rapport-building potential. Invite/require your kids to work alongside you as you work to complete household chores or special projects. This not only builds their competence, it lets them know you value their help. Most important, it makes them feel like they are a valuable part of the family team (sometimes whether they want to be or not). And of course, young children love the big feeling they get inside when they can help mommy and daddy do "big people jobs."

6. Pray Together

As the saying goes, "The family that prays together, stays together." Praying together is an essential part of family life that fosters family relationships however you do it. The following are some special ways you can use prayer to reinforce the rapport and affection in your home.

First, every morning or evening, take some time to bless each other. As parents, "lay hands" on each child (i.e., pray over them), thanking God for him or her, and ask God to help the child "grow up to be the man (or woman) God wants him (her) to be." Then invite your children to return the favor by asking them to lay hands on you and pray for God's blessing. Our children love this, as they feel they are receiving a special gift from us and giving a special gift to us. And we are not alone. We hear similar endorsements from other families who practice this blessing.

Likewise, when you are being affectionate with your children, remind them that "I love you more than I could ever say, and God loves you even more than I do." And, when you tuck your children in at night, make the sign of the cross on their foreheads and pray that God will send His angels to guard them in their sleep.

Finally, make sure that at least once a week your family spends some special time in prayer, as well as Bible or catechism study. In these special times of prayer and reflection, give thanks for each family member, ask God to show you His will for your lives, ask Him to supply your needs, that, as Scripture says: "He might show the immeasurable riches of his grace in his kindness to us in Christ Jesus" (Eph 2:7 NAB). Feel free to occasionally ask your children to lead this special worship-time. Such actions show the children that you value their input and that prayer really is a family thing, not just a grown up thing.

7. Be There

Make a point of attending the activities your child is involved in. Of course, you must be there for the important things like the big game, recitals, plays, and other especially significant activities, but as much as possible, make a point of "being there" even for the simple things like watching gymnastics or karate practice. It doesn't matter if your child pays you a lot of attention, or technically *needs* you to be there. They will appreciate the effort.

Of course, beyond simply showing up for your child's life, it is important to be mentally present to them when we are physically present. Make sure to listen to your children. Too often we tune them out because we think they don't have anything to say that is relevant to whatever is going on in our own lives, but when we do this, we are missing an important opportunity to bond with our kids. When your children are talking, force yourself to look them in the eye. Give appropriate feedback. Ask questions about what they are saying. Compliment them on their insights when they offer a particularly good one. Your efforts to respectfully and actively listen to your child will pay off in their willingness to listen to you.

8. Be Welcoming

Every neighborhood has a home where all the kids gather to play. Try to see that yours is that home. Be hospitable to your children's friends. Make them feel welcome. Equip your home for their games. Be on hand to congratulate them on the successes in their lives, and lend an ear in difficult times. Your efforts at displaying Christian hospitality will go a long way toward helping your kids, especially your teens, feel like you understand them.

9. Respect Their Space

Being an affectionate parent is not the same as being an in-your-face parent, or even a parent who doesn't know when it's his cue to leave. Sometimes affection means respecting a child who says, "I need some time alone, please." Affection and love are supposed to help your child develop a firm, healthy foundation on which to build his own life. Make sure that even while you are keeping an eye and an ear out for problems, you are giving your kids the room they need to grow.

10. Make Rapport a Two-Way Street

Some parents make the mistake of thinking that parent-child rapport is a one-way street. Such parents kill themselves taking care of their child and waiting on him or her hand and foot, without ever asking the child to demonstrate the same level of respect and service in return. Don't misunderstand us, we place a high priority on parental service to children, but at the same time, parents are not to set themselves up as their children's slaves and whipping posts. As far as the Church is concerned, every family member is called to serve every other family member as generously as he or she is able. Teach your child this lesson first by modeling it, then by requiring him or her to follow your lead. Rapport is a two-way street, just as real love is reciprocal. Make certain that you are teaching your child to give love and service as well as receive it.

11. Have Regular Family Meetings

Once a month (or more often if you prefer) meet as a family to discuss any issues that are affecting all of you. We offer the following format for your consideration:

Begin with a prayer.

Thank God for each member of the family and ask for His wisdom and peace to reign in your home.

Express your gratitude.

Think of one thing each family member did since the last meeting to make life easier on the rest of the family. Be specific. Thank them for it. The parents should take the lead in this and then invite each child to participate in turn.

Raise any concerns.

This is not the time to address problems with individual family members. Generally speaking, such correction should be done privately, unless that person is being a nuisance to all. This time ies best used to address any upcoming events or circumstances that might be affecting the family as a whole, or to set goals that the family would like to work toward.

Discuss any questions.

Make sure everyone is on board before closing the discussion. If any familys members have been particularly quiet, remind them how important their input is and invite their response.

Close with a prayer.

Thank God for His guidance in your lives and ask for His grace to love one another, as He loves each of you.

Have a family meal/snack and fun time.

After a good relational workout you need some social time. Serve fun food like pizza or tacos or something else that is completely non-nutritious while you play games or watch a movie together.

It is also important to have some rules in these family meetings. Specifically, no name-calling or picking on anyone, each person should listen attentively to whoever is speaking (no interrupt-

Can I Increase My Affection Connection?
A Quiz

Check as many as apply to you.

_____ I am comfortable giving physical affection to my kids.

_____ Every day, I tell my children I love them.

_____ Every day, I spend time playing with my kids.

_____ I don't complain about my children publicly.

_____ I compliment my children publicly.

_____ At least once a month, I plan some special one-on-one time with each of my children.

_____ When my children talk to me, I look them in the eye and really listen.

_____ I am kind and welcoming to my children's friends.

_____ I tell my children that I am proud of them.

_____ I take the time to learn about my kids games, interests, and ideas.

_____ At least once a month, we have family meetings to talk about the direction of our lives together.

_____ I require my children to offer the same level of service and respect I offer them.

Scoring
10-12 Checked
Keep up the great work!
6-9 Checked
You're doing pretty well, but try to be a little more attentive to the affection and interest you show in your kids lives.
5-0 Checked
You need to work harder on your capacity to express affection and attention to your children. Without taking corrective action soon, you run the risk of losing rapport and having to resort to punitive measures to increase compliance (which will simply undermine the relationship more).

ing or parallel conversations allowed!), and everyone must participate.

Family meetings can help remind you that your family is a team, called together by God to love one another and lead each other to heaven.

Before we take a look at the last and most powerful secret, use the "Can I Increase My Affection Connection?" quiz on the preceding page to discover ways to increase the basic affection and rapport between you and your child.

Questions: Discuss the Following with Your Family

1. Think of one time that you especially enjoyed as a family in the last six months. Make plans to do it again.
2. Think of another family you admire. Name one family ritual they have that you would like to incorporate in your family.
3. Each evening, each family member should take turns answering the following question, "I'm grateful to God for this family because...."

Affection in Action

At a family meeting, give each family member a sheet of paper. Have each person answer the question, "I really feel loved by this family when...." Some examples may include things like "When you say you love me"; "When Dad takes me out for ice cream"; "When Jimmy lets me take the first turn," etc. Each person should list as many things as possible. Afterward, make copies of the lists and give them to each family member, as well as post them in a public area. Ask each family member to do at least one thing on someone's list each day. At dinner time, share what each of you did, and how it made you feel.

The Affection Connection: A Master Class

Now that we've taken a look at the eleven basic ways to increase affection and rapport between you and your children, we would like to invite you to the master class. The last step is a doozy, and it has the potential to help you always know the best ways to reach out to your child.

12. Know Their Relating Style

A "relating style" represents the specific way a person gives, receives, and understands love from and toward another person. To get a better grasp of how your and your children's relating styles can make or break family rapport, we need to take you back to school for a minute (but don't worry, we'll come back after just a moment).

Teachers spend a great deal of energy trying to discover your children's "learning styles." These styles represent the easiest ways your children can learn new things and communicate with others. They are all based on the particular sense (sight, sound, touch) that is most acute in your child. So, if your child has a visual learning style (i.e., his sense of sight is the one he relies on the most to learn and communicate), he probably learns best through reading and other visual presentations like videos, or show-and-tell-type activities. Alternatively, if your child has a more auditory learning style (i.e., his sense of hearing is the one he relies on the most to learn and communicate), your child may learn best by being talked through certain tasks, or by singing educational songs and listening to read-aloud stories (and for older children, classroom lectures). Finally, if your child has a kinesthetic (kin-es-THET-ic) learning style (i.e., his sense of touch is most acute) he probably learns best by doing hands-on projects. He may also be a "slower" learner who has a hard time sitting still in class and doesn't enjoy reading very much — unless the stories are action-packed and short, like comic books.

Learning Styles and Family Relating

"So," you might ask, "what's this got to do with parenting?"

Learning styles, because they are neurologically based, aren't just relevant to the classroom. They translate into the ways people need to give and receive love as well, and in this context, they are called "relating styles." In order for people with more visual relating styles to feel loved, they need to be able to see the things you've done to show your love (like giving cards or notes, or other special, tangible tokens of affection). People with a more auditory relating style need to be talking with you to feel connected — if you aren't listening or conversing, you aren't being loving. Finally, individuals with a more kinesthetic relating style appreciate more physical displays of affection. They are also grateful when a parent takes the time to quietly work on projects together. Understanding and becoming fluent in your child's learning/relating style has a major impact on both your child's behavior and the amount of peace you can experience at home. The following two examples might help illustrate this concept.

Danny was a six-year-old boy who was referred to the in-home family-therapy program I was working in while I was a graduate intern. The most immediate issue was that Danny was throwing horribly violent tantrums which frightened his mother. On separate occasions during his many tantrums, Danny pulled a knife on his mother and even kicked the family's television set, breaking it. One time, Danny threw a tantrum in front of me and my pregnant supervisor, threatening to "Kick her tummy and kill the baby!"

Our first reaction was that Danny wasn't getting enough attention from his single mom. The only problem with this hypothesis was that his mother was very affectionate. Each day when Danny would come home from school, she would spend a good deal of time telling him how much she loved him, looking at his work for the day, and talking about all the things he did. All-in-all, it seemed as if she was pretty clued in to her son.

We decided to back up and attempt to assess the intention behind the violent tantrums by asking, "What does this mom do differently when Danny throws a tantrum than she normally does?" What we discovered was that when Danny had a tantrum, his mother would have to get off the couch and physically restrain him. This was no small feat for the woman, who was permanently disabled with chronic back problems. Not having much else to go on, we suggested that perhaps Danny was not getting enough kinesthetic (touch) attention from his mother (who had a more auditory relating style). That is, she loved him by talking to him, and his tantrums were actually a very clever adaptive response he had developed to meet his need for increased touch.

We explained our theory to the mother and offered the following suggestion. When Danny came home from school, she was to continue their usual ritual of looking at his schoolwork and telling him she loved him (visual and auditory attention). But from now on, she was to do this while he sat on her lap and she cuddled him, giving him physical affection for as long as he would stay.

The mother took our advice and ran with it. Even though it made her physically uncomfortable, she held Danny, rubbed his back, stroked his head, and cuddled with him — sometimes up to an hour — while she talked to him and reviewed his day. Amazingly, within a week, the tantrums decreased significantly. Within a month, they were gone completely.

While there remained other issues for treatment, understanding and attending to Danny's relating style enabled this mother to prevent his imminent placement in foster care and establish the control and safety needed to build a new relationship with her son.

The second example is of the Ashford (not their real name) family, whom I saw in my private practice. The father was having a very hard time with his wife and one of his daughters. The major point of contention was trying to find a balance between work and play in the family. The father had a more visual relating style, in that he had a hard time relaxing and playing until the domestic chores were completed. As he put it, "I can't relax if everywhere I look I see something else that needs to be done." On the other hand, his wife and one of his daughters were more kinesthetic (feeling-oriented), saying, "We don't have a problem doing work; we would just like to feel we're a team, instead of being grouchy the whole time. If we could do something fun first, then we'd feel closer as a family and be able to take on the work with a better attitude."

Neither side could understand the other's position because, neurologically speaking, they weren't wired to. As far as a more visual person is concerned, doing anything *other than* "clean up the visual field first, then enjoy yourself" just doesn't make sense. (Literally. It is not appealing to his sense of sight.) Likewise, to the kinesthetic person, doing it any way *other than* "work up some energy and good feeling by doing fun things first, and then take on the stuff you don't feel like doing" doesn't make sense. To the more kinesthetic person, feelings (physical and emotional) are everything.

Once I articulated these differences to the family we were able to come up with some solutions. We developed a plan that made sure both the kinesthetic and visual members of the family were getting their needs met every week. To begin, I asked the family to consider the following question: "How many hours of play and how many hours of work per week does it take to make our family run smoothly?" After

Part One: The Visual Relating Style Quiz

Give yourself one point for each item that describes you MOST of the time.

_____ Learns best through independent reading and/or visual aids (notes, lists, posters, movies and videos, etc.)

_____ Nothing says "I love you" like giving or receiving letters, cards, or other things I can see.

_____ Clothes are important. Looking good is more important than comfort or practicality.

_____ Desktops and visible surfaces neat as a pin. Desk drawers and closets, however, may be a disaster. Out of sight, out of mind.

_____ Always making plans/inventing creative scenarios and coming up with new ideas. Usually very productive. Can mentally track 100 projects at once.

_____ Good at visual arts (photography, painting, drawing, writing, etc.)

_____ Organized.

_____ Thinks more clearly when house/workspace is neat.

_____ Daydreams a lot/gets lost in thoughts.

_____ Speaks quickly. Uses a lot of words.

_____ Tends to be "anal retentive" (i.e., uptight/high-strung/detail-oriented).

_____ Enjoys books with vivid descriptions/pictures.

_____ Loves to keep journals, makes plans, and write lists.

_____ Uses visual metaphors in speech like, "See my point," "I've got to focus," "Imagine that," "It seems vague," "It seems clear," "I can see right through you," "I'm seeing things in a new light," "I'm drawing a blank."

Tabulate your scores for your Visual Relating Style:

_____

_____

_____

Part Two: The Auditory (Hearing) Relating Style Quiz

Check the statements that describe how you are MOST of the time.

_____ Learns best when talked through how to do things.

_____ Nothing says "I love you" like taking the time to listen and talk with me.

_____ Talks constantly about everything./ Has an opinion on every subject.

_____ Likes hearing and saying "I love you" half-a-million times a day.

_____ No such thing as a "rhetorical question"; they answer everything.

_____ Likes music, poetry, etc.

_____ Very sensitive to other's tones of voice.

_____ Hums, whistles, talks to self, perhaps constantly.

_____ Radio or TV on at all times, "Just for the noise."

_____ When arguing, doesn't know when to stop. May follow other person from room to room talking, whether or not the other is listening.

_____ When moderately stressed you try to talk about it. When maximally stressed, quiet is the only thing that will restore you.

_____ Phone permanently connected to head.

_____ Always wants the last word.

_____ Uses auditory comments, "Hear me out," "I could tell by your tone," "I need some feedback," "We need to talk," "Just listen to me," "It made me want to scream," and other auditory metaphors in speech.

Tabulate your scores for your Auditory Relating Style:

_____

_____

_____

Part Three: Kinesthetic (Touch) Relating Style Quiz

Check the statements that describe how you are MOST of the time.

_____ Learns best by doing. Likes hands-on projects/work. Often a slower learner at school.

_____ Very physical with affection. Likes being touched, held, or engaging in affectionate rough-housing.

_____ Dresses for comfort. Appearance secondary if considered at all.

_____ Easily overwhelmed in verbal conflict. Often feels picked on. "I never know what to say…." May either shut down or pick physical fights as defense in conflict.

_____ Has a hard time making decisions. Tends not to reason things out. Gives "gut reactions" to things.

_____ Poor organizer. Lots of unorganized piles. "Don't touch my mess. I'll never find anything."

_____ Gestures, grunts, shrugs more than talks. Conversations should have a purpose and be over when the purpose is served.

_____ Works off stress physically (e.g. working out, fighting, napping, baths, etc.).

_____ Loves sports or other physical activity.

_____ Tends to be impulsive or spontaneous.

_____ Sometimes hard to motivate them because they can't get past how they feel right now, in that particular moment.

_____ Doesn't like to read, or prefers books and movies with "action."

_____ Tends to be a slob. Doesn't see mess unless they trip over it.

_____ Says things like, "Get a grip," "I'll handle it," "Take it easy," "We really connected," "I just feel that way, that's why," and other physical metaphors in speech.

Tabulate your scores for your Kinesthetic Relating Style:

_____

_____

thinking about it for a week, the Ashtons concluded that in those weeks in which they felt the best about each other, they engaged in about eight cumulative hours of "family working-together time" and about ten cumulative hours of "family talking-and-playing-together time." They decided that in the future, they would keep a casual count of the amount of time they spent in each activity (work or play) throughout the course of the week, making sure that both quotas were met as closely and as consistently as possible. In this way, all family members felt that their visual and kinesthetic needs were being attended to, and regardless of what they were doing at any given moment, the good of the entire family was the over-reaching concern at all times.

The exercises on the previous pages will help you identify your own relating style, as well as the relating style of each family member. They will also offer some specific suggestions for ways to build a stronger rapport with those family members whose relating style is different from your own. (For a more specific discussion of how relating styles effect marital relationships, please see the chapter on "Love Languages" in *For Better ... FOREVER!*)

Relating Styles Exercise

Do the "Relating Style" exercises on the previous pages together with your family. Read each item aloud. On a separate sheet of paper, have each family member keep track of their score for each of the three sections of the quiz.

How to Interpret your Score

Chances are you checked some items in each category. To the degree that most everyone has five senses, everyone has some capacity for each of the relating styles. However, each individual will be more attuned to one or two of the relating styles. Examine your scores for each section. The relating style with the most points is your "primary relating style." This means that you prefer to communicate and receive affection through this style more than all the others. You are capable of giving and receiving affection through the other styles, but the ones you experience through your primary relating style will be the most meaningful to you and seem the most "natural" to you. Your second and third highest scores identify your secondary and tertiary relating styles, respectively. Affection given to you through these styles may or may not be appreciated, but regardless, they will be less meaningful to you than those presented to you in your primary style. Like Danny in the earlier example, even if you are given an abundance of affection in your secondary or tertiary style, your relationship with another family member could still break down if you are not receiving affection through the sense to which you are most attuned.

Some readers will wonder why, if these styles are really based on the five senses, there aren't five relating styles. The simple answer is that for most people, their senses of smell and taste are simply not as refined or as practical when it comes to communicating affection. For most folks, the olfactory and gustatory senses are secondary relating styles at best.

It is interesting to note that generally speaking, different relating styles tend to be dominant at certain ages. For example, the kinesthetic style is dominant up until around the second grade, at which time, due to the emphasis on developing reading and spelling skills, the visual sense begins receiving greater stimulation at school. Incidentally, this is also the grade where primarily kinesthetic kids begin being misdiagnosed as having Attention-Deficit Disorder (ADD). They are still trying to learn kinesthetically while the rest of the class has moved on. While ADD does exist and is a problem for some children, what these children need is practice with their visual learning skills, not drugs like Ritalin. This emphasis on visual learning continues until adolescence, when the auditory sense begins to express dominance in many people (as evidenced by the switch to a lecture format in high school and the teen's love affair with the phone). The reason we share all this is that it will be important not to pigeon-hole your children at a young age, saying "You are visual" or "You are kinesthetic." This may be true of your child today, but this may change tomorrow as their cognitive ability and neurological facility expands with greater experience and maturity. In adulthood, relating styles tend to be more static, but even there they can change dramatically over the years. (For more information on this last point, please see *For Better ... FOREVER!*)

In order to maintain rapport with all the members of your family, it will be important for you to become fluent in all the different languages spoken (i.e., relating styles expressed) by your mate and your children. It is not uncommon for one parent to have a great connection with one child, but feel completely out of sync with another. Often, this is due to mismatched relating styles. When this happens, arguments about the "right" way to approach tasks, the "right" timetables in which those things are to be done, and the "correct" perceptions to have about certain situations abound. The auditory child overloads her kinesthetic father with all her talk about "nonsense." "She never shuts up!" he complains. "He doesn't care enough about me to listen," she responds. If the mother is auditory as well, the father is in for a rough time, as the mother and daughter gang up on dad to lecture him about how he never talks about his feelings — and dad just gets quieter in response. He doesn't know what to say.

Likewise, the visual mother may fuss about her kinesthetic son's table manners or appearance. "Why do you have to be such a slob?!"

"I'm comfortable. I like being this way."

Both may pick at each other constantly about such things and think of the other as an idiot for being "concerned about stupid stuff" or "not caring about the most important things," depending upon their own perspective.

The only answer to such differences is realizing that if you love somebody and want them to know it, you must love them through their unique relating style, even if it makes no "sense" (literally) to you. Loving a person with a different relating style than your own will feel unnatural to you, and at first, it will take a sincere act of will and commitment to remember to follow through. However, if you do stick with it, the payoff is twofold. First, you will become more fluent in that other person's relating style, opening yourself to a whole new world of experiences and insights of which you were previously unaware. Second, as you become more fluent, the rapport between you and the other person will skyrocket. The following are some ways you can express love or care to a person with a particular relating style.

Increase Your Relating Style Fluency

Visual

Because people who are most proficient with the visual relating style tend to be most interested in things that *show* love, concentrate on more visual expressions of affection. For example, put a card in your child's lunch that says "I love you." Write a note or letter to your child telling him how proud you are of a particular accomplishment of his or how much he is maturing. Show your support for the more visual family members by actively helping keep the house clean and less cluttered (visual people feel ill at ease when their environment is disordered.) Sometimes, do work before fun, so the visual person can enjoy himself more when the fun comes. Encourage and support any artistic interests he or she may have. Sit down and plan a calendar of activities so that visual person doesn't feel lost or confused without his or her schedule. Give him or her a diary to encourage the writing or drawing of thoughts and feelings.

In short, do what you can to express affection in ways they can see, and do your best to keep your home orderly and regular.

Auditory

The easy answer to the question of how to love the more auditory members of your family is to talk and listen. Engage them in conversations. Listen attentively to their answers. Ask thought-provoking questions. Tell them how much you love them every day. Music is always a good gift — find out who their favorite groups are. Educate yourself so you can talk about these groups, or any other subject that interests them to show you care. Collect jokes and interesting stories. Try not to criticize them for talking too much. And respect their need to talk things out when stressed, or their need for quiet when they are super-stressed.

Kinesthetic

Kinesthetics tend to either be the most mellow or the most physically active members of the family. In either case, kinesthetics appreciate being quiet together and/or working on family project and hobbies. They thrive on physical affection. They also love presents that help them make their bodies feel good. For example, toiletries, exercise equipment, and similar gifts for the body-conscious. Be patient with their impulsiveness and spontaneity. Respect the fact that they are not and perhaps will never be fashion plates due to their value of comfort and practicality over appearance.

Regardless of your own relating style, you will benefit in many ways by learning to communicate more fluently with the other members of your family through their. Relating styles are much more adaptable than most people tend to think at first. It would be a mistake to believe, "I AM visual (or auditory, or kinesthetic), and that's that." It is more true to say that you prefer to communicate and relate visually, but because God gave you five senses, you have untapped potential to express yourself through all the other styles as well. It takes some effort, but it is worth it. The payoff is a more harmonious home-life and a more well-rounded personality as you open yourself up to new experiences, and those experiences make you a more vital, attentive, and joyful person.

Affection is the fuel that makes a family run well. Practice the eleven basic affection strategies and challenge your own ability to be "multi-lingual" when it comes to relating styles. By working to give more of yourself for the good of each family member and encouraging your children to do the same, you will be well on your way to creating the "civilization of love" Catholic families are called to be.

Now let's examine what it takes to build a practical and effective discipline program on top of this foundation of parent-child rapport.

Chapter Two

We Are F. A. M. I. L. Y. —
Daring to Discipline the Catholic Way

Now that we've given you some basic ways to maintain the strength of your family relationships, it's time to talk about discipline. Specifically, we want to answer the question: "How can I develop a system of discipline that is firm and effective, but at the same time protects the intimate relationship the Church asks me to build with my child?" This is more than an impossible mission, and finding practical answers to this question has far-reaching effects, especially for your children's future adult relationships. For example, in my marriage book *For Better ... FOREVER!* I talk about those exceptional couples whose arguments do not feel like boxing matches so much as they do deep-muscle massages, in that they may be uncomfortable while the couple is going through them, but they leave the relationship more intimate and more flexible afterward. Ideally, the training for such mature arguing begins in childhood. When a child grows up under the mature, firm, but compassionate discipline system we will outline in the next few chapters, he will be more likely be able to handle marital and relational conflict in a similar mature, firm, and compassionate manner as an adult. We know this because couples who naturally gravitate toward this "deep-muscle massage" style of arguing report being parented in a manner similar to what we will describe, and they credit their ability to do this to the way their parents treated them.

As we begin our mission of developing a method of discipline that will enable your family to experience "a respect for others, a sense of justice, cordial openness, dialogue, generous service, solidarity, and all the other values which help people live life as a gift" ("Gospel of Life"), we need to explore the differences between discipline and punishment. Most people use the terms "discipline" and "punishment" interchangeably, but in fact they refer to two completely different things. This isn't merely psychological hair-splitting on our part. The words themselves have different origins and meanings. "Punishment" comes from the Latin *punire*, which means "to inflict pain," while "discipline" comes from *discipuli*, the word for "student." ("Now class, let's practice our conjugations! *Amo, amas, amat....*") As the etymology suggests, discipline assumes a teacher/student relationship, while punishment assumes a police/suspect relationship. In the words of Fr. Leo Trese, the late but well-known Catholic apologist and child psychologist, "Many persons confuse discipline with punishment but the two words are not synonyms. Punishment is a tool which is sometimes used in the exercise of discipline, but it is one of the lesser tools. Discipline takes in a much wider field than punishment." Like salt in a cake recipe, punishment may play a limited role in effective discipline, but it cannot be the main ingredient.

Parents with a punitive mindset tend to define their primary job as "stopping bad behavior." Such parents — though perhaps well-intentioned — find themselves spending significantly less time teaching their children Christian virtues, self-control, and appropriate behavior, than they spend trying to come up with ever-more-creative punishments to get their children to stop behaving badly. Or, alternatively, these parents are forced to obsessively seek out more and more creative ways to shield their children from the world, often suffocating them in the process. One such set of parents once brought their thirteen-year-old daughter, Allison, to me for counseling. She was incorrigible, to be sure, but in response to her offenses, her parents had virtually kept her a prisoner in the house for going on six months, and it still wasn't working! Allison was becoming even more disrespectful as time went by and was sneaking out of her bedroom window two or three times a week.

In contrast to punishment, effective discipline is an entirely different animal. Represented by the acronym F. A. M. I. L. Y., the following summarizes the six reasons why discipline is superior to punishment. Discipline allows parents to:

F = Focus on a vision (not mere correction)
A = Act proactively (not reactively)
M = Make your relationship the agent of change (not manipulation)
I = Imitate Christ's way to "command" obedience
L = Look for ways to train the will, not break it
Y = (Say) "Yes" to methods that increase internal control.

Ready to take a closer look? Let's go!

Focus On a Vision

Effective discipline requires parents to have a vision; or if you prefer, a lesson plan for the values you wish to teach your children. To this end, we encourage families to develop a "family identity-statement," an enumerated list of the values, virtues, and ideals that are most important to your family accompanied by specific suggestions for how to practice those qualities in your daily lives together. Through baptism, every Christian is given a "mission from God" (as the Blues Brothers put it) to live out Christian virtues in their own unique way. A family identity-statement (also called a family mission-statement) helps each member of the family support the others in clarifying and fulfilling the purpose of their lives.

On the following pages, we'll examine the five benefits your family can receive by creating a family-identity statement, and you'll be given a chance to develop one o fyour own. Let's look at those benefits now.

The Five Benefits

1. It will give you, the parent, a lesson plan to follow in your work to build a family that not only avoids problem behavior, but also exhibits virtue and moral strength.

When John Paul II challenges families to practice "solidarity," he's not asking us to house Polish workers in our basements. We believe he is calling families — children and their parents — to help each other grow in holiness, to work together daily to practice the values, virtues, and ideals that were imprinted on our hearts at baptism. The whole point of the sacraments, most of all the Sacrament of Marriage on which the family is founded, is to help us bring the virtues God shares with us at baptism into everyday life.

Looking back on my own Catholic education, I am sad to say that sometime around confirmation, I learned the list of virtues (for example, the twelve fruits of the Holy Spirit) that I was supposed to practice in my Christian walk. I say that this was "sad" because I only memorized a list. I never really understood the significance of things like "piety," "counsel," or "fear of the Lord," much less did I have any clue what any of these qualities had to do with everyday life. I figured it was enough to "try to be the kind of person Jesus wanted me to be." But without a proper understanding of those "technical-sounding" virtues, I found that I lacked a blueprint for what being the kind of person Jesus wants me to be really meant in certain circumstances. By working together as a family to develop and live out a family mission-statement, not only will your children learn to identify Christian values and virtues, but they will also understand what they look like in daily life.

Many families very often have only one goal in mind: "Please God, help us make it through the day without anyone killing anyone else — or the dog." But when a family develops an identity statement, it helps get them out of crisis mode, and allows each family member to concentrate on building character, as opposed to merely putting out fires.

2. It will help your child develop internal control (the ability to do the right thing on one's own rather than because of fear of punishment).

A family mission-statement helps children develop internal control by giving them specific virtues against which to check their own behavior. For example, when our young children begin snapping at each other or fighting over a toy, we will remind them that "our family works to make kind and loving choices." While they sometimes need a little extra help clarifying what this means, it is amazing to watch how creative they can be finding solutions to their own problems given simple parameters like these.

I recall one time in particular when our son came downstairs to tell me that he and his sister were fighting over who got to use a particular toy. I listened to him explain his frustration and then said, "It sounds like this is a really tough problem you've got. Can I make a suggestion?"

Son: "Yeah?"

Greg: "You may handle this problem however you choose. But whatever choice you make you must remember to be generous."

Son: "Can't you just go upstairs and yell at her?"

Greg: "Well, I could. But I think you're big enough to figure this out for yourself."

He looked disappointed that I wasn't going to solve this for him, but he knew what being generous meant, and he knew he was expected to be it. How, specifically, he chose to manifest that generosity was entirely up to him, but that he would be generous was not debatable. I kissed him and he went upstairs. Keeping an ear out, I heard him tell his sister that she could play with the toy first, but that she had to "be generous too and give me a turn when I ask." Not only did his — at the time — two-and-a-half-year-old sister agree, she actually followed through when he reminded her of their deal ten minutes later.

If I had solved this problem for them, they would have continued to rely on my wife or me to be their arbitrator every time they had a problem. On the other hand, I couldn't just ignore the situation and leave my children completely to their own devices. They might have clobbered each other. By requiring our children to solve their own problems within certain parameters that Lisa and I set and supervise, we are not only teaching them the virtues that would be useful in a given circumstance, we are encouraging their creativity and the development of their own moral consciences.

3. It reminds you that family life is first and foremost a spiritual endeavor, empowered by the Sacrament of Marriage to play a role in the perfection of each family member (parents included).

Thinking of family life as a spiritual exercise does not require you to be some kind of super-pious person with a fourteen-foot neon crucifix in your family room (unless you were wondering what to do with that space over the sofa...). It simply means that as Christians, we need to be aware that we are preparing for something bigger than this world and that we should use whatever circumstances we are given to prepare ourselves.

Not so long ago, I had a Catholic family in therapy, and I helped them develop a family mission-statement. A few weeks later the father gave me the following feedback: "I've always been active in our parish community, but I don't think I realized how much I could grow, spiritually, in my family. I've tended to think of my family obligations as something that distracted me from my spiritual life, but this 'family identity-statement' thing has helped me begin to see that family life is my spiritual life."

The whole point of prayer is to grow closer to God, to learn to participate more fully in God's grace. By developing a family mission-statement, parenting to it, and living it out in your own life, you begin to see that each interaction between family members is another opportunity to grow in grace — from taking out the trash to playing video games with the kids. It allows you to experience up close and personal what it means to worship in the "domestic church."

4. It will make your family work more closely as a team. Each family member will come to see the family as providing the greatest opportunity to become the people God wants them to be when they grow up.

In a family, everyone's behavior affects everyone else's behavior. Usually, this happens for the worse. Little Smedley is fighting with his sister, Brunhilda, over who gets to shave the dog's head first. This irritates mom, who yells at dad, who yells at everyone, and so on, and so on. Wouldn't it be nice if, for a change, you could all influence each other for the good? When you have a family identity-statement, you can do just that.

Marylin, a former client, shared this story with me. It seems that she was trying to get her children to practice being more sensitive to others' feelings. "I heard the kids arguing in the other room about something. I was just about to go in when I heard Emily [age eight] say, 'Hey! We're supposed to make loving choices.'

"Things got quiet for a few minutes, which had me wondering what they were up to. I went down the hall to check up on them and there they were playing as nice as could be. I asked them if everyone was okay and James [age ten] said, 'Me and Emily wanted to build our puzzle but MaryBeth [age five] wanted to play too, so we decided to play school 'cause she could play and that would be a more loving choice, right, Mom?' "

Marylin told me, "I nearly fell on the floor. It made me feel so good to find them playing that way. I told them how proud I was of them for working so well together. And it made me feel like maybe I was doing something right for a change."

Another way an identity statement helps your family become a team is by establishing house rules for everyone, including the parents. The Cirrillos (not their real name) were coming for family therapy. One of several issues they were discussing was the daughter's lack of respect when talking to her parents. When the father confronted her about this in session, she retorted, "You don't speak respectfully to me, either!" At first, the parents were understandably irritated by this outburst, but after the daughter explained herself, they had to admit that, in fact, no one in the family had been being very respectful for a fairly long time.

In that session, the Cirillos added the following to their mission statement: "We are a family that speaks and acts respectfully toward one another." Additionally, the family talked about ways that they could — respectfully — keep each other on-task when one or the other of them returned to less considerate ways. Over the next few weeks, the family made steady progress. As the mother put it, "We've each caught ourselves being less than kind to each other, and each time, we've made a consistent effort to do better. I think the kids appreciate that Jim [the father] and I are being accountable for our own behavior — at least they can't use the 'you-don't-do-it, why-should-I' excuse — and I know that they have been trying harder too. I think all of us working on it together has been helpful. I guess whenever you work cooperatively on anything, it's easier to get the job done."

Working together to "get the job done," especially when the job is growing in virtue, is the essence to the family solidarity which John Paul II calls families to exercise. A Catholic family needs to be a team whose primary job it is to support each other in "running the race," as St. Paul put it, so that each member of the family win the crown of eternal life.

We are aware that some parents bristle at the idea of letting their children call them on certain character flaws. But we have found that this is often because these parents confuse power with proper parental authority. In administering justice in our homes, parents do have dominion over children, but this is different from power. John Paul II defined the difference between authority and power when he wrote, "Man's lordship is not absolute ... [it is] ministerial: it is a real reflection of the unique and infinite lordship of God. Hence man must exercise it with wisdom and love, sharing in the boundless wisdom and love of God" ("Gospel of Life").

Power is absolute; doing what it does, "because I can," but Christian authority acts with love; a sincere desire to will and work for the good of another. When parents work to set and safeguard the values and ideals their family stands for, they are exercising proper parental authority. When safeguarding these values and ideals includes a willingness to subject oneself to the same, even at the risk of one's own pride, then parental authority is being exercised "with wisdom and love."

5. It increases gratitude.

As you work together to fulfill your family identity-statement, you will become more and more grateful for each other's influence, learning to appreciate even the struggles as opportunities to grow in personal strength, family solidarity, and intimacy.

After her car accident, Jennifer, the mother of four, was laid up for several weeks. Though this was a difficult time for all concerned, the family spent time talking about how their mission to be "a family that practices love, service, and joy together" required them to respond to these circumstances. As Jennifer later said, "I would never want to go through anything like that again, but the family really pulled together. My husband had the two youngest decorate my room with pictures of the family and with paper flowers, and they each made me a new get-well card every day. The walls were plastered with construction paper! Ed [her husband] and the all the kids — especially the older ones — talked every day about the chores that needed to be done and made sure to do them. My son even volunteered to ask the coach for some time off from basketball practice to help more around the house. Of course we told him not to, but I was genuinely touched by his offer. It might sound strange, but I came out of that whole, terrible time feeling kind of grateful; it really showed me what this family is capable of."

Having a family identity-statement turns your family into a team that has something to aspire to on a daily basis and rally around in times of crisis. In *For Better ... FOREVER!* I wrote that the secret to a successful marriage is believing that you have a better chance with your mate than without him or her, of becoming the person God wants you to be at the end of your life. The same goes for family. When a family is functioning as God intends it to function, then each person is able to say that, on a daily basis, he is becoming more of the person God wants him to be because of each other's influence. If this is true about your family, then you have something for which to be extraordinarily grateful. If you cannot say this about your family, then designing your family identity-statement is a good place to start.

The "Fostering Family Identity" exercise, on pages 62-64 marks the beginning of your family identity-statement, but it is just the beginning. You should revisit it frequently to check your progress and add new challenges as you achieve your earlier goals. Post your mission statement somewhere prominent in your home so that everyone in the family will have an ongoing reminder of the goals you are working toward.

Now that you have a clearer sense of your own family identity (the "F" in our F. A. M. I. L. Y. acronym), let's consider the remaining five differences between discipline and punishment.

Act Proactively, Not Reactively

Parents must constantly fight the temptation to practice what we call "*Ex Post Facto* Parenting." This is a parent's temptation to leave our children to their own devices until there is a problem, at which point we go into crisis/punishment mode trying to solve a now-intractable problem that could have been prevented had we only been paying attention in the first place.

Allow us to use an almost universal example to illustrate the difference between proactive discipline and reactive punishment. Let's say your child never brings home assignments from school, but when you ask, he says he's doing "great" in all his classes. Because you are busy attending to other things in life that happen to be going wrong at the moment, you decide to take him at his word despite lack of any supportive evidence. Then one day, report cards come home and the results are something about ten-thousand miles south of "great." All of a sudden you feel shocked — *shocked* — that your little angel would not only be so irresponsible, but also could be either so clueless or deceitful about it. Then you dust off parent lecture #573 ("You are a very intelligent young man, but you need to apply yourself if you want to get anywhere in life..."), ground him for a couple of weeks, and hope for the best. Of course, this rarely works. Fortunately, there is an alternative.

The more proactive, discipline-oriented approach would be to address the problem early on. Rather than saying, "Johnny says things are going fine, and so there isn't any reason for me to get involved," the effective disciplinarian realizes that when a child isn't bringing home assignments the real problem is that by not bringing his books home (a) the child isn't acting responsibly, and (b) there is inevitably going to be a breakdown communication between the parent and teacher. That Johnny is or is not doing well in class is entirely beside the point. Effective discipline in this case would require the parents to both do what was necessary to help the child behave more responsibly (i.e., bring home assignments) regardless of his actual school performance (after all, education isn't just about getting the grades to get by, is it?) and find ways to stay in touch with the teacher. By handling the problem this way, Johnny learns that you are paying atten-

Fostering Family Identity: An Exercise

Use the following steps to develop your family mission-statement. Don't try to do it all in one sitting. Take your time and thoughtfully consider the input of all family members. I would encourage you to work through these questions over the course of several family meetings.

1. Take some time to talk about the virtues each of you was given at baptism, as well as other qualities you consider to be closely identified with the Christian walk. The qualities listed below are a good place to start:

The Theological Virtues
The three theological virtues are gifts God gives us to help us understand his own life and makes it possible for His life to be intertwined with ours.

Faith: A free gift from God that allows you to be aware of His presence in your life and invites you to want Him to become a greater part of your life.

Hope: Confidence that God will never abandon you or forsake you because neither death, nor life, nor any living creature, nor circumstance can come between you and God's love.

Love: Your willingness to work for the good of another, whether or not you "feel like it." The greatest of all virtues, practicing this empowers you to act as God Himself acts.

The Cardinal Virtues
From the Latin word for "hinge" (*cardine*) these are the four virtues on which our ability to lead solid, Christian lives hinge.

Prudence: The practical "know-how" that helps you apply all the Christian virtues to the specific circumstances of your everyday life.

Justice: Your desire to help others achieve all that God wants them to have; and your personal commitment to work for the common good of your family, Church, and community.

Temperance: Your ability to enjoy good things without letting them become a distraction or obsession.

Courage: (a.k.a. "fortitude") Your willingness to live Christian virtues even when doing so causes you to risk personal discomfort, or rejection/persecution from others.

The Twelve Fruits of the Holy Spirit

These qualities especially are the ideals every Christian family wants to encourage and nurture in their home-life:

Charity ("self-donative love") ... Joy ... Peace ... Patience ... Kindness ... Goodness ... Generosity ... Gentleness ... Faithfulness ... Modesty ... Self-control ... Chastity.

Other Virtues of Value

Solidarity (being a team/being willing to make sacrifices in your pursuit of a common goal.) ... Hospitality ... Openness ... Knowledge ... Creativity ... Respect ... Intimacy ... Obedience ... Service Attentiveness ... Wisdom ... Understanding/compassion ... Counsel/support ... Fear of the Lord (joyful awe and respect of God's goodness and power) ... Piety (an acknowledgement of the respect we owe God — and things sacred — throughout our day.)

List others here:

_____

_____

2. Which of the virtues listed above does your family do well? Feel free to list several. As you consider this, invite each family member to offer examples of how he or she witnessed those virtues in the family. Complete the following statement: Dad/Mom/Brother/Sister, you really showed (virtue) when you:

_____

_____

3. Which virtues are confusing or disturbing to you? How will you learn more about them so you can be sure that you aren't missing out on an important aspect of the Christian walk?

_____

_____

4. Which virtues do you consider desirable, but your family needs more practice with? List as many as you like:

_____

_____

Discuss the following questions about the virtues you listed above:

1. What specific situations in your family life would benefit from your practicing these virtues?

2. If you were to practice these virtues in your family life, what would each of you need to do differently?

3. How can you support each other in your struggle to exhibit these behaviors?

4. How will you respectfully keep each other on task when you revert to your old ways (both parents and children)?

5. Imagine the family you could become if you exhibited these virtues on a consistent basis. How would you feel about belonging to such a family?

6. Complete the following:
We, the _____ family, are pledging to work together to grow in _____ (list virtues here).
We promise to help each other practice these virtues by making the following choices on a daily basis:
(List answers to question #3 here.)

_____
_____
_____
_____
_____
_____
_____
_____
_____
_____
_____
_____

tion, and that his school responsibilities are not restricted to maintaining good grades, but also include facilitating communication between his teacher and his parents. This approach also circumvents what I call "R. C. S. S.," or "Report Card Surprise Syndrome," which afflicts most American homes at one point or another.

Parenting must be about more than stopping eruptions of bad behavior. We can't think of ourselves as firemen who are only activated when the house is burning down. An effective parent, especially an effective Catholic parent, is more like a wise ship's captain, who knows that as soon as you let go of the helm, especially in a storm, you should expect trouble. Not because the ship is "bad," mind you, but because the ship, being what it is, needs continuous guidance to get it to go where you want it to go. We are not suggesting that you should attempt to control every aspect of your child's life, far from it; but more than simply putting out fires, it is the effective Catholic parent's job to keep the family on course, moving each member, yourself included, toward your destination — perfection in love. Stopping bad behavior is parenting at its most basic and least rewarding — like plugging leaks on your ship. To be effective Catholic parents, we must work to be aware of the virtues we and our children need to practice the most and then look for opportunities to practice those virtues — like making sure the ship stays seaworthy in the first place. Instead of waiting for little Hildegarde to show us how irresponsible she can be, we want to give her a million ways every week to practice responsibility. Instead of yelling at our children when they don't share well, we look to manufacture a million opportunities for them to practice sharing and then reward them for a job well done. Instead of screaming "Why can't you people just get along for a change?!" and then sending everyone to their rooms after an optional paddling, we want to create opportunities in which the children can practice getting along well, and we want to positively comment on each time the children spontaneously get along well. This lets the children know we are paying attention, and it encourages them to work to please us because they know we can be pleased. Likewise, when our own children (or the child of a client) persist in an undesirable behavior, rather than punishing him more and more severely for that behavior, we are first going to try to find out what he is trying to accomplish by doing that obnoxious thing. Does he not know how else to get his sister's attention? Does he not know how to vent his frustration or anger in an appropriate way? Does he gain some reward by doing this irritating thing? Once you know the intention behind an obnoxious behavior, you can teach your child a more respectful and hopefully more efficient way to meet his intention or need. Discovering the intention or need which underlies an undesirable behavior is not meant to excuse the behavior. It is simply the first step in changing it.

If punishment is mostly concerned with stopping bad behavior once it starts, the cardinal rule of good discipline is that it is nine billion times more important to teach a child what to do in the first place than it is to teach them what to stop doing.

Make Your Relationship the Agent of Change — Not Manipulation

Discipline means knowing how to trade on your strong relationship with a child to inspire good behavior, but parents with a more punitive mindset are always looking for the next technique or punishment that can make their children behave. What such parents do not learn, often until it is too late, is that you cannot manipulate good behavior out of your child — at least not for long. Once, a woman brought her teenaged daughter to counseling. Exasperated, she said, "I don't know what else to do. I've used every lecture, she's been grounded for going on four months, and I've taken away every privilege except air." Knowing that the key to compliance is strong attachment and good rapport with a child, I asked this mother to tell me what she and her daughter did together that was pleasant or interesting. She looked at me as if an alien baby had suddenly burst out of my chest. "We fight. And when we're not fighting, we stand around waiting for the next argument. I can't honestly say that there's anything else we do *except* yell at each other."

Effective discipline requires you to think of your relationship with a child as if it were an emotional bank-account. When you compliment your children, "catch them being good," spend enjoyable times together, work together on family projects and chores, show interest in their lives and games, and engage in other similar rapport-building activities, you make deposits into the emotional bank-account you have with your children. When you correct them, challenge them, ask them to change, or criticize them, you make withdrawals. Its okay to make withdrawals, that is what the "money" is there for after all, but it is important that you not withdraw so much that you overextend your credit, and damage your credibility with your children.

As Fr. Flanagan wrote, "Finding fault with a boy, criticizing him, and constantly reminding him at home of his mistakes will never improve his condition. But if you encourage him, praising him for the little signs of improvement you see in him, he will soon begin to think he is not so bad after all, and it will give him greater incentive to try harder and harder."

As we suggested in the last chapter, good discipline requires us to build a relationship that is so strong and loving with our children that they would be loathe to do anything to risk the intimacy they share with us, just like the father of the prodigal son did upon his son's return. As parents, we need to shun the police/suspect relationship that a more technique-oriented, punitive mindset leads to, and instead embrace the intimate teacher/student relationship to which Christ and His Church call us.

Imitate Christ's Way to Command Obedience

In the introduction you saw the difference between Christian obedience, which is based on self-donative service, and blind obedience, which is based on fear. Punishment/technique-oriented parenting tends to increase blind obedience on the part of children ("I won't do [insert inappropriate behavior here] for fear of what my parents will do to me.") Effective discipline, on the other hand, seeks to command obedience by strengthening relationship.

Alex and Marylin had a seven-year-old son who was giving them an especially hard time when it came to back-talking. On their own, the parents had tried "everything," from sending him to time-out, to lecturing, to — as of late — washing his mouth out with soap, and even spanking him once or twice. One particularly bad day, the son absolutely refused to do anything his parents asked and even called the mother a few names. Rightly, they sent him to his room after this outburst, but that evening in session with me, the parents asked me what they might do to stop the behavior, as opposed to merely punishing it.

I suggested the parents do the following. First, because the mother was tired of handling this crisis on a day-to-day basis, I suggested the father take his son out for breakfast the following morning, at which time the father was to simply tell his son how his son's behavior was making him feel about him, assess what his son was trying to accomplish by the behavior, and, based on the information he got, discuss specific things the son could do to meet this intention more respectfully.

The next morning, over breakfast, the father began — not to lecture his son as usual — but to really talk. As the father later told me, "I told him how much I loved him, but I also told him how much his behavior was letting me down. I talked about how, when he was a baby, I was sure I would always be proud of him no matter what, but that lately, I was so sad to actually find myself being ashamed that he was my son. I started to cry then and he looked shocked. I told him that if I, or his mother, did anything to make him think that the only way to get through to us was to be disrespectful, then we were sorry, but that it had to stop now.

"He actually came over and hugged me. He said that when we punished him he thought we were just being mean. He didn't realize he was actually hurting us by the things he did. He started to cry too, and we talked about the ways he needed to talk to us when he was angry or frustrated with the things we asked him to do. He also said that sometimes when we asked him to do things, or corrected him, he felt like we didn't love him. He said he knew we did, but he just sometimes didn't feel it. I told him that if he ever felt that way, instead of yelling or talking back to us, he should ask us 'Do you love me?' or ask for a hug. I explained that we weren't going to let him off the hook for doing what we asked, but that I understood how everybody needs a little reassurance now and then.

"He really surprised me with the mature way he responded to all this. I won't say that he became perfect overnight, but with reminders here and there, his behavior improved one hundred percent almost immediately. As I see it now, I really underestimated his desire to do good. I used to think that all kids were just brats and you needed to stay on top of them. Of course, you do need to stay on top of things, but I think I understand better how to do it like an attentive teacher would, as opposed to the way a policeman would."

By taking time with his son, showing his true feelings about his son's behavior instead of merely lecturing the boy, and taking time to listen to what the child needed from his parents to do better (the reassurance of their love even when they were angry or critical of him), Alex learned that the key to good discipline was constantly working to build a stronger and stronger relationship. He learned by experience that before he could make a large withdrawal from his son's emotional bank-account by asking him to change his behavior, he had to make an equally large deposit by putting in the time, the willingness to share his genuine feelings, and the willingness to listen. And he learned that — though he was initially suspicious — his investment was a wise one.

Look for Ways to Train the Will, Not Break It

A parent with a more punitive mindset tends to view misbehavior as an expression of the innate badness or the manipulativeness of children. Considering this view, it is understandable why some parents might seek to break their children's will, dismissing a child's various needs out of hand as being mere attempts to manipulate the parent. The baby crying at night must be ignored, or the misbehaving child must be decisively punished, so that he will know he can't get one over on the parent. But this attitude is inconsistent with the more optimistic view of the will held by the Church. Further, you may recall from the introduction that children raised by parents who held this pessimistic view of their children's will and nature were more likely to grow up to fall prey to evil influences (e.g., Nazi collaborators and bystanders in the Holocaust). Considering this, it would seem to us that this attitude would be something we Catholics would do well to avoid in the future.

While the will can certainly be stubborn and must be trained, we believe that based on the Church's remarkably positive opinion of our personhood, that the Catholic response to the will is to respect it and teach it more appropriate ways to meets its intentions. A police officer might not care a fig for the positive intention behind a criminal's behavior (that's really not his job, after all) but a good teacher is always concerned with discovering the intentions behind obnoxious, immature behavior and teaching more appropriate, godly, and efficient alternatives. Which role would you rather play with your children? Or perhaps more importantly, which role do you think is more consistent with the Catholic call to practice self-donative love?

(Say) "Yes" to Methods that Increase Internal Control

Internal control is a technical term that really refers to building a child's own conscience. Certain parenting methods contribute to healthy conscience formation, while others definitely detract from it, despite the intentions of the parents using them.

The more you use punitive methods with a child (lecturing, removing privileges, spanking, grounding, screaming, etc.) the more you set yourself up as your child's conscience, so he or she never learns to develop his or her own. This is not to say that there won't be times when some of these more punitive methods (e.g., grounding, rescinding privileges, and perhaps the occasional lecture) may be appropriately used. We are simply suggesting — to refer to a metaphor we used earlier — that when you're baking a cake, you don't want to use too much salt in the batter.

The discipline methods you will read about in this book are primarily concerned with teaching a child to exercise and develop his own, strong sense of right and wrong so that even when he or she is without you, he or she will be able to stand up for what is right. As child psychologist and Catholic apologist Fr. Leo Trese wrote, "The ultimate fruit of discipline is self-discipline."

When our son was six he had an experience that made us feel especially proud of him, and we believe it serves as a good example of what we mean by internal control. If you don't mind, we'd like to share it with you.

Lisa recently took our kids to one of those places inspired by those things you put a pet gerbil in when you were a kid (no, not your sister's underwear drawer). You know, those popular indoor playgrounds with plastic tubes, ball-rooms, climbing nets, slides, and the like. Human Habitrails — as it were.

Anyway, our son disappeared inside one of these things for over an hour and when he finally emerged — all sweaty and jazzed on adrenaline — my wife asked him if he was having fun.

Son: "Yeah. Guess what?"

Lisa: "What, honey?"

Son: "We [he and the other human gerbils] had a club, and every room was for doing a different thing."

Lisa: "Really? Like what?"

Son: "We had a singing room, and a screaming room. And there was an S.W. room."

Lisa: "What's an S.W. room?"

Son: "The 'swear words' room."

Lisa: (gulp) "A swear words room?"

Son: "Yea, but I didn't want to go in, so I started an N.W. room."

Lisa: (fearing the answer) "What's that?"

Son: "A 'nice words room' where we could sit and tell stories, but only using nice words. And anybody who wanted to be with me had to only use nice words in my room."

Lisa: "And did anybody want to be with you?"

Son: "Oh, yeah. I started telling my stories and then everybody wanted to be with me and I wouldn't let 'em in until they promised to use nice words, and they said 'okay' and we all told stories and played and stuff."

Lisa: "Really?"

Son: "Uh, huh. And the boy who had the S.W. room wanted to play with us but we wouldn't let him, so he said 'I'll only use nice words' so we let him play too."

Lisa: (giving him a kiss on the cheek) "I'm really proud of you."

Son: "Uh, huh. Thanks. Can I play some more?"

As we demonstrated earlier, some very well-meaning parents trip all over themselves trying to come up with ever more creative punishments and ever more restrictive environments to control their children's behavior. Eventually these punitive strategies wear thin and children become sneaky and deceptive in an attempt to "get one over" on mom and dad. But because effective discipline strategies rely less on an exterior scaffolding (the fear of punishment) than on an interior structure (the child's conscience) to uphold a child's moral character, compliance is more likely and more consistent, even when the parent is not around to make it so. Admittedly, discipline strategies are not nearly as flashy as their more punitive cousins. But they work better — so what's to complain about?

Now that you have a clearer idea of the goals your family is working toward, we invite your to join us in discovering the powerful educational tools that every Catholic parent can use to teach the lessons that must be taught in the "school of love" that is your family.

Chapter Three

Tools of the Trade: Everyday Discipline That Makes a Difference

In the last chapter, we examined how, generally speaking, good Catholic discipline differs from mere punishment. In this chapter and the next, we are going to examine some of the actual techniques used by parents who view themselves as teachers in the family school of love (as opposed to wardens of the family pokey). For the sake of clarity, we have divided the list of discipline techniques into two categories: those which are relational and educational in nature (we'll cover these in this chapter), and those which are corrective in nature (which we'll cover in the next chapter).

Relational/educational discipline techniques are concerned with both strengthening the relationship parents have with their children (so that their advice/counsel will be accepted by the child) and proactively teaching the values and virtues parents want their children to exhibit.

The techniques we will present here are not flashy, but don't let their unassuming nature fool you. They are the most powerful change techniques available because they teach you how to use your very self to nurture growth and change in your children. In this sense, they rank high on the self-donative scale. In fact, many of the techniques you will learn here are similar to the way God uses the gift of Himself to constantly call us into a deeper, more powerfully transformative relationship with Him. They are drawn from my clinical training and practice, Lisa's experience as a teacher, our meditations on the "parenting style" of the Church in her sacraments, and the wisdom we have gained by listening to those parents who, many times over, have demonstrated remarkable effectiveness and rapport with their own children.

When You C. A. R. E. Enough to Parent Your Very Best

In the last chapter, the acronym F. A. M. I. L. Y. explained why discipline is superior to punishment. Now we want to review the four ways to making discipline truly effective. These four parenting "musts" are represented by the acronym **C. A. R. E.**

Consistency is key.
Acquire a firm but gentle style.
Remember not to lead your children into temptation.
Expect the best from yourself and your children.

Consistency is Key

Children become confused in the absence of consistency. To not have consistent rules, expectations, and consequences sets you up for future power struggles with your child. If everything is negotiable on a daily basis from bath times to homework to chores to "you name it," then the likelihood is that nothing will get done in an efficient manner and you will be forced to engage in a constant diet of "When are you going to get this done?" arguments. Fr. Flanagan once said, "When discipline is lax, or when it is applied in a haphazard manner so that the child doesn't know what to expect, parental authority breaks down and the child's mind is thrown into a state of chaotic confusion." Consequences too must be enforced consistently; otherwise children will never know whether to take you seriously when you correct them.

Likewise, it can be important to establish fairly regulated routines for when and how your family works together to get things like house-cleaning or homework done. For example: "Saturday mornings the family works together to get the house in order" or "After dinner is when our family does the homework/take-home office work/other educational activities together," or "Sunday is the day we do special family things together." Or even, "The family has a Scripture and catechism study for a half-an-hour on Tuesday evenings."

Establishing family routines and rituals establishes and maintains the importance of working together to build solidarity and fulfill your family identity-statement.

Acquire a Firm but Gentle Style

It is a parenting cliché to say that we must be both firm and gentle with our children, but well known as this statement is, it can be difficult for people to explain what it means in practice.

One way to conceptualize this balance is to say that the Christian values of love (i.e., willing and working for the good of another) and justice (giving a person all that is his due) require us to address our children's misdeeds, but to do so in the least offensive, most respectful, and most efficient manner possible. In other words, you shouldn't hunt rabbits with an elephant gun.

Take the following quizzes to see if you exercise enough of both qualities in your discipline style. Scoring follows both quizzes.

Scoring

If you scored six or more points in both categories, your discipline style most likely reflects a good balance between firmness and gentleness.

If you scored six or more points on firmness and five or less points on gentleness you may run the risk of coming across as a bully — or at least as

---

Firmness Quiz

Answer T (true) or F (false) to the following questions.

_____ I have high expectations for my children's behavior.

_____ Our house rules are clearly stated and consistently enforced.

_____ My children know that consequences will be enforced when they break the rules.

_____ I do not let my children argue me out of their consequences.

_____ It is less important to me that my children like what I say than that they comply with my request.

_____ I require my children to do chores/help around the house as much as their age and ability permits.

_____ My "yes" means "yes" and my "no" means "no."

_____ I am not threatened by my children's attempts to argue with me because I know that I am in control of the situation.

_____ I require my children to speak to me respectfully even when they are upset or frustrated.

_____ I am able to get my children to comply with my requests/rules even when they don't like them.

Give yourself one point for each true answer.

Firmness Quiz Score_____

Gentleness Quiz

_____ I am sensitive to my children's feelings.

_____ I listen respectfully to my children's opinions even when differ from my own.

_____ I show my children an abundance of affection daily.

_____ I encourage open dialog in my family.

_____ I am patient with my children's questions.

_____ I try to consider my children's age and capabilities when establishing rules and consequences.

_____ I actively look for ways to build up and encourage my children.

_____ I take pains to let my children know I love them even when I don't approve of their behavior.

_____ I take time every day to play with my children.

_____ I actively work to develop a close and loving relationship with my children.

Give yourself one point for every true answer.

Gentleness Quiz Score:_____

insensitive — to your children. This will only undermine your rapport and solidarity, decrease their compliance, and increase the number of power struggles you encounter over time. Be careful not to mistake mere power with true authority. Work on your ability to give affection to your children, to be respectful of their feelings, and to solicit their opinions even when they differ from your own. The payoff will be greater respect and compliance both now and in the future.

If you scored five or less points in firmness and six or more points on gentleness you may run the risk of being a doormat for your children. You may find yourself in never-ending, futile discussions with your children in which you try to convince them to see the value of your rules. You must learn that a child's approval is not a prerequisite for his or her compliance. Clarify your rules and consequences and stick to what you decide.

If you scored five or less points on both quizzes, you have some serious work to do. You may tend to treat parenting as a hobby, or as just another chore that you get to as you have time. Both you and your children deserve better. Do what you have to do to become an affectionate and deliberate (as opposed to merely reactive) parent.

Hopefully, this exercise gives you a clearer picture of what it means to be both firm and gentle. Good discipline is a balancing act. Whatever your scores on the quizzes, work to bring your capacity for both firmness and gentleness into equilibrium.

Remember Not to Lead Your Children into Temptation

In the Lord's Prayer, "… and lead us not into temptation" is our request for God to not give us any greater burden than we can handle, and to give us the grace we need to handle the burdens we currently carry. There is a lesson for parents in this.

A Christian parent must be careful not to give his or her child any greater responsibility than that child is developmentally capable of handling or has been trained to handle well. Case in point: Some parents recommend giving your toddler a smack on the bottom for running into the street or physically endangering himself in some way. On the surface this makes sense; after all, we don't want our children killing themselves. But the problem is that by not adequately understanding, respecting, or compensating for our toddler's developmental abilities, we sometimes lead our children into temptation and then punish them for accepting the invitation.

As parents, it is our job to avoid putting our children into situations they are simply incapable of handling. Toddlers try to run into the street because they are cognitively not able to consistently connect actions with consequences. But toddlers succeed at running into the street because a parent was asleep at the wheel. Think of it this way: If you were a shepherd, and you let one of your sheep get squished by an oncoming chariot, it wouldn't be the sheep that the master would be giving a whipping to that night — if, indeed, the master was going to whip anyone at all.

The only developmentally appropriate way to solve the toddler-running-in-the-street problem is to use the "hold hands or hold you" rule. This is where the toddler or younger child must either hold a parent's hand while he is walking out-of-doors, or be held by the parent. Period. The child doesn't have to like it, he just has to live by it until he has developed the ability to control his desire to run into the street. By practicing this rule, the parent sends the message to the child that "I know you think your legs are neat new toys — and they are — but you must learn to use them appropriately, and until you do, I am going to supervise you."

This intervention has worked extremely well with our own children as well as with those parents to whom we have recommended it. No doubt there are some readers who will think this is a bit over the top. But consider this: if a parent gave a child a BB gun, gave him no training or supervision in the use of that gun, and then punished that child for indiscriminately shooting things in the neighborhood, would you think well of that parent? If a father gave his child a car and let her drive it without a license or proper training, could he then justifiably punish his child for later wrapping the car around a telephone pole? Of course not. Chances are, if you ever met such a parent, you would say to yourself, "This parent is an idiot." (You know you would.) Why then, would any parent in his right mind give a toddler free and unlimited access to a mode of transportation as dangerous as legs? And then punish him for using them indiscriminately? By using the "hold hands or hold you" rule, the child learns to stick close to the parent, to walk with the same caution mom and dad use, and to develop the self-control necessary to "walk responsibly" — as it were. And, when the child is having problems with self-control, he or she knows that the parent is going to help them regain control by holding him or her — even if he or she doesn't like it. Again, to an adult, this may seem like much ado about nothing. But to the toddler, it communicates a deep level of respect. It says, "Mom and dad understand my needs and they want to help me learn how to use my feet."

Of course, all the stages of childhood are filled with examples like the above. We will attempt to help you develop a greater understanding of the developmental capabilities of your children in part two of this book. But for now, it is enough to know that as Christian parents, we are obliged to know what our children are capable of, and hold them responsible for that. No more, no less.

Expect the Best from Yourself and Your Children

Once we know what our children are capable of, we have a responsibility to expect our children to be the best they can be at that level. This is a delicate balance, but as parents, we are obliged to constantly seek it.

The way we try to find that balance in our own parenting adventures is by reading books on child development and by looking to other families we know and seeing what other children in the same age bracket as our own are capable of. We don't do this to keep up with the Joneses, we do it to make sure we are really expecting the most we can out of our "students" — our children. As their primary educators, we don't want to give them a shoddy formation.

When we see a child or family exhibiting a behavior or ritual we would like to practice in our own home, Lisa and I ask ourselves some important questions. For example: Is it possible to encourage this trait in our children at this stage of their lives by using loving, self-donative means only? (As opposed to smacking them around or verbally terrorizing them.) And, if it is possible to encourage this behavior or ritual through self-donative means only, what exactly do my wife and I have to do to make this possible? What investment of time would it take? What kind of supervision would it require? Is the outcome really worth the effort? Or would our energies be better spent elsewhere? By asking these questions, we find that we do not only require the best from our children, but we also constantly push ourselves to become better people by becoming better parents.

When we share this attitude toward parenting with others, sometimes we get an odd reaction: "Aren't you making parenting harder than it needs to be? Why do you have to think so much?" The fact is, Catholic parents have little choice but to think this much about their mission. The Church tells us that parents' "role as educators is so decisive that scarcely anything can compensate for their failure in it" (*Gravissimum Educationis*, no. 3). Likewise, Thoreau said that the key to success in life is to "live deliberately." This is true about parenting as well. To parent well, we must parent deliberately, constantly asking more of ourselves and our children. We do this, not because we're anal-retentive people who want our kids to be show ponies and our home to make Ozzie Nelson's look like Ozzie Osborne's, but because we're on a mission to activate the grace of marriage — on which the family stands — to help us and our children to become perfect as our Heavenly Father is perfect; perfect in love.

Discipline That Teaches and Builds Relationships

Having examined the four "musts" that serve as the foundation for a healthy attitude toward discipline, let's start looking at the first set of discipline techniques, those which proactively educate a child in virtue and build relationships which have the power to transform through love.

Technique One: Build Rapport

Though we have talked about the importance of parent-child rapport in general, the following is a good example of how building rapport itself is a powerful discipline technique.

In her book *Raising Catholic Children*, Mary Ann Kuharski, a mother of thirteen, tells the story of a family who was having a terrible time with a teenage son who was all but completely estranged from the family. They had tried "everything" and even went from counselor to counselor with no success, until they finally found one therapist who suggested that the first thing the parents needed to do was stop all verbal communication but increase the amount of physical affection they gave their son. As the mother told Ms. Kuharski:

> After two weeks of virtually forcing a daily hug I saw no real warmth or change.... Late one evening of the second week, however, he came up behind me while I was reading a newspaper.... I asked him what he was looking for. He shrugged and sheepishly said, 'Aren't you forgetting something?' (referring to the 'good night' hug I'd usually given him). It worked! When talking, screaming, crying, and nagging had done nothing but aggravate a hostile situation, a daily hug had melted hearts and broken down the barriers.

As you saw in this dramatic example, affection and rapport is everything. (Incidentally, I highly recommend Ms. Kuharski's book, especially chapter twenty, from which this story is taken.) We have also noticed that affection can be more attention-getting than yelling. Taking a younger child on your lap and correcting him quietly in his ear, or sitting down to a calm, intelligent conversation with an adolescent often has a surprisingly powerful impact on behavior, much more than screaming ever will.

When we talk about building relationship and rapport with your child, we want to make it abundantly clear that we are not suggesting that you become your children's buddy. Your children have plenty of friends. They need a teacher. Yes, they need a lovable, wise, affectionate, and even fun teacher, but they need a teacher nonetheless. Most of us can think of someone in our lives who has most closely mirrored Christ to us. A person whose wise counsel we have followed, and whose wisdom we respected. A person who generously gave of himself or herself, whom we would willingly follow to the ends of the earth. That is the kind of person our children need us to be to them. Affection and gentle, loving correction play an important role in helping us become such people.

Technique Two: Write It Down

One mother of six I counseled was having a hard time with her youngest three children. It seems that they were constantly breaking the house rules, and this mother was spending entirely too much time arguing with and yelling at them. After a few sessions, this mother had an important insight. "I just realized this week that the younger kids really don't know what the rules are. I used to be so conscientious about posting the house rules and teaching the kids what they were, but as the family got bigger, I just figured the little ones would learn that stuff by osmosis. Boy, was I wrong."

The following week, that mother did a very important thing. She sat down with her children in a family meeting, reviewed the rules and wrote them down on a piece of paper. Each member of the family (parents included — these were, after all, house rules) signed their names to the list, which included things like "speak respectfully to each other" and "do chores daily without being asked twice." Then she posted the paper on the refrigerator.

"It's funny," she told me later, "once I was clear about what I expected and I communicated that to everyone, things improved a lot. I still had to correct them sometimes, but they didn't act as surprised or hurt, because they knew where I was coming from."

In the book *How to Talk So Kids Will Listen and Listen So Kids Will Talk*, Faber and Mazlish offer a creative turn on this idea of writing down the rules. They suggest that when a parent needs to correct a child, or redirect inappropriate behavior, instead of doing it verbally, the parent should tell the child to "please go look at the rules list." This way the child learns what the rules are, learns when they most need to be followed, and learns to take responsibility for himself in applying the rules. This technique is the behavioral equivalent of asking your fifth-grade teacher how to spell a word and being told to "look it up."

Incidentally, Faber and Mazlish's technique works with pre-readers too. You just have to use pictures instead of words. For example, when our children were smaller, we had a rule, "no loud playing while mommy or daddy is on the phone." To reinforce this, we had the kids draw a picture of a phone, as well as symbols of all the things they could do — like draw, look at picture books, play in their rooms, etc. — while someone was on the phone. Then we posted this in the family room. Later, when the telephone rang, Lisa or I would say, "Kids, the phone's ringing, please look at the rule," and they would know what games they could and could not play for the next few minutes.

One of the primary reasons children misbehave is that parental expectations are not stated clearly enough. Make certain yours are.

Technique Three: Redirection

It is not enough to tell a child to stop doing something. We must offer suggestions for what a child can do instead of the inappropriate activity in which they are currently engaged. Redirection is a simple technique that forms the cornerstone of good daily discipline. Redirection allows parents to help kids learn to channel their youthfully indiscriminate energy into productive, respectful, and appropriate channels. When you see your child doing some unacceptable thing (say, running around the house screaming at the top of her lungs), give your child the choice to either do that thing in a more appropriate place ("Honey, if your want to use your outside voice, please go outside."), or offer suggestions for alternative things to do ("... Or if you'd prefer not to go outside, what could you do that would let you use an inside voice?")

There are several benefits to parents for using redirection as one of the more important tools of everyday discipline. First, it teaches your children to respect your needs, because you are constantly modeling respect for theirs. Second, it teaches your children to come to you when they can't figure out how to meet a need in an appropriate way. Redirection seems rather silly and mundane when applying it to the problems encountered in early childhood, but it sets a powerful precedent that allows your teenager who, having been respectfully redirected by you in a million ways over the last sixteen years or so, trusts you enough to come to you and say, "I really love Biff. And all my friends are saying that if I really love him, I should have sex with him, and honestly, I kinda want to. But I know that's not right, so what do I do with these feelings?"

Some people may think this is unrealistic, but we know parents to whom this exact thing has happened. It only happens in homes where a child's needs have been respected and, when necessary, redirected. It tends not to happen in homes where a child's needs or intentions have been ignored or denied; homes in which the child has experienced sixteen-plus years of interactions that look like this:

Child: (doing inappropriate thing)

Parent: "Knock it off!"

Child: "But I was trying to...."

Parent: "I don't care what you thought you were doing, I said stop!"

Child: "But...".

Parent: "I said NO! GO TO YOUR ROOM!"

Of course there are times when we must say no. Period. But most times it really is possible to help a child find the appropriate context to do the thing he wants to do or help the child find something he would enjoy doing that much more. It takes more effort, more self-gift, than the more simple, dramatic, fist-on-the-table, "NO!", but over the years, redirection is more effective, encourages a child to practice internal control, and builds relationship and communication between parents and their children.

Technique Four: Restating

When children say something in an obnoxious way, use the restating technique by asking them to rephrase their statement or ask them to repeat a more appropriate phrase that you suggest to them. For example:

Child: "Give me that toy!"

Parent: "Let's try that again."

Child: "I want that!"

Parent: "How about, 'May I have that, please?' "

Child: "May I have that, please?"

Parent: "Thank you. Much better."

Then, and only then, should you feel free to say "yes" or "no" to the original request. Just remember that just because they asked nicely does not mean that you must give them everything they ask for. For example:

Four-year-old: "But I want to use the chainsaw!"

Parent: "How about saying, 'May I use the chainsaw, please?' "

Child: "May I use the chainsaw, please?"

Parent: "Thank you for asking so nicely, but no, honey, you may not."

This is a silly example, but the intention is to show that asking nicely has absolutely nothing to do with your eventual choice to grant or deny the request. The child must learn to be respectful whether or not she thinks she is going to get anything out of it. Your child's "reward" for "asking nicely" is the approval and affection you give them for making a good choice. It is not giving in to every fool thing they ask for.

Technique Five: "Do-overs"

As kids, a "do-over" was what we would ask for when we blew it at bat and wanted another turn. There is a similar meaning here. Just like restating addresses inappropriate speech, a "do-over" addresses inappropriate behavior. For example:

Child: (Throws a toy at brother instead of handing it to him.)

Parent: "Please pick that up and hand it to your brother — GENTLY."

Child: (Complies.)

Parent: "Thank you. Now please say, 'I'm sorry for throwing.' "

A good "do-over" has two steps. First, tell the child what to do and how to do it (i.e., "gently," "more slowly," "carefully," or insert your own adverb here: _____). This helps a child learn specifically what you want and also helps him make an experiential connection with the specific qualities you are trying to teach (i.e., gentleness, care, attentiveness, etc.). Second, supervise the child as he or she works to fulfill the request to your satisfaction. Feel free to require a child to "do it over" as many times as necessary for him or her to meet your specifications. In considering whether to require your child to do something over more than once, remember that on the one hand, you shouldn't be superpicky, but you also shouldn't let your child get away with a less-than-sincere effort. Be gentle. Be firm. And use your discretion.

With redirection, restating, and do-overs, the trick is consistency. When you are trying to change some behavior in your child, you must have him practice a more appropriate alternative every time you catch him doing the inappropriate thing. This is the only way your child will get enough practice to change.

Technique Six: Choices

It is extremely important to teach your children that they are responsible for both the choices they make and the consequences that accompany those choices. The best way to do this is to present your rules in the form of a choice to your children.

For example:

You: "If you choose to not eat your meal then that means you are choosing not to have dessert."

Child: "But I want dessert!"

You: "Then you should choose to eat your meal. It's your decision."

Or:

You: "If you decide to continue this tantrum, that means you are choosing to leave your friend's house right now. If you decide to stop and calm down, I will be willing to listen to what you have to say. What's it going to be?"

Child: "No! I don't want to leave now!"

You: "Then what choice do you need to make?"

Child: (sniff) "I'll stop."

You: "Fine, now what can we do about this problem [that caused the tantrum]?"

Use this technique liberally whenever it looks like your child is making poor behavioral choices. First, it reminds the child of the consequences he is facing while he still has a chance to avoid them. Second, it reinforces the lesson that your child has complete power over the choices he makes and, ultimately, the consequences he experiences. Finally, in those times when you do actually have to enforce a consequence, you can use the experience to reinforce your child's sense of internal control. How? By saying to the child as he is pouting about the consequence, "I am very sorry you made this choice. If you are unhappy with your decision, please choose differently next time."

When parents do not use the choices technique, consequences can seem to come out of nowhere to some children. This pattern, repeated thousands of times over the life of a child, can create rebellious adolescents and passive, resentful, defensive adults. Alternatively, by using the choices technique, children learn that in life, consequences are what they are, and while there is little that can be done about that, a person does have the power to make choices that lead to pleasant consequences instead of unpleasant ones. This is the essence of internal control; knowing that one has the power to choose well or choose poorly and knowing the rewards or setbacks that accompany such decisions. Do your children — and yourself — a favor by teaching them the power of their choices to affect their happiness throughout life.

Technique Seven: Reviewing/Rehearsing

Before a test, a good teacher goes over all the information to make certain that there are no questions and that the students have a clear understanding of the information they are going to be tested on. It doesn't matter that the teacher has already taught this material and that the students "should know it"; the teacher wants the students to do well and so is willing to put in a little extra time to ensure their success.

In the same way, we must review the lessons of good behavior with our children, especially when we are putting them in a situation where they will be "tested." That is, where good behavior is especially important. For example, I once did a series of phone consultations with a mother who took her five-year-old, Chelsea, to story time at the local library. Unfortunately, the child was not used to sitting still and listening to stories. She wanted to jump about and play games while the librarian was reading, which caused no small amount of clucking from both the other mothers and the library staff. The mother was incensed at the adults' reactions: "What do they expect from a child?"

I acknowledged this mother's desire not to stifle her child's spirit, but I suggested that she was not doing her child any favors by approaching the problem this way. She was well within her rights not to take her child to such events if the expectations offended her sensibilities, but if she was going to take her daughter, she was also going to have to teach her the rules — or else she would set herself and Chelsea up for criticism by the other parents whose children who did play by the rules. Somewhat grudgingly, the mother saw my point. But under the circumstances, it wasn't going to be enough to tell Chelsea to sit still during story hour at the library. The mother was going to have to teach her daughter to do this at home first.

That week, the mother explained to Chelsea that they were going to practice sitting still so that they could go the next time. Each day, the mother sat reading with the child on her lap. For increasing periods of time each day, the mother and daughter rehearsed sitting still and listening to stories, until the daughter had more or less worked up to the amount of time story hour required. The following week at the library was a much better experience for all concerned. "She did beautifully," the mother told me. "I used to think it was unrealistic for a child to be expected to sit that long. I always figured the other parents must have had to beat their kids or something to get them to stay put, but now I see I was selling Chelsea short. She really could do it."

As another example, one family we know liked to eat out, so they taught and reinforced "restaurant manners" by rehearsing them at home, where the children could make mistakes without incurring the wrath of a watchful maître d'hôtel.

Of course, rehearsing could be as simple as reminding your kids — in the car — how to behave when Great-Aunt Bertha May serves them a heapin' helpin' of her famous kelp and tibuli pie. The point is this: Be a good teacher. Review and rehearse compliance with the rules before subject your kids to the test.

Technique Eight: Transitions

Due to their ability to get easily lost in their own worlds, children do not do well moving right from one thing into the other without any warning. Parents often set themselves up for a tantrum by walking in on their child in the middle of some activity and announcing, "Time to go!" or "Time for bed!" or "Okay, say goodbye to your friends!"

This is the mental equivalent of tying a rope around your kid's neck and jerking it really hard. It is a recipe for disaster. Next time, give your child fair warning. Tell her, "We're going to be leaving in ten minutes. Start thinking about cleaning up." Then give her five-minute, two-minute, and one-minute reminders. I used this technique once with a client's child, who went from throwing horrible tantrums when it was time to leave his friend's house to actually getting his shoes on — by his own choice — at the two-minute warning.

Though this approach seems a bit protracted and redundant to adults, it helps kids adjust slowly to a new thing, and teaches them to be better stewards of their time. Plus, it decreases the frequency of those public "I don't wanna!" tantrums. That alone is worth the price of admission.

Technique Nine: Be a Supermodel

You cannot underestimate the power and importance of modeling. Whether you want your children to be more polite, more respectful, more responsible, or more anything, you have to learn to do it on a daily basis yourself first, because you can't give what you don't have.

In a particularly moving passage of *Mere Christianity*, C.S. Lewis suggests that even God Himself is not exempt from the "can't give what you don't have rule." In his discussion on the necessity of the "atonement" (i.e., Jesus dying to "pay our debt"), Lewis notes that every quality we humans exhibit is directly "lent" to us from God's own Self. "When you teach a child writing, you hold its hand while it holds the letters: that is, it forms the letters because you are forming them. We love and reason because God loves and reasons and holds our hands while we do it."

But, says Lewis, after the fall, the one thing people needed to do to be saved was to surrender to God's perfect will. Unfortunately, considering our entire dependence upon Him for every good thing we do and are, we couldn't surrender, because nothing in God's nature allowed Him to surrender. God couldn't hold our hands while we did it, because God, being God, never had much call to surrender to anybody.

But supposing God became man — suppose our human nature, which can suffer and die, was amalgamated with God's nature in one person — then that person could help us. He could surrender His will, and suffer and die because He was man; and He could do it perfectly because He was God. You and I can go through the process only if God does it in us; but God can only do it if He becomes man. Our attempt at this dying [surrendering to God's will] will succeed only if we men share in God's dying, just as our thinking can succeed only because it is a drop out of the ocean of God's intelligence: but we cannot share in God's dying unless God dies; and He cannot die except by being man.
— C.S. Lewis, *Mere Christianity*

It would seem that, at least as far as C.S. Lewis was concerned, God has precious little use for "do what I say, not what I do" parenting models. Modeling, as a parenting technique, plays a significant role in our ability to access the transformative graces of marriage upon which family life stands, because modeling constantly calls us to challenge our own weaknesses and grow in our Christian identities. Further, it teaches our children — by our loving example — to share in that same process of surrender that defines the chief work of the Christian walk.

While every parent knows the importance of modeling good behavior to their children, you can also use modeling to correct obnoxious behavior. When your child uses unacceptable language, or demonstrates an unhealthy habit, or makes a questionable choice, ask yourself first, "Do I do that?"

Granted, you may not be given to jumping on the couch, calling the baby "dooty-head," or doing something more serious like blowing off your homework, or coming home drunk. But there are probably times when you did something similar; for example, times when you were disrespectful of your children's property (e.g., "Get this junk outta here!" as you kick the Lego pieces/ninja stars out from under your feet), called someone an unkind name, sat around watching TV when you should have been doing some chore, or even behaved in a more seriously irresponsible manner. Use these experiences. Ask your child to be your partner in overcoming these shared flaws. Call each other on them, share ideas about more respectful solutions. You can use these discussions as a springboard to address a host of issues. For

Supermodel Quiz

Answer T (true) or F (false) to the following questions.

_____ I display good manners and make an effort to say "please" and "thank-you" when making requests of my children or spouse.

_____ I am quick to admit my mistakes — even to my children — and apologize for them.

_____ Every day, I make an effort to lovingly and cheerfully perform acts of service that are above and beyond my regular duties.

_____ Every day, I make some time for individual and family prayer.

_____ I am comfortable working with my child to overcome a shared flaw.

_____ I make an effort to speak respectfully to my children, even when I disagree with them, or think their ideas or feelings are silly.

_____ I make a point of expressing my gratitude for even the simple things others (including my spouse and children) do for me.

_____ I regularly turn to God to thank Him on the good days and ask for help in the difficult ones.

_____ I express my emotions In honest and healthy ways.

_____ I am generous toward my family with regard to my time, energy, financial, and emotional resources.

Give yourself one point for each "true" answer.

8-10 — "Pout for the camera, baby. You're a supermodel!" Keep up the good work.

4-7 — Pretty good. You need to expand your modeling portfolio. Work on your consistency and your willingness to cooperate with your children to overcome shared flaws. Supermodel status is within your grasp if you only practice a little harder.

0-3 — Well, what can I say? Your modeling career is "runway impaired." Stop looking at the speck in your children's eye and concentrate on getting the plank out of your own. If you need help, call me at the Pastoral Solutions Institute.

Good modeling is absolutely essential for effective parenting. Develop your modeling skills and reap the rewards!

example: learning more appropriate ways to express anger, discovering more efficient ways to get household chores done, or more responsible ways to live life in general. Partnering with your children to overcome shared flaws reinforces that each person in the family is responsible to help the others grow in holiness, and it respects the God-given authority you have over your children without neglecting the fact that you too are a child of God who struggles with imperfection. Of course it is absolutely necessary to model good behavior in the first place, but if you learn how to use modeling to address shortcomings and teach healthy humility as well, then — move over Cindy Crawford — there's a new supermodel in town.

James and Michelle are the parents of two children. Their oldest son, Jimmy (age nine), has a very negative attitude and regularly gets into arguments with his parents when they try to correct him for it. When we applied the "supermodel" technique to Jimmy's behavior, James admitted, "I'm a pretty negative person. I have a tendency to find fault with everything. I guess he sort of gets some of that from me."

The fact is, the personality traits we most dislike in our children are often the same traits we despise in ourselves. But instead of admitting this to our children and using it as an opportunity to grow in solidarity by overcoming the offensive trait together, most of us try to punish the habit out of our children while letting ourselves off the hook, as if it were too late for us to change. Unfortunately, this attitude runs counter to the Catholic idea that the primary mission of family life is pursuing perfection in love.

In the week after that session, James sat down with his son and not only brainstormed several ways to try and approach life more joyfully, but also came up with several ways they could help each other get back on track when one or the other of them reverted back to their old, critical ways. Says James, "I would always tell him that his negative attitude stank, so now, when one of us starts acting like Eeyore [the depressed, grumpy donkey in Winnie-the-Pooh] the other grabs his nose and makes a scrunchy face as if to say 'P.U.' Now, instead of yelling at each other, we crack up laughing and try a little harder to be pleasant. This thing that used to come between us is drawing us closer as we are both working harder against our shared enemy."

Family solidarity at work. It's a beautiful thing. How good a model are you? Take the quiz on the page 89.

Technique Ten: Use Your Emotions

Chuck, an eight-year-old client, was working toward becoming the *Guinness Book*'s world-record-holder for "longest tantrums." According to the parents, regardless of what they did (and they had tried everything from time-outs, to grounding, to spanking, to everything in-between) the child would continue kicking, screaming, pouting, and whining for hours on end. In fact, the week before their first appointment, the child had pitched a whopping, eight-hour-long fit. He didn't even stop for bathroom breaks!

In response to such inappropriate displays, therapists often suggest that an alternative way to express one's self needs to be taught. In this case, I told the mother that when her child began to have a tantrum, she should take him immediately to a chair, give him a box of crayons, and tell him to write or draw whatever he was feeling. She was to then sit with him until they worked out whatever needed to be worked out. Mostly, I was doing this to see what information I could get out of the child, but I also hoped that Chuck and his mother might be able to use this exercise to communicate more effectively. In the following session, the mother reported that she had used my suggestion, but in a slightly different way.

When Chuck started to have a tantrum, she took him to the kitchen table, gave him a box of crayons and a stack of paper, and told him to show her how he felt. He refused to play along. He just sat there and stared at her. Then the mother said, "Fine. I'm going to show you what I feel like when you throw these tantrums." As the mother told me the following week, "I took a black crayon and I just scrawled on the paper so hard I ripped it. Then I scrawled all over another sheet and another. Chuck just looked at me as if I was crazy. His eyes were bugging out of his head. I went through about ten sheets of paper and I had no intention of stopping when I saw Chuck take a crayon and start writing. When I finished destroying my next page, he handed me his paper. On it, he wrote two words: 'I'm sorry.' "

Chuck and his mother had a long talk that night about strong feelings and how to handle them in respectful ways. In that talk, Chuck was able to explain the reason for his tantrums (Chuck's father tended to be physically and emotionally distant. The tantrums forced him to be home more often and more present when he was home), and his mother was able to suggest some better ways to meet those needs (scheduling a father-son night once a week; having dad be more involved in counseling). The family still needed some additional support from me, but by their sixth session, they had progressed enough that they felt they could handle things on their own. And incidentally, Chuck was tantrum-free since the second week of treatment, ever since "the night of the black crayon," as the mother called it, because it was that night that Chuck first felt his needs were understood and he was able to break through his own pain to begin working with his parents to solve his problem, instead of just venting the hurt and loneliness. As this example shows, while expressing your emotions well to one another solves few problems directly, it creates an atmosphere in which problems can be solved.

It is important to be respectfully demonstrative with the feelings you have about your children's behavior, both positive and negative. Lisa and I work very hard to be just as effusive with our grateful and approving feelings when our childen please us as we do of our sad and angry feelings when they disappoint us. However, it is critical to remember that you must never direct your negative emotions at your child, but only at your child's behavior. It is never appropriate to unleash a torrent of anger on a child. It is, however, completely appropriate to show your anger about what your child has done. This is the difference between, "You little brat! Who do you think you are?" and "That choice you made really disappointed me. I am so angry I could scream. Please go to your room while I cool down." Hopefully it is obvious that the second way is the preferred method.

Some people believe that it is somehow inappropriate to show your angry, sad, and/or hurt feelings to a child, but we have found that when done respectfully (i.e., no name-calling, threatening, or physical displays such as slamming things or hitting), it can be an important part in teaching a child the relational consequences of their choices, as well as presenting a wonderful opportunity for the parent to model emotional control to a child. Just remember what we wrote in the chapter on rapport. You must be careful to be five times as demonstrative of warmth and affection toward your child as you are of the more "negative" emotions like disappointment or anger.

Assuming this positively-to-negativity ratio is in balance, your strong emotions — and how you handle them — can be powerful teaching tools for your child. Every child knows what it feels like to be so angry that they want to hit someone; to be hurt so deeply that they want to cry all day or hurt someone else just as badly; to be so disappointed that they can think of nothing else but to throw a tantrum. What every child doesn't necessarily know is that every adult feels this way at one time or another, too. By taking the opportunity to say to our children "When you did _____ I felt so angry/hurt/ disappointed/sad/ etc. that I felt like [doing some inappropriate thing]," but then when demonstrating a healthier way to express those powerful feelings, we model respectful, healthy ways to work through negative emotions. Compare this to the more typical parental reaction of simply punishing inappropriate emotional displays to the point of discouraging their children from ever sharing their feelings — and then come to counseling saying, "We used to be so close. Why won't she talk to me?" — and you'll see what we mean.

If you, the parent, need tips on getting your own emotions under control, we refer you to the chapter on problem-solving in *For Better … FOREVER!* We'll address tips for teaching your child emotional control later in this book in the chapter on early childhood.

Technique Eleven: Labeling

We once saw a cartoon that showed a man taking to his dog. The first frame used the headline, "What Man Says to Dog" and read, "Now Fluffy, don't mess on the carpet, Fluffy. Do you understand me, Fluffy? Be a good dog, alright, Fluffy?" The next frame showed the headline, "What Dog Hears" and read, "Blah, Fluffy, blah, blah, blah, blah, blah, Fluffy. Blah, blah, blah, blah, Fluffy? Blah, blah, blah, blah, blah, Fluffy?"

Sometimes interactions between us and our kids are very much like this. We say, "I expect you be more responsible/considerate/generous/thoughtful/attentive/etc." without having really explained in practical terms what those qualities mean to us, and so all our children end up hearing is, "I expect you to blah, blah, blah…."

Labeling gives us a way to teach what it means in specific, concrete ways to exhibit certain qualities. It also allows us to use experiences of everyday life, the examples of others, and even the television programs and movies we watch as vicarious learning experiences. Labeling simply means pointing out virtue, or perhaps even inappropriate behaviors, when you see it. There are several ways you can do this. Katrina Zeno, a contributor to several Catholic publications and co-founder of Women of the Third Millenium, practiced labeling from the earliest years of her son's life by asking him if he thought his, or his friends', behaviors reflected a "good choice, " "bad choice," or a "neutral choice."

Lisa and I use this technique extensively. By catching our children being good (for example: "Thank you for making such a responsible/ loving/generous/kind/brave/etc. choice") we label specific, concrete ways they can demonstrate the particular qualities we value in our family. When we see a friend or even a stranger exhibit a behavior we want to reinforce in our children, we point it out. (For example: "Eddie made a very responsible choice when he volunteered to help you clean up after your play date). And — though we try very hard not to ever point out the negative behavior of other children — when we watch a television show or video, or read a book in which a character makes an unhealthy or unkind choice, we label it and point that out too. ("That was a very selfish thing to do, don't you think?"; "He's speaking very rudely.")

Labeling gives younger children a practical, concrete way to relate to all those big words we throw around when we're correcting them. If Lisa and I consistently point out responsible behavior (or other positive traits) in our children, their friends, and characters we see on TV and the movies, then when we say, "I need you to be more responsible" our kids know exactly the kinds of behaviors we are talking about. But they wouldn't have a clue about what we meant if Lisa and I didn't make the effort to point out and label these qualities one-hundred times a day.

Another way to practice labeling is to use "virtue tokens." This is especially helpful with small children. First, take some small stones, bingo chips (Bingo chips — This really *is* a Catholic parenting book!), or other small items, and write various virtues on them. (For starters, refer to the list in the family identity-statement exercise at the end of the last chapter.) Each day, take turns drawing one of these tokens out of a paper bag — have your kids decorate it if you like — and that becomes the quality that everybody works especially hard at that day. (Of course, you still have to live out the other virtues, you're just putting extra effort into the "virtue of the day.")

Young children especially like this because it has a certain Sesame Street quality about it: "Today, the Popcak family is brought to you by the virtue ... peace! (And the letter "Y" and the number "2."). Sure it's corny, but why not? It makes the concept of pursuing virtue more accessible to children, and a little bit more fun to boot.

Technique Twelve: Storytelling
This was one of Jesus' favorite ways to make a point, and not being one to quibble with our Lord, we're kind of partial to it ourselves.

There is a temptation to think of storytelling as a technique for small children, but counselors use it with adults too (only we rather stuffily call it "therapeutic metaphor"). The fact is, everybody loves a good story.

It works like this. When your child exhibits a certain problem behavior (say, lying, for example) you may either make up a story or find an appropriate book in which the main character tells lies, suffers a natural consequence, and learns not to do it anymore. You may also use this technique proactively, identifying certain qualities you would like your children to display and reading stories — or making up your own — about characters who exhibit those qualities in the face of extreme danger. To this end, nothing beats stories from the Bible — check out the original parables, they're keepers — and the lives of the saints. Some very good resources for the latter include Ignatius Press's *Visions Book Series Saints for Youth* (call 1-800-651-1531 to order). Also, Our Sunday Visitor (1-800-348-2440) has some very nice resources for children available.

Of course, there are a slew of good, generically Christian entertainment choices suited for this purpose as well. At the top of the list of videos, I highly recommend the "Veggie Tales" series, hysterical, musical morality plays performed by computer-animated vegetables that are just as entertaining for adults as children. Also, the Nancy Rue series of historical fiction published by Focus on the Family are excellent stories of challenge and courage in the daily life of several generations of the Hutchinson family. Written on a fourth-grade to junior-high reading level, they are also wonderful read-aloud books that even our three-year-old can follow with some help. For other suggestions of books that build character, check out the Kolbe Academy reading list at http://www.kolbe.org.

Storytelling is a wonderful intervention that builds relationship and teaches lessons in an easy-to-digest way. There are reams of psychological data to support the benefits of "vicarious reinforcement." That is, learning from the successes and struggles of others. Utilized properly, books and other media can be an important part of educating your children in virtue.

The twelve techniques we've outlined in this chapter represent the meat and potatoes of basic, everyday discipline. All of them are focused on helping you use your relationship with your child to encourage good behavior and Christian virtue. In the next chapter, we will cover those discipline techniques, which are more corrective in nature, but before we do, complete the "Everyday Discipline Quiz" on page 98, then answer/discuss the questions on page 99. On page 100, use the "Making a Change" exercise to help you make specific changes in your child's behavior and attitudes.

Old MacDonald Had A Farm, EIEIOOOOOOO!

In some ways, parenting has a lot in common with gardening (except, of course, that I like parenting). Plants need good soil, sunlight, and water to grow, and "climbing plants" (which, I think, are most like children, considering their mutual ability to grow all over the place and get into all kinds of unexpected, undesirable places) need a trellis, a structure that helps them grow in the right way and the right shape. Everyday discipline provides the nourishment and structure children need to grow in age, wisdom, and grace. Everyday-discipline techniques are effective because they provide kids with an abundance of the one thing they need to grow up well: the "self."

Experienced counselors talk about using "the self" in therapy to help their clients progress through treatment. Essentially, this means learning how not to rely on manipulative techniques, but rather on your strong relationship with a client to move things along. Parents, too, as they become more experienced, learn how to put away all the creative punishments, all the star charts, the token economies, the spanking, the bribing, the cajoling, and all the other more technique-y ways to "make" their children change, and become more skilled in how to use their relationship with a child to nurture change on a daily basis in the simple interactions of every moment.

This chapter was meant to be a primer in the "use of self" in parenting. As God Himself has shown us through the self-emptying act of His Incarnation, as well as through His passion, death, and resurrection, the most powerful change technique is having a "close encounter of the loving kind" — i.e., an intimate, transformative relationship — with someone who is daily willing and working for our good.

But sometimes, plants need more than nurturing to grow well. They need pruning, too. In the next chapter, we'll examine some powerfully simple corrective-discipline techniques that can help you trim the odd-looking growths off of your child's budding moral character. You just might get to grow some per fect kids after all! Grab your gardening gloves and let's get to work!

Everyday Discipline Quiz

Are you a master of everyday discipline? Are you taking advantage of the transformative power of your relationship with your children? Take the following true-and-false quiz to find out what you do well, or can do better.

_____ I engage in constant power struggles with my kids.

_____ My children act like they are disgusted every time I open my mouth.

_____ My children "forget" or ignore even the simplest house rules, no matter how many times I tell them.

_____ My children tell me that they think I don't love them or am always picking on them.

_____ I don't enjoy being with my children.

_____ I get a sick feeling in my stomach when I have to ask my kids to do anything, because I know it's going to be a fight.

_____ My children obey me, but they are very tight-lipped about their feelings, thoughts, and the circumstances of their daily lives.

_____ My spouse and I regularly argue about our different parenting styles.

_____ I yell at my children more than I would like.

_____ I feel like I don't really know my kids.

Scoring

Give yourself one point for every "true" answer.

0-2 — Looks like you're in pretty good shape. To maintain your course, make sure that you take some time to develop your family identity-statement (see chapter one). Also, review this chapter and exercise for more tips on how to continue to expect the best from yourself and your kids.

3-5 — Your parenting relationship is probably not as effective or rewarding as it could be. Take some time to develop your family identity-statement, and review this chapter and exercise for additional tips on how to expect the best from yourself and your children. You may also benefit from some assistance in applying these tips to your unique set of circumstances.

5 or more — Your relational bank-account is seriously overdrawn. First, STOP EVERYTHING. Place a moratorium on all the yelling, lecturing, creative punishing, cajoling, bribing, begging, etc. Concentrate on re-establishing relationship and increasing affection, and limit yourself to enforcing the most important one or two rules (no more!) without which your family cannot function.

Discussion Questions

1. What can you do to increase the credit in your emotional bank-account? Talk to your children, one by one. Ask each of them, "When do you feel most loved by me?" Solicit as many responses as you can and write them down.

This can be helpful in two ways. First, it will automatically give you a step-by-step plan for building and maintaining your relationship with your children. Secondly, it will let you assess the depth of your child's understanding of what "love" really is. Are their answers all material things? Perhaps you have unintentionally taught them to think of you as a wallet, instead of a parent who invests time and energy. Are their answers "indulge me"? Perhaps you are not as good at showing your love on a daily basis as you are on your "days off" or special occasions. Assume that whatever answer they give, they learned from you. Then use open discussion and modeling to lead them to the truth about love; that it is the willingness to work for the good of another on a daily basis. Their answers might just lead you to a teachable moment.

2. Are your rules clear? How could they be clearer? Should you write them down? Have your younger children draw pictures of the rules. Discuss them in a family meeting? Develop your family identity-statement?

3. Are your expectations developmentally appropriate? What are other children the same age as your own capable of? Can you get your kids to do the same without torturing them?

4. Are you consistent with the rules and enforcement of consequences? What do you need to do to make it even more consistent? What resources (other people, books, counseling, support groups, etc.) will you use to help you achieve your goal?

Exercise: Making a Change

The following five steps will help you make specific changes in your child's behavior and attitudes.

1. Identify a behavior that you would like to change in your child:
   _____

2. Circle the everyday discipline techniques you think might help you nuture this change:

   Increase affection   Write down the rules   Redirection
   Build rapport   Modeling   Labeling
   Do-overs   Virtue tokens   Storytelling
   Use your emotions   Restating family identity-statement
   Choices   Reviewing/rehearsing
   Catch them "being good"

3. Write how you will specifically utilize these techniques to meet your goal: _____
   _____

4. Talk to your child about what you are going to do. Ask for their input. Write your plan down or — if they are too young to read — have them draw it: _____
   _____

5. Give it two weeks. Follow your plan consistently. Assess your level of success:
   • Problem resolved. Congratulations! Keep following your plan to maintain and reinforce your success.
   • Problem partially resolved. Are you being consistent? Is there at least some steady progress being made? If you answered "yes" to both questions, give yourself another week and reassess. If you answered "no" to either question, go to "Problem unresolved" below.
   • Problem unresolved. There are a few possibilities here. The first possibility is that you have not been consistent enough. Have you? If not, give it two more weeks and try harder to discipline yourself. If you have been consistent, then there are two other possibilities. Your child may not be developmentally ready to address this problem, or the problem is more difficult to correct than you previously thought, and you are going to have to refer to the corrective-discipline techniques discussed in the next chapter.

Chapter Four

Mutiny on the Bounty!
Corrective Discipline for Stormy Seas

In the last chapter, we concentrated on those techniques which prevent problems from occurring in the first place and can correct minor disturbances to daily life. Here, we are going to examine those techniques designed to correct problems once they've gotten a foothold.

So far we've compared parenting to gardening and piloting a ship, but sometimes parenting is like this: You are the captain of a ship. Onboard, you have a couple of beloved, fast-growing, stubborn, but nonetheless beautiful plants that tend to grow everywhere and get into everything. You are now in the middle of a storm. Your job is to lash yourself to the mizzenmast, pilot the ship through rough seas, hold onto the plants so that they don't fly overboard, prune the plants as they try to wrap themselves around your legs and toss you into the drink just to see what would happen, and at the same time, try to stop the one plant from shoving Milk Duds up its brother's nose.

Corrective Discipline

This chapter is about tending your garden in stormy seas. Like their everyday-discipline cousins, the techniques outlined this chapter are deceptively simple, but used together have the power to transform your relationship with your kids into a powerful instrument for growth — yours and theirs.

As with all the techniques discussed in this book, corrective discipline tends to work best when there is good rapport between a parent and child. Likewise, it is best to reserve these techniques for more serious problems when simpler relational discipline has failed because some of the techniques in this section do withdraw more "currency" from your emotional bank-account. Regardless, used properly, consistently, and with a charitable spirit, they are efficient and respectful ways to address problem behavior.

Let's take a look.

Technique One: Cool-down Time

Use: For those occasions when emotions are beginning to run high in discussions between a parent and child.

In my Catholic-marriage book *For Better ... FOREVER!* I outline several steps that couples can use to turn arguments into problem-solving sessions. One of those tips is learning to take respectful breaks. Such breaks serve to decrease tension and increase creative problem-solving as the couple takes time apart to reflect on their own responsibility for solving the problems at hand and come back together — ideally — in a more cooperative mood. As basic as this idea is, it often comes as a shock to couples in counseling, because they never had this experience in trying to resolve conflict with their parents when they were growing up. Most of my marriage-counseling clients who have problems in the arguing department fall into one of two categories. The first group is made up of those people who were raised by overindulgent parents who let them get away with all manner of childish behavior and tantrums, often rewarding such displays by giving in to the child's demands. In adulthood, these individuals tend to become very frustrated at the first sign of not getting their way and employ an arsenal of childish, manipulative techniques to win the fight.

Sheila was one such person, a self-proclaimed "spoiled brat." Sheila was given to "withholding privileges" from her husband, like domestic service or sex, when she was upset. Likewise, she would often lock herself in her room or simply leave the house in the middle of an argument when it was apparent that things were not going her way.

The second group is made up of people who grew up in overly punitive environments in which blind obedience (as opposed to Christian obedience) was demanded and their needs were not respected. As adults, these people tend to become either extremely passive in arguments, rarely talking about what upsets them until they can't keep it in any longer, at which point they erupt in a rage which is disproportionate to the problem at hand. Or, they become extremely defensive and volatile in arguments. Such individuals may be the sweetest people in the world when they are not arguing, but in conflict they often become capable of remarkable cruelty.

What both groups of people need to learn is a way to interrupt their unproductive discussions and gain control of their more rational selves. Parents who understand that interactions between themselves and their children will be repeated in their children's future marital relationships try to approach conflict in a way that would transfer to adult relationships. One of the techniques that does just this is what we call "cool-down time."

Cool-down time is different from the well-known time-out (see below), because rather than it being something you do to a child to get them to calm down, it is intended to help both you and your child regain control of yourselves and come up with more respectful solutions to the crisis at hand.

Imagine that you could measure your "emotional temperature" on a scale from one to ten, with "one" representing you on heavy tranquilizers, "four" representing you as you read this book, and "ten" representing you scaling a clock tower with an AK-47 strapped to your back. On such a scale, no effective problem-solving goes on between a parent and child over a "6.5." At that point, your fight or flight response is kicking in and your heart rate is quickly escalating to one hundred twenty beats per minute (compared to eighty at rest). Cognitively, you begin thinking how nice it would be to send your child to that boarding school in Tibet and/or wondering why more animals don't eat their young. To make matters worse, your children are beginning to think similar thoughts about you. Obviously, this is not a good place to be.

When either you or your child's emotional temperature begins approaching a 6.5, it is essential to interrupt the process by taking a respectful break from the conflict. Sometimes a simple hug or other gesture of affection will do; sometimes it takes sending yourself and your child to separate corners of the house. Either way, the breaks should not last any longer than it takes for both of you to cool down so you can get back to the work of problem-solving. Remember, the point of cool-down time is not to punish anyone, but to interrupt an unproductive discussion so that you and your child can regain your composure and return to solve the problem in a healthier frame of mind.

Mark and his fourteen-year-old son Devin regularly got into arguments that were poisoning the relationship. Both often had legitimate points to express, but both tended to state their positions in a fairly hostile way, which would have caused anyone to respond defensively. Over the course of several weeks of therapy, I used a number of different techniques with this father and son, but one of the first things I suggested (besides increasing affection and pleasant times together) was making increased use of cool-down time when either of them felt they were approaching a 6.5 on their emotional thermometers. Two weeks later, they had this to say:

Mark: "The hardest part about using your suggestion was remembering to do it. But after a few false starts we got the hang of it."

Devin: "Dad totally blew me away the other day. He was on me about my chores and we were starting to get into it like we usually do, when all of a sudden he said, well...." [Devin trailed off.]

Mark: "I think Devin is a little embarrassed. I said, 'I'm really afraid this is going get to out of control and I don't want to forget we're trying to work together. Would you mind if I gave you a hug?' I don't think he knew what to do with me."

Devin: "Well, its like, I wouldn't mind giving him a hug or anything, but right then I was too ticked off. So I told him I didn't want to."

Mark: "At first I was a little put off, but I decided to play it cool. I just told him that I needed a break. I suggested we come back and try again in half-an-hour. I used the bathroom, and tried to get my head together, and Devin played video games. After about twenty minutes or so, I went upstairs and asked I could join him. We blew away some aliens...."

Devin: "I skunked him!"

Mark: "Devin beat me. And then we talked for a while. It was a good talk for a change and I think we really solved some things."

Devin: "It was pretty cool."

By taking the lead in this process, Mark was not only able to resolve some of the problems he and Devin were having in the moment, but he was also able to begin teaching his son an important lesson about problem-solving in adult relationships — that rather than being like a boxing match where two people verbally pound on each other, good problem-solving is like fishing in that involves striking a healthy balance between tension and release until you've made your catch. In this case, a tailor-made resolution.

Technique Two: Time-outs

Use: An intervention that stops bad behavior in the moment and offers the child an opportunity to think about healthier alternatives.

Everyone knows about time-outs, but not everyone knows how to use them effectively. There are six steps to the traditional time-out. We'll review these first and then I'll briefly explain some tips that can make them even more effective.

Six Steps for Traditional Time-outs

1. Interrupt the inappropriate behavior. Tell your child exactly what he or she had done wrong, even if you think they ought to know.
2. Send your child to a place where there are no distractions (i.e., no toys, TV's, video games, etc.). Some good places include the stairs, spare rooms, and/or bathrooms. If you use the latter, make sure that all dangerous chemicals are safely out of reach. Also, with younger children who try to use "passive resistance" (when they fall down to the ground and refuse to go to time-out) it is acceptable to gently but firmly carry them to their time-out place.
3. Require the child to stay in the time-out place one minute for every year of age. (For example: Two years old = two minutes. Ten years old = ten minutes.)

Use an egg timer to keep track of their time. This prevents those "Can I get out now?" questions.

4. Do not start the timer until all the arguing and physical tantruming has stopped. It is not necessary — nor is it remarkably useful — to require a child to sit silently at attention. But your child must be sitting calmly and relatively quietly before you start the timer.
5. Take a break and cool down while your child is in time-out. DO NOT stand over them commenting on every move they make and word they mutter. You are only asking for trouble.
6. After his or her time is up, give affection to your child. Ask your child to apologize, offer your forgiveness, and talk to him or her about your expectations for the next time. Also, if necessary, discuss any additional consequences your child may have incurred. (See "Logical Consequences" beginning on page 108 for help in this area.)

While the above summarizes the steps for a traditional time-out, I would suggest one change that Lisa and I practice with our own children and I recommend to my clients. We have some minor issues with the arbitrary amount of time that kids are in time-out for. It has been our experience that many kids — instead of thinking about what they have done wrong and what they must do to change their behavior — simply "serve their time" and expect it all to be done and over with when they "get out." In fact, the hard work, developing a plan to change future behavior, is just beginning when a time-out ends. To correct this problem, we suggest letting the child be in charge of how long the time-out lasts. In other words, instead of saying, "Sit here until the egg timer goes off," you can say, "Please go to time-out and stay there until (1) you are calm, and (2) you have figured out how to act the next time your sister disagrees with you/I ask you to do something/you have to share/you feel frustrated/etc." We have found that this approach reinforces internal control by giving the child an added motivation (shorter time-out time) to think of their own solutions to their problems. Used this way, a time-out may take three seconds, or it could take fifteen minutes, but it is entirely up to the child because it all depends upon how long will it take the child to calm down, review the lessons he or she has been taught, and come up with a possible solution to the problem. After all, the real point of time-out is not to punish the child for the sake of saying you did something to her, but to teach her how to make more appropriate behavioral choices in the future. It is our opinion that the quicker a child can move from inappropriate behavior to more respectful alternatives the better.

Allow us to offer two qualifying points. First, we do not normally require a child — especially a younger child (say, three to six years old) — to come up with the final answer to a behavioral problem. What we do insist on is that they show some real effort at trying to come up with ways to change themselves. For example, if our three-year-old daughter, after thirty seconds in time-out, says that the solution to her fighting with her brother is "selling him to the neighbors," we send her right back into time-out. But if after thirty seconds she came down both calmer and with at least one semi-practical suggestion for how to change her behavior — "I should share/be nicer/ask for help instead of hit/etc." — then we would move to step six and help her identify the specific changes she needs to make (e.g., "Well, that's a good start, but what would you have to do differently if you 'acted nicer'?") It would be ludicrous to expect our children to come down with their own completely developed behavior plan ready to be filed in triplicate. But it is absolutely appropriate for us to require our children to make a sincere effort, exercise whatever insight they may have, and come up with at least some plausible — if not entirely complete — solutions to their problems.

If you decide to use this suggestion instead of the standard egg-timer approach, then we need to offer one more qualifier. Sometimes children really do get stuck trying to figure out a better way to handle a problem. Because of this, we don't really recommend making a child stay in time-out for longer than ten to fifteen minutes tops, regardless of their age. If a child is going to come up with an answer, he is going to come up with it sooner than later. Making a child "sit there until you figure it out" is usually just giving them an invitation to piddle the day away and entertain themselves by watching your head explode as they do nothing. If, after a few minutes, the child is calmer but no closer to finding his or her own answers to the problem, feel free to move to step six and engage them in a problem-solving discussion.

Occasionally, a parent will complain that neither the traditional nor our revised time-outs work for them. The most common reason is that they are violating one of the six steps. But there is another possibility, and that is that the parent does not have an adequate attachment or rapport with the child. Time-outs assume that your child will feel emotional and physical estrangement when he or she is apart from you. Basically, this feeling of "I'm on the outs with mom and dad and I am longing to repair the damage to our relationship" is the corrective mechanism of any effective time-out. But unfortunately, more and more parents are spending less and less time with their children (studies show forty percent less time than in 1960). As a result, rapport and attachment suffer, and discipline fails to work. In other words, when a child spends ten or more hours a day not interacting with his parents, then what's the big deal about spending five, six, seven, or more minutes of not interacting with them in a time-out?

By contrast, our own children, and the children of parents who practice the kind of relationship-building discipline we are describing in this book, act as if you are trying to cut off their heads with a spoon when you send them to time-out. The reason for this dramatic effect is that when attachment and rapport is strong, it hurts like hell to be away from the person to whom you are attached. Think about it. When you have been most in love with your mate, didn't you ache when you were away from him or her — especially after a small tiff? Didn't you feel his or her absence in the pit of your stomach, anxious to make things right again? The same is true for children who are well attached, who value the relationship with their parents so much that it pains them to have to be away when they have done something to damage the rapport. (Incidentally, this is how God disciplines us. He builds attachment with us, and when we sin, we experience the pain of estrangement which calls us back to Him.) In sum, time-outs work. But in order to work well they must (1) be applied consistently, (2) the six steps must be followed, and (3) there must be adequate rapport between the parent and child in order for the child to care enough about being separated from the parent to change his behavior.

Technique Three: Logical Consequences

Use: To help the punishment fit the crime, a parent will use logical consequences when necessary to teach a child the effects of poor behavioral choices and to reinforce future good behavior. Also, logical consequences can be used to short-circuit the amount of yelling a parent has to do to enforce compliance.

The word "consequence" literally means "with order." Sometimes, our children make choices for which they must experience a consequence. Unfortunately, most of the consequences parents attempt to use with their children are decidedly out-of-order insofar as they seem arbitrary to the child, don't logically follow the child's misbehavior, and don't teach any lesson beyond "don't get caught in the future."

Elisa absentmindedly left a can of white paint uncovered. Her six- and four-year-old sons got into the paint and spilled the open can onto the wood floor. Understandably, Elisa was upset, but rather than requiring her children to help clean up the mess they made (a logical consequence), she spanked them. While her response may have been understandable, it was not logical, and she missed an opportunity to teach her children a valuable lesson. What the children did learn was a lesson in external control ("Don't do that because it will make mommy mad!") when they could have learned an important lesson in internal control. ("I shouldn't do that again because it makes a mess that I will have to clean up.") You might think we are making too fine a point, and if this was the only time this child experienced an illogical consequence in his life, we would indeed be making a mountain out of a molehill. But multiply such lessons by a million times over the life of a child and you end up with two different kids. The first one — the child raised with external control — learns that it's okay to make messes (literal or figurative) as long as no one gets mad or he gets caught. The second child — raised with logical consequences that reinforce internal control — learns that it's not okay to make messes (literal or figurative) because that just makes life complicated for himself, whether or not anyone else is inconvenienced by it.

When looking for a logical consequence to address their child's misbehavior, a parent's mindset must not be "What can I do to the little creep so that he will learn to never do this again!?" But rather, "What must my child do to clean up the mess (literally or figuratively) they made?" It is unrealistic to think that there is any "one thing" a parent can do to a child that will get them to "never again" misbehave in a particular area, any more than it is possible for the best teacher in the world to do anything to a child "to get" them to never again misspell a word, any more than it is possible for God to do anything to us to make us never sin again in the same way? In all of these cases, the only thing God, the wise teacher, and the effective Christian parent can do is love the child, leave him to experience and overcome the sad consequence of his action, and give him the opportunity to try again.

A logical consequence is not something a parent adds on to "teach my kid a lesson." A logical consequence is what a child must do to correct the immediate effect of his action or choice. For example:

- The child who tells a lie must be required to admit the truth and ask forgiveness.
- The child who breaks something must be helped to find a way to fix it, replace it, or work off the debt.
- The child who doesn't do his chores must not be allowed to go anywhere or do anything until he is done (and then be free to go about his business).
- A child who "back-talks" must be required to restate himself more respectfully.
- The child who does not complete his school work or other responsibilities on his own must be given a structure which teaches him to manage his time and responsibilities appropriately.
- A child who does not take care of a particular toy (or items he borrows from you, like tools) may be required to lose the privilege of playing with it until he demonstrates responsibility in other specific ways. (Or, if his neglect results in the item being lost, stolen, or broken, then he must be required to replace the item with his own money or work off the debt to you.)
- If a child is unkind to another child at school, you might wish to require him to arrange a play date (supervised by you) in which your child hosts the other child for an afternoon as a way of making up and trying to build understanding. Or, at the very least, the

child should be required to do something concrete (buy him a soda, carry her books, etc.) to make the other child's life more pleasant, in addition to apologizing for the offense.

• If the child is unkind to a grown-up neighbor, you may wish to supervise your child as he or she does some act of service (cutting the lawn, raking leaves, shoveling the driveway, etc.) to make up for the offense. (Your supervision is especially important to make sure the work is done properly and to make sure your child is safe.)

• If your child steals from a store or a neighbor, he must be required to return item, offer to pay for it anyway, and possibly do some other act of service to try to make up for the ill will he caused.

These are all examples of simple, logical consequences that not only correct inappropriate behavior, but teach an important lesson. Namely, "You can't escape your responsibilities. You've got to clean up your own mess and not look to anyone else to save you from your own stupidity."

A child cannot escape a logical consequence, because it is logical. It is the mess (literal or metaphorical) that is caused by a poor choice and must be cleaned up before life can be gotten on with. Likewise, a child does not resent a logical consequence, because it is just. That's not to say that your child will happily go about repairing the damage he or she has done. Your child may very well complain a great deal about having to face the consequence of his or her actions, but this is different from the change-inhibiting resentment a parent faces when he or she tries to enforce an illogical consequence.

For example, say your child does not complete his chores in a timely manner — or at all. The logical consequence would be to require him to complete those chores before he gets to do anything else at all — including playing, sleeping, or eating. (Of course, immediately after the chores were done he would be allowed to do all three. Remember, discipline requires justice. That is, doing no more or less than is required to effect the change the circumstances require.)

But imagine that this isn't enough for you. You want to teach your child "once and for all" to "do her jobs when they're supposed to be done." So, in addition to requiring her to complete her chores, you ground your child, or throw a screaming hissy-fit, or spank her, or take away her bicycle for a week, or any and all of the above. Now, most of these consequences (except spanking) could be logical consequences under different circumstances. For example, if your child was using his bike to try to run over the other kids in the neighborhood, taking it away would be a completely logical response. Or if your child was having a difficult time resisting unhealthy peer-pressure, then grounding might be absolutely logical (see below). But in this case, such interventions make no sense, because they are in no way connected to the offense and do not attempt to teach the child anything other than "don't get caught in the future." As any experienced parent knows, the more you try to enforce "inconsequential" (i.e., "out of order") consequences, the more energy your child will spend resenting you (and trying to figure out ways not to get caught in the future) than on thinking about how to change their own behavior.

Logical consequence can also be used to help you escape those energy-draining arguments you have with your children about compliance. There are three steps to this process: (1) Tell your child what your request, limit, or rule is. (2) Tell them the consequence for not obeying that request, limit, or rule. (3) Leave them alone. If your child doesn't comply, let the consequence do the talking. Let me give you an example.

Sharon, a telephone client of mine from Chicago, was having difficulty getting her twelve-year-old son, Jeff, to comply with her requests. "He never listens to me. Anything I ask him to do is always, 'I'll do it later, mom' or 'Do I have to?'. Then we get into a big argument. Sometimes he'll do it after that, but just as often I get fed up and do it myself. It just isn't worth the aggravation."

When I explained how to use logical consequences to increase Jeff's compliance, Sharon was delighted. And she was even happier the following week when she called to report her progress.

"Well," she said, "this was really interesting. We only had one incident earlier in the week and I think the way I responded really made a difference. I followed your steps. I was cleaning the house and I asked Jeff to help by cleaning the upstairs bathroom. He responded in the usual way, that he would 'get to it later.' I didn't react. I just told him that it needed to be done before I took him to his karate class that night. He said, 'Yeah, all right.'

"Normally, I would have been on him the whole time — 'Did you do it?' Not this time. I stayed out of his way and concentrated on cleaning the rest of the house and getting dinner together. After we ate, Jeff went upstairs and got his ghi [karate outfit] on. I knew he hadn't cleaned the bathroom, but I still didn't say anything. In fact, I pretended not to notice that he was standing by the door waiting for me. Finally he said, 'C'mon, Mom, we're gonna be late.'

Mom: "For what?"

Jeff: "Karate."

Mom: "You can't go yet."

Jeff: (shocked) "Why not?!"

Mom: "You tell me."

Jeff: "I dunno."

Mom: "Well, sweety, you think about it and let me know when you figure it out."

Logical Consequences Exercise

1. On the lines below, write down a behavior that you believe is serious enough to warrant a logical consequence.

2. What would your child need to do to either adequately fix the damage or effectively heal the hurt caused by this behavior or choice?

3. The above represents a preliminary idea for a logical consequence. Ask yourself: Does this consequence adequately address the damage or hurt caused by the misbehavior? Have I (the parent) been careful not to use this consequence to inflict revenge? Remember: The point of a logical consequence (or any good discipline) is to restore the moral imbalance caused by a misdeed and educate the child about proper conduct in the future. It is not to "teach them once and for all never to do that again." The latter is a parenting fallacy.

4. Take some time with your child to educate him or her about the more appropriate behavioral and emotional choices you expect to be made in the future. If it seems helpful, role-play the problem situation again with the child making the better choice this time. Practice this role-play once or twice. Give your child affection and compliment him or her on a job well done.

Jeff: "This is about the bathroom, isn't it?"

Mom: "What do you think?"

Jeff: "But Mom, I told you I'd get to it later!"

Mom: "And I told you that I'd take you when it was done. If you start now, you'll still be able to get to your lesson before its over."

Sharon stood her ground and added what I believe was a master's touch. It was twenty minutes later before Jeff got done, but rather than excusing Jeff from his lesson, she fulfilled her promise to take him. When he arrived late, he was forced to explain to his karate instructor why he was late for class. The karate instructor proceeded to remind Jeff that karate was about discipline, and that if he didn't show good self-discipline at home by obeying his mother, then he would not be permitted to continue the class. Said Sharon, "Jeff was mortified. It was worse than anything I could ever have done to him myself. But after that, Jeff knew I was serious."

Over the next few weeks of phone counseling, Jeff tried to test his mother's resolve a few more times, but the power dynamic had changed to the point that by the end of the fifth session, Sharon told me that she felt ready to discontinue treatment. "I know Jeff's going to try and pull stuff now and then, but he knows now that I mean what I say, and I feel in complete control of the situation. I can't believe how much better we feel about each other now that I'm not chasing after him and fighting with him all the time."

When a consequence is called for, use a logical consequence that inconveniences your child more than it does you, and let that consequence do the fighting and teaching for you. And as an added bonus, treat yourself to a movie with the money you saved in aspirin purchases.

Technique Four: Positive Intentions

Use: When a behavior is resistant to change or simple correction. This technique enables the parent to get to the heart of the problem and teach the child more efficient, respectful ways to meet his or her needs.

Sometimes simple redirection or corrective measures don't work because they don't address the intention behind the child's misbehavior. For example, a child who throws tantrums may not know a more appropriate way to deal with strong emotions. A child who doesn't complete homework assignments might be lacking healthy study skills. And a child who tends to get into playground fights may need to be taught better ways to resolve conflict, or make himself feel powerful.

In other words, sometimes children misbehave because they don't know any more honest, appropriate way to get their needs or most important wants met. No amount of corrective discipline will work in these cases, because the child lacks the skills to do anything different than the inappropriate thing he or she is doing to meet his or her needs. The result is that you get a child who, when you say "Stop that!" will stop that for an hour, and then do that exact same thing over again. When this happens it is up to us parents to teach our children the most efficient and respectful ways to meet their wants and needs, because if we don't we will — no matter how inadvertently — encourage deceitfulness and deviance in our children. Let me give you an example of how this works.

Fred was a fifteen-year-old client of mine who had been arrested for shoplifting a pair of one hundred dollar running shoes from a local department store. Furthermore, he had confessed that this was not the first time he had done such a thing. He had good, Christian parents who were understandably distraught about the situation. When I talked with Fred, he explained that he was sorry for what he did, but that the other kids at school were making fun of him to the point of threatening to beat him up because he didn't have those "phat" (read: "good") shoes. Fred's intention behind getting the shoes — in fact, all his stealing — was not only to save his hide, but like all adolescents, he desperately wanted to find his place and fit in — even if doing so required him to steal.

His parents understood, but explained that they thought it was foolish to spend that kind of money on "a pair of sneakers" and besides, they didn't have that kind of money even if they thought it was worthwhile.

I asked Fred to wait in the lobby of my office while I spoke to Fred's parents alone. I explained that I completely sympathized with their opinion and I agreed with them that one hundred dollars was a ridiculous amount of money to ask them to spend on a pair of shoes. But I also suggested that they might be missing out on a great opportunity to teach Fred a lesson in responsibility. I asked them to tell me how much they felt was a fair price to pay for a good pair of sneakers. The father told me, "Well, if it was up to me, ten bucks. But I guess I could go up to forty."

I then suggested that they tell Fred that they were willing to give him forty dollars toward the pair of shoes, but that if he wanted to spend more, he would have to work for the difference. I asked Fred's parents if there was any way Fred could earn some extra money — preferably not from them. It happened that Fred's uncle was a plumber, and the mother knew that he would be glad to have Fred along on Saturdays as an assistant. I suggested that she set this up, and then I called Fred back in and had his parents explain the plan to him. Fred seemed thrilled that his parents were going to help him get his shoes, even though he had to earn most of the money himself.

Several things happened as a result of this intervention. First of all, he learned the role hard work and responsibility play in helping you get what you want out of life. Interestingly enough, as Fred developed his responsibility and earned a little more money, his circle of friends changed. He said he didn't want to hang around with "those losers" any more. "All they want to do is party and stuff anyway. They're not goin' anywhere in their lives." Also, he decided not to buy the shoes after all. Having to spend his own money clarified things for him a bit. As he put it, "I figure if they just like me for my shoes, then they don't really like me anyway. I don't need that."

Helping Fred meet the intention behind his behavior — finding a place he could "fit in" and giving him some control over his purchases — made more changes than I ever expected to make in Fred's life. The nice thing about this technique is that it works with any age group. To discover the intention or need behind your child's misbehavior try the "Positive Intervention" exercise on the next page.

You may need to repeat this exercise more than once to completely address any one particular behavior, because several intentions may be at work. But this process is a very effective change technique because it actually builds rapport with your children while getting them to change their behavior! How can this be? Because while you are asking them to make a change, you are taking the time to listen to what is really important to them and offering to help meet that need or intention in a more hassle-free, respectful manner. Such concern will be greatly appreciated by a child, who will marvel at your ability to not only hear what he or she is saying, but also really understand what he or she means.

Incidentally, looking for the intention behind a behavior is a very Catholic idea. One of the major reasons people sin is because of something the theologians call "concupiscence." This is the longing for the mud that remains even after we have been washed clean by the waters of baptism. To put it more technically, the *Our Sunday Visitor's Encyclopedia of Catholic Doctrine* defines concupiscence as the tendency

Positive Intervention Exercise

1. Identify something your child does that drives you crazy. (The more resistant to your efforts to correct it, the better.)

_____

2. Ask yourself, "How does my child benefit by engaging in this behavior?" Ask your child the same question. When trying to figure out the intention, try to think like a kid, not a parent. Write your ideas below.

_____

3. If you can't figure it out yet, and your child won't tell you (or "doesn't know") his intention, ask yourself, "What is the immediate result of this behavior?" (e.g., "I get angry." "He gets grounded." "She gets thrown out of class." "He pushes me away from him." "She forces me to drop what I'm doing and deal with her crisis du jour.") Write your answer below.

_____

4. Now ask yourself, "What could my child enjoy/what benefit could (s)he receive from this natural consequence?" For example: If you yell at him, could he be looking for ways to make you angry because he's angry with you? If he is grounded, what temptations might he be trying to avoid in the "outside world"? Or, what is it about getting alone time with you that is so important? If she is getting thrown out of class, what is she trying to avoid? Or, what is she in such a hurry to get to? If he is pushing you away, perhaps he needs to learn healthier ways to gain some independence. If she is forcing you to come to her aid, perhaps she needs healthier ways to draw you in. And so on. Write your thoughts here:

_____

5. At this time, the above represents your best guess at the positive intention or need that underlies the behavior. Begin brainstorming alternative ways to help your child meet this need or intention. For example: How could he approach you when he's angry with you? How could he get more time with you without having to get in trouble and be grounded to meet this need? How could she develop the skills she needs to succeed in class (socially or academically) so that she doesn't have to run away from it? Write your ideas here.

_____

to "choose a lesser good over a greater good." So, for example, while it is a good thing to want to feel happy or satisfied, it is an even better thing to know how to satisfy oneself in a manner that is respectful to the people in one's life. Satisfying oneself in a manner that is disrespectful to others is often sinful. That's not to say that the pleasure itself is bad, but rather the means used to acquire that pleasure is bad — or at least less good than a more respectful means. So the Church teaches us not to settle for lesser goods, but for the greatest good: finding our fulfillment in a manner that is respectful of our own dignity, as well as our relationship to others and to God. In this way, the Church respects the intention behind our sinful desires (i.e., fulfillment) but constantly asks us to leave behind the false paths to fulfillment and pursue the greatest good: loving, serving, and knowing God in this life so that we may be happy with him in the next.

Further, the idea of working with the positive intention behind a inappropriate or even evil behavior has a biblical precedent. When Jesus was dying on the cross, He said, "Father, forgive them. They know not what they do." Jesus knew that their intention was not to attempt to kill the Son of God, but rather to kill a blasphemer. Because He knew what was arguably the positive intention behind many of His persecutor's evil deeds, He was able to extend Divine Mercy, even to them.

Saying that one should look for the positive intention behind offensive behavior is not an attempt to excuse that behavior. Rather, it presents an opportunity to reach out in love and begin changing even the most awful conduct, just as Jesus did, and the Church encourages us by her example in the Sacrament of Reconciliation even today.

Technique Five: Solution-Focused Questioning
Use: To ask questions that help us focus on the solution to the problem.

Imagine that you take your car to the shop. The mechanic says, "I know exactly what's wrong."

"Good!" you say. "So, you'll be able to fix it?"

"No," replies the mechanic. "It's much too soon for that. First we have to figure out exactly how and why it got broken in the first place."

I don't know about you, but I really don't care how it got broken in the first place. I mean, it might be an interesting bit of information, but it really has little to no bearing on the repair process. If you know what's broken, fix it already, and let me get on my merry way.

Problem-focused questions are like this. They yield a great deal of fascinating, but utterly useless, information. Too many parents are problem-focused when it comes to parenting. We ask questions like "Why do you do that?" and ""What's wrong with you?", staying focused on what's wrong, why it's wrong, and how it got broken. Such questions may make us feel as if they were doing something useful, but they do little to solve the problem even if the child would answer them.

Alternatively, solution-focused questions confront misbehavior by asking: "What is different about the times when my child does behave well, or I get the desired response from my child? Does my child

Problem-Focused Questions	Solution-Focused Alternative
1. What's wrong with you?	1. What does my child gain from doing this? What would be a more efficient/respectful way to get that same or similar benefit?
2. How many times have I told you...?	2. What can I do to help you remember? Let's come up with a plan.
3. Are you stupid, or do you just not pay attention?	3. I know how smart you are. How can you use some of that intelligence (or other quality) to solve this problem?
4. Why doesn't he ever listen/do his homework?	4. What is different about the times he fulfills his responsibilities, etc.? Does he listen/do his homework/fulfill his responsibilities? How can we exploit that difference to increase his compliance?
5. What's wrong with you? Why can't you just understand...?	5. This is what I need from you.... What can I do to help you make that happen?
6. Why does this keep happening?	6. How (specifically) will things be when they are better? What needs to happen to get to that point?

behave better when he or she is well-rested? Am I using a different tone of voice or a different technique, or a different set of consequences? Does he/she behave better for someone other than me, and if so, how can I use a similar style? How can I use that difference to my advantage?"

Look at the list on page 118 to see the difference between problem-focused and solution-focused questions.

While asking problem-focused questions keeps you stuck in an interesting parlor game of "diagnosis," asking solution-focused questions helps you concentrate on your end goal and the steps that must be taken in order to accomplish that goal. Most importantly, they help you identify "the difference that makes a difference." For example, even when a child misbehaves "all the time," there are some times when he doesn't misbehave — or misbehaves less. Solution-focused questions first allow us to focus on those things that are different when the child behaves (for example: diet, general health, parenting method, tone of voice, which parent makes the request, etc.) Having found some possibilities ("Well, on the days Johnny behaves better, he eats less sugar, gets a full eight hours of sleep, does his homework as soon as he gets home as opposed to after dinner, and mom or dad — as opposed to the sitter — supervises all this.") you can then start testing these variables out one by one to see which is the most influential for increasing Johnny's chances of behaving well today. Once you've found out which factors seem to matter the most, you can make the appropriate changes and help both Johnny and yourself have many more better days.

George and Tina are the parents of four children. They were coming to me because there was a great deal more fighting between the siblings than they were comfortable seeing. I asked them to concentrate on times in the last few months when their children didn't fight, or at least fought considerably less than usual. After some thought, the parents realized that during the weeks when the parents were able to each get some one-on-one time with the children, the children fought less. Likewise, in the weeks when they were too busy to take this time, their children fought more. The parents then saw that they had a choice. They could either give greater priority to taking individual time with their children, or on weeks when this just wasn't possible, they could expect that the week was going to be more difficult and prepare themselves for it. Over the next few weeks, the parents tested their hypothesis, making a greater effort to give their children the focused attention they seemed to need, and predictably (based on the family's past experience), each of those weeks the fighting decreased significantly.

More than anything else, it is solution-focused questioning that helps me find answers to even tougher behavioral problems in my practice. Assuming there are no other serious emotional problems accompanying them, the family that presents for treatment of a behavioral problem can be ready to go after as little as four weeks of treatment just by making use of the solution-focused questions I have presented here. Don't underestimate the power of looking for answers instead of overanalyzing problems.

Technique Six: A New Twist on Grounding and Restricting Privileges

Use: When a child is abusing a privilege or is unable to resist certain instances of peer pressure, this twist on traditional grounding or restricting privileges can be an opportunity to teach a child the proper ways to exercise his or her freedom.

I do not have a problem with grounding as corrective discipline, but I do have a problem with the way some parents use it. It has always stuck me as odd that the same parents who want to have a close relationship with their children use spending time with their kids as a punishment. Of course, that is not the intention, but that's the way it comes across. "You really did it now, kid. I sentence you to a fate worse than death! You are going to have to spend two weeks trapped in the house with your mother and me! HA HA HA HA!"

"Oh NO! Please! Anything but having to RELATE to you! ARRRRRGGGG!"

I'm all for using your relationship as a discipline tool, but somehow, this approach strikes a sour note. The funny thing is that kids often use grounding to meet their own unspoken needs. In my practice, it is a fairly common occurrence for parents to come and tell me that their child has been grounded "forever" and go on to say that their child continues to commit the offense — and be grounded again and again. The parent usually finishes this complaint with, "It's almost as if (s)he likes being grounded." I often respond that perhaps he or she does.

Grounding presents an interesting opportunity for teens who on the one hand want to be independent of their parents, and on the other hand often have a difficult time with the responsibilities that accompany independence, as well as the emotional complications of separating from mom and dad. For some children, grounding presents a win-win opportunity to spend extra time with their parents — a guilty, and rarely admitted, pleasure of adolescence — and also avoid temptation they don't think they can handle. For example, say your child is being tempted by his peers to do something he knows he shouldn't but lacks the courage to say "no" to. He could, in effect, plead guilty to a lesser offense — as it were, be grounded for it, get to spend time with mom and dad, and still get to look cool to his friends. "No, I can't go to the party. My stupid parents grounded me." In this case, the parents actually are rewarding bad behavior (although it is an admittedly lesser evil) by grounding the child.

Grounding works best when it is an open acknowledgement of the fact that the child needs to be "grounded" in the love of the family. We need to stop thinking of grounding as the time a child spends in the family pokey, and start thinking of it as a kind of "summer school" for developing life-skills. The way I prescribe grounding to the parents in my practice is to say to their children: "You are obviously having a hard time handling the responsibility I am giving you. I am going to spend the next few weeks working with you to learn how to handle yourself better." The parent then breaks down the task at hand into two to four steps and practices one of those steps each week of the grounding. If the child demonstrates greater competence at the one step for a week, then the child gets that portion of his or her privileges restored and begins working on the next step, and so on, until he or she has mastered each of the skills needed to successfully handle this problem in the future.

Fifteen-year-old Carolyn was having a difficult time juggling her relationship with her friends and her boyfriend with her school and extracurricular responsibilities. Her parents finally had enough when she failed a test and they received a call from her cheerleading coach that she had skipped practice later that same week. In session, we worked out a way to ground Carolyn so that she would be able to grow into all the responsibility she had taken on in her life. The process would unfold over at least four weeks, though it could take longer depending upon Carolyn's compliance with the program. The first week was the hardest. She was prohibited from seeing her friends out of school or participate in extracurricular activities. She was allowed to call her friends or boyfriend, but only after she finished her daily chores and her homework had been completed and checked by her parents. The second step was that she could engage in extracurricular activities, if she kept up with her homework and chores. At this level, she was still restricted to in-school or telephone contact with her friends and boyfriend. The third step was that she would be permitted to go out with her friends if she maintained her home and other responsibilities, and her boyfriend could visit her at home, as long as the parents gave permission for the visit. Finally, if she did well at all these levels, full privileges would be restored. Each week the parents were to meet with Carolyn to determine if she had fulfilled her responsibilities well enough to move to the next stage — or if the present stage would have to be extended another week. Carolyn was made to understand that she had complete control over the length of the process. The whole thing would take at least three weeks, but it could take longer depending upon her attitude and compliance. She wasn't happy about it, but what could she do? It was the best deal she was going to get and she knew it. She agreed.

Carolyn worked very hard to earn her privileges back. By breaking it down into steps, she was able to concentrate on regaining control of the most important aspects of her life first, and integrate the rest of her life piece by piece until she got it all back. Within the three weeks, she was back on-line, balancing her home and school responsibilities with her active social life. Did she need occasional reminders? Of course, she is a teenager after all, but she was definitely on the right track — and stayed there.

Grounding a child or suspending privileges in this manner works better than traditional grounding because it actually builds skills. Forcing a child to merely serve his or her time in "family jail" and go out into the world no more prepared than he or she was a week ago to handle the same problems is — forgive me — idiotic. It is a recipe for failure and frustration. But grounding in this manner teaches children to handle more and more responsibility in bite-size pieces until they have mastered the skills they need to handle their lives with true aplomb. Also, where traditional grounding is arbitrary, too focused on external control ("You're grounded until I say so!") and humiliating, grounding in the manner I described above serves a purpose, gives a child a chance to save face by working toward responsibility, and builds internal control by making the child responsible for the length of the grounding.

Finally, this kind of consequence is just, because it seeks to correct the moral imbalance caused by the misbehavior; no more, no less. Use grounding and the suspension of privileges as a kind of "summer session" in the family school of love, not as "doing time" in the family pen.

Technique Seven: Token Economies

Use: For reinforcing positive behavior and virtues.

"Token economy" is the technical name for "star charts" and other reward-based systems for encouraging good behavior. While they do work, I am not a huge fan of them because their overuse tends to cultivate a "what's in it for me?" attitude in children. That being said, they are a good way to clarify specific expectations and "catch children being good." If you are going to use a system of discipline in which you give your child stars or tokens to trade in for certain privileges, I suggest doing it to build virtue rather than simply specific behaviors. For example, instead of giving your child a star for "picking up my clothes," make the assignment "being responsible" and then list two or three ways the child could demonstrate responsibility (e.g., pick up your clothes, do your homework right away when you get home, do your chores without being asked). Then give your child one star or token for each way he or she demonstrated responsibility (or another quality) that day. While I confess that this is entirely my own opinion, I prefer this method over the more behavioral approach, because it gives the parent an opportunity to reinforce good behavior, and also to teach a child in practical terms what certain qualities or virtues mean. It is one thing to say, "Be generous." It is another thing to be able to point to a chart that indicates that generosity means to "share with my sister," or "offer to help around the house by doing chores that aren't specifically mine to do."

Technique Eight: Practicing

Use: When a child is capable of exhibiting a particular behavior but, for some reason, repeatedly chooses not to and is resistant to more sensitive attempts to change his behavior.

This technique ought to be used fairly rarely, as it tends to expend a great amount of emotional dollars in a fairly short amount of time. But it can have very powerful effect on behavior. It is most effective with children ten and under — although it could possibly be altered by a creative parent to work — in a more subtle form — with pre-adolescents and younger teens. Basically, this is the behavioral equivalent to writing "I will not pull Emma's pig-tails" one hundred times on the blackboard.

Ann was having a hard time getting her seven-year-old son, Angelo, ready in time for school in the morning. It was a constant battle that left her exhausted and irritated. Finally, she decided to practice his morning routine with him on a Saturday. Employing solution-focused questioning, she noted that on his best days, Angelo was able to get ready for school in twenty minutes, although most days it took him close to an hour or more. As Ann explained to me, "Every day I start out in a rotten mood because of his lollygaging around. He's making me late for work and I've really had it."

Friday morning, Ann gave her son one last warning. She told him that he had to get ready in twenty minutes or she would require him to attend "getting-ready-for-school practice" the following day. That morning he got ready in fifty minutes with her yelling at him the whole time. She said nothing for the rest of the day, but the next morning, Saturday, she rousted him at seven a.m. — his usual school time — and announced it was "getting-ready-for-school practice." She informed the groggy child that he had twenty minutes to get ready for school, that he would be "getting ready for school" at least four times in a row that morning so that he would be able to do it correctly during the week, that nothing else would happen until he completed "getting ready for school practice" and that he should get started — NOW!

Ann told me in session, "I worked really hard to keep my cool the entire time. I didn't want to come off like a drill instructor, so I kept trying to imagine being his soccer coach when he's really intent on getting the kids to learn a new skill. I stood over Angelo 'coaching' him the whole time. I was like, 'Wash your face! Go, go, go! Two minutes! Dry off, now! C'mon, you can do it! Three minutes! Brush your teeth! Brush, brush, brush! Atta boy! Ten minutes!' all the way through getting dressed and then I said, 'All right. Twenty minutes! Back in bed! Do it again, and I want to see some real effort this time!' And I made him do it all over again — three more times.

"I worked hard to be cheerfully obnoxious. The best way I could put it was to say that I was probably a little like Jack Nicholson doing an imitation of Kathie Lee Gifford playing 'the Gipper.'"

It was a lesson Angelo would not soon forget. As Ann told me later, "He was exhausted by the end of practice — poor kid. I spent time with him afterward, telling him that I loved him too much to let him treat me the way he had been and that I was happy to help him practice responding to my requests in a timely, respectful manner. We cuddled for a while, I made him his favorite breakfast, and we spent the day doing things that he liked as a reward — I told him — for practicing so hard that morning.

"The following week was perfect. I woke him up and he didn't even give me a hard time. Anytime he looked like he was dragging, all I had to do was sweetly ask if he wanted me to schedule another practice for the weekend and he was off like a shot. He learned that I was serious, that I loved him too much to let that go on any longer, and I think he respects me a lot more now."

I have used this technique to help parents do everything from successfully potty-train a reluctant four-year-old (after a medical examination determined no physical problems), to helping children learn how to complete specific chores in a timely manner to their parent's specification, and many other things. However, I usually use this as one of my last-resort methods and only after several other more sensitive methods have been tried consistently for several weeks and failed. If you are going to use this technique you must keep the following in mind:

1. Do not use this technique unless the child has demonstrated the desired behavior at least a few times in the past. Using this technique with a child who simply does not have the ability to meet your expectations is nothing short of cruel. We must hold children responsible for exhibiting the highest level of behavior they are capable of, but we must not brow-beat our children into giving us more than their ability or developmental capacity allows.

2. Try everything else first. This is not a first-line technique. It is a specific intervention designed to attack a specific problem after other, more gentle methods have failed. This technique makes a child work very hard, and there is nothing wrong with this as long as you have the money in the emotional bank-account to pay for their effort. But use it sparingly.

3. Do not use this in a spiteful way. Practicing is not a punishment. It is not an opportunity for you to exact revenge upon your stubborn child. Ann's metaphor was a good one. If you can bring yourself to use this technique as your child's coach — firm, direct, no-nonsense, matter-of-fact, but with love — then by all means use it when you must. But if there is any part of you that is angry or spiteful, put off using this technique until your heart is in the right place. Remember, St. Paul wrote that love does not gloat over

another's wrongs (see 1 Cor 13:4-6). Love your child into good behavior, don't brow-beat him or her.

4. Reward your child for his/her effort. When you use this technique you are not a taskmaster, you are a coach. Act like one. Stand there and cheer them on to victory. Yes, this is obnoxious, and in part that is the point, but it obnoxious in a supportive way, not a destructive one. Likewise, after a good practice, be prepared to spend some extra time complimenting your child on a job well-done. Treat him like he helped the team win the game. You don't have to make a huge production out of it — that would simply be embarrassing. But give him a little special attention both as a reward for his effort and to reinforce the idea that this behavior is important to you. By doing this, you make sure to replace the withdrawal you made earlier from your child's emotional bank account and ensure that there will be "funds" left for future behavioral "purchases."

Technique Nine: Physical Redirection

Use: A technique that can be used with younger children to assure compliance with, and decrease arguing over, certain tasks when simpler methods have been tried and failed.

Sometimes you can talk and talk to a child and it just doesn't get through. This is especially true of children under three, who sometimes have a hard time understanding requests (or sometimes, just enjoy saying "no"), but it is also true for any child who, feeling uncooperative or overwhelmed, simply prefers not to do something you have asked him to do.

The gentle answer to this problem is physical redirection.

Marcia's toddler son was refusing to put his blocks away after several reminders. Rather than screaming at him or swatting him for his non-compliance, Marcia got down on the floor, made sure she had eye contact with her son, and calmly said, "Micah, will you put these blocks away yourself? Or do you need mommy to help you do it yourself?"

Micah said, "No!" so Marcia decided that she needed to help him comply with her request. She gently took his hand, moved it toward a block, helped him pick up the block, walked him over to the toy box, and deposited it. Then she said again, "Micah. Would you like to do this by yourself? Or do you want mommy's help to do it yourself?"

Micah responded, louder this time, "I don't wanna!" so she led him through the process one more time and then repeated her question. Finally, he said, "Do by-self." As Marcia told me later, "And don't you know? He picked up every last block without any more fussing. Afterwards, I spent some time cuddling with him. I asked him how he felt and he said, 'Angry.'

"I told him I was angry too, and sad that it had come to that, but that next time he could choose to be a big boy and do it by himself the first time. He seemed to like this idea, and pretty soon we were laughing and tickling each other. The best thing about this technique is that any time after when he refused to comply with a request, I simply gave him the choice to either do it by himself or have me 'help' him comply. He always chose to do it by himself. It's a big difference."

An example of how this technique can work with slightly older children is Cynthia and her eight-year old son, Taylor. Taylor simply refused to clean his room, and Cynthia was at her wits' end. The last episode of her ongoing struggle ended up with her screaming like a banshee at her son, removing the junk-filled drawers from his dresser and dumping them on the floor, after which she was so angry that she had to go out for a while. Of course, when she got back, the room was no better than when she left it.

After I described the physical redirection technique to Cynthia, and cautioned her not to use it if she felt she would get into an altercation with her son, she decided to try again. Later that week, she reminded her son that it was time to clean his room. He responded, as usual, that he would "do it later." This time Cynthia was ready. She asked the "Would you rather do this yourself or have me 'help' you do it yourself?" question. Taylor just said, "Whatever."

I'll let Cynthia tell you the rest in her own words.

"I said, 'Good, then I will help you comply with my request.' I took his hands in mine and moved them toward a sweater lying on the floor. Apparently the element of surprise was on my side, because he let me close his hands around the sweater without fighting me. Walking him through it step-by-step, I helped him fold his sweater, and then walked him over to the drawer and had him put it away. Then I asked him again, 'Do you need me to keep helping you listen to me, or will you listen to me all on your own?'

"Taylor apparently got the message. I'd never been so calm and so forceful at the same time with him before. He started cleaning his room while I supervised.

"Later, I asked him why he listened to me. He said, 'You were really serious, weren't you?' I told him that I was, and if he doubted me, he could test me out the next time I asked him to do something. But I also said that I would prefer he simply listen the first time.

"I've had to stay on top of him, but since that time, he has listened to me so much better. He knows that putting me off is not a choice any more and it benefits him to listen and do it himself, because its going to get done either way."

This technique has five steps:

1. Speak directly to the child. Make sure you have good eye-contact. State your request.
2. If the child refuses, give him a choice between doing it by himself or having you "help" him do it by himself.
3. If the child either refuses to answer or chooses to have you help him, gently but firmly take his hand and walk him through part of the task. DO NOT use this technique if your emotional temperature is over a 6.5. Over this point, this technique could be used in an abusive manner that is completely counter to good discipline. While you will have to use a firmer attitude and approach with this technique than with the others, you must not under any circumstances drag your child kicking and screaming through a particular task. (If you are at this point, use time-outs or cool-downs to restore order, then restate your request to the child).

   When using physical redirection, the image in your mind must be that of a loving teacher who is going to lead your reluctant child through a task that — for whatever reason — seems difficult for him at the time. If you can think about your role in this technique this way, then feel free to use it. If not, table the technique unless or until you are more confident in your own ability to keep your cool while being challenged. Or if there is no such time in your life, don't use this technique at all
4. When you have successfully led your child through part of the task, ask him if he would like to complete the remainder of the task on his own, or if he wants you to lead him through it again. Some children will find it funny the first time you lead them through, but by the second or third time, it gets less humorous. Regardless, when the child tells you he would rather do the rest of the job himself, back off and let him.
5. Debrief. Thank him for doing a good job and for obeying even when it is difficult. Allow him to vent whatever feelings he may have.

Corrective Discipline: An Exercise

Making a Change

1. Identify a behavior that you would like to change in your child.

   _____

2. Have you tried to address this problem by using everyday discipline? If you haven't, review the exercise at the end of the last chapter before continuing.

3. Circle the corrective-discipline techniques you think might help you nurture this change:
   Cool-down time • Time-out • Logical consequences • Seeking the positive intention • Solution-focused questioning • Grounding • Restricting privileges • Practicing • Token economies • Physical redirection

4. Write how you will specifically utilize these techniques to meet your goal:

   _____

5. Talk to your child about what you are going to do. Ask for the child's input. Write your plan down or — if he or she is too young to read — have your child draw it.

6. Give it two weeks. Follow your plan consistently. Assess level of success:

   • Problem resolved. Congratulations! Keep following your plan to maintain and reinforce your success.

   • Problem partially resolved. Are you being consistent? Is there at least some steady progress being made? If you answered "yes" to both questions, give yourself another week and reassess. If you answered "no" to either question, go to "Problem unresolved" below.

   • Problem unresolved. There are a few possibilities here. The first possibility is that you have not been consistent enough. Have you? If not, give it two more weeks and try harder to discipline yourself. If you have been consistent, then there are two other possibilities. Your child may not be developmentally ready to address this problem, or the problem is more difficult to correct than you previously thought. Re-evaluate the importance of addressing this problem at this time in your child's life. If you continue to believe that this issue must be addressed, then try to develop an alternate plan or consider seeking professional assistance.

Share your feelings. Talk about how to avoid having to do this in the future.

Physical redirection is not something to be done on a daily, weekly, or even monthly basis. We have only used it twice in our children's lives (when they were toddlers), and clients tend to only need to do it once or twice before order is restored and the less-intrusive techniques we have described up to this point are effective. Use physical redirec-

A Quiz: Could I Benefit From Professional Parenting Help?

Take this quiz to see if your family might benefit from some counseling. Answer T (true) or F (false) to the following questions.

_____ My child(ren) and I often engage in power struggles.
_____ I do not enjoy my child(ren) nearly as much as I would like.
_____ My child(ren) do(es) not listen to me.
_____ My child(ren) and I argue more than anything else.
_____ My spouse and I disagree over parenting styles.
_____ No matter what I do, my child(ren) keep(s) getting into the same trouble, over and over.
_____ My child has certain undesirable habits that resist my attempts to correct them.
_____ I often lose control of my temper with my child(ren).
_____ My spouse often loses control of his/her temper with our child(ren).
_____ My child is very defiant and stubborn.

Scoring (number "true")
0-1 — You're doing great! Keep up the good work.
2-3 — You may need to concentrate a bit more on your relationship and your consistency. Review the last two chapters of this book with an eye toward improving these.
4-plus — I would suggest an evaluation with a family-friendly counselor. Call the Pastoral Solutions Institute at (740) 266-6461 for assistance.

tion once in a while to make a point. Then reinforce your message by consistently using everyday discipline and less-intrusive corrective-discipline techniques.

The last two chapters have been our attempt to summarize some of the most effective discipline techniques we employ in our home and in the counseling practice. While this list is incomplete, it will hopefully give you an idea of the kinds of methods that are both effective and yet consistent with the self-donative discipline and deep intimacy the Church asks us to celebrate in our homes. The exercise on page 129 will help you apply the corrective-discipline techniques we've just covered to remove the more stubborn, behavioral weeds from your family's garden.

Putting It All Together

Some parents believe that loving-guidance forms of discipline (the category the last two chapters fall into) are too "soft and squishy" to be effective, especially with more difficult behavioral problems. But these individuals are mistaken.

While every parent has been tempted at one time or another to run around the house looking for "a spoonful of whup-ass to make the medicine go down" (with apologies to Mary Poppins), giving in to such temptations diminishes both the parent and the child. On those days, it is the rare parent who would say that he is acting like the person he wants to be when he grows up, the person God is calling him to be. Worse, on those days, parents will notice that the light in their child's eyes dims — if only for a moment — in a way that we do not believe is at all what God wants to see in our children. Tertullian wrote, "Look at those Christians, see how they love one another!" and Scripture has it that "by their fruits you will know them" [Mt 7:20]. If this is true, then loving guidance is the only way to go, because the fruit borne by it is a greater willingness to become the people God wants us and our children to be when we grow up. It enables us — each member of the family — to use the simple interactions of everyday life to be perfected by God's own, holy, transformative love.

It has been our intention to show you over the last few chapters that good discipline is less about what you do to a child to make them behave than it is what you share with a child that increases their desire to make a gift of their good behavior. To some of you this will seem an unusual way to think of discipline, but this is exactly what occurs when these methods are lovingly and consistently used. We have had the privilege of witnessing their effectiveness in both our own home and with children of all ages in my practice. While other, more punitive, techniques lose their effectiveness or appropriateness over their years due to their unhealthy reliance on either novelty or force, the methods we have described in the last two chapters do not lose their power over time because they rely on building an increasingly stronger relationship with your child. Such techniques assume a teacher/disciple relationship, as opposed to the police/suspect relationship so many more popular discipline strategies reinforce. If you would like to learn more about these techniques or others like them, we highly recommend the following books *How to Talk So Kids Will Listen and Listen So Kids Will Talk*, by Adele Faber and Elaine Mazlish, and *Raising Your Spirited Child* and *The Discipline Book*, both by Dr. Bill Sears and Martha Sears, R.N.

The next section of this book is going to walk you through the ages and stages of childhood. As you review these stages, we will offer suggestions for teaching those most Catholic of virtues, love and responsibility, at every turn of your child's life — from infancy to adolescence.

So, do you want learn how to have the kids that every other parent wants their kids to be like? (You know you do....) Do you want to make everybody at the office sick with how much you love your kids — and they love you? (Ditto!) Would you like to learn how to suck the marrow out of every stage of your life as a parent, to discover the secrets of turning the woeful ones, the terrible twos, the taxing teens, and the exhausting everything-in-betweens into the fabulous five phases of childhood? (Yep. You betcha!)

Well then, you are cordially invited to turn the page.

Part Two

The Five Fabulous
Phases
of Childhood

Introduction

Helping Your Child Grow in Age, Wisdom, and Grace

Have you ever noticed how some parents find a way to hate every single stage of their children's lives? Infants are "so demanding"; toddlers are "terrible! Always getting into things"; school-age kids "never do what I tell them to do"; and teenagers — "don't even get me started …". Early in my career, a mother told me — in all seriousness — that she knew her seven-year-old son was going to be trouble while he was still in the womb, because he once kicked so hard that she fell off the edge of her chair.

Catholics can do better than this. Why? Because we are empowered by grace to experience truly joyful, intimate relationships with our children; to find real meaning and fulfillment in the joys and heartaches inherent in parenting; to thank God every day for another opportunity to share both life and faith with our "closest neighbors" — our children. But to take full advantage of this grace, you are going to need to know how to apply the attitudes and techniques we've covered so far to the five major phases of your child's life: infancy to toddler years (birth to age three), early childhood (ages four to six), the elementary-school-age child (seven to eleven), pre-adolescent to adolescent (twelve and over). Over the next few chapters, you will also be acquainted with some of the most important issues facing your child at each stage, including faith development, sexuality and socialization, and overcoming major developmental crises. Finally, you'll discover powerful tips for teaching your child two of the most important virtues for Catholic life in the next millennium: love and responsibility.

You might wonder why — out of all the possible virtues we could pick — we would choose love and responsibility as the two most important. First of all, these two virtues have been a major theme in the life and ministry of Pope John Paul II. We figure if the Holy Father likes 'em, they can't be all bad. In fact, before he became pope, Karol Wotyla penned a book entitled *Love and Responsibility*, which came to serve as the foundation for much of his later writing on marriage and family life.

Second, as Mercedes Arzu Wilson, a member of the Pontifical Academy for Life and founder of the World Organization for the Family, illustrates in her book *Love and Family*, a proper understanding of both love and responsibility provides the basis for the development of healthy sexual attitudes both before and after marriage. Obviously, passing on such a healthy, responsible attitude toward sexuality is an important consideration for any Catholic parent. But beyond this, since the whole point of discipline is to teach your children how to have healthy, intimate relationships with God and eventually their own mates and children, you would be hard-pressed to find two virtues more important to such relationships than love and responsibility.

Last but not least, in the introduction (you did read the introduction, didn't you?) we talked a great deal about the virtue Catholics call self-donation. Self-donation is a responsible love in that it gives us the "ability to respond" generously to the physical, mental, emotional, and spiritual needs of each other. Considering that love and responsibility serve as the pillars upon which self-donation rest, we are going to pay special attention to discovering opportunities to nurture these very special virtues in your child as he or she grows in age, wisdom, and grace.

I AM a Good Parent! I AM a Good Parent!

People get a little paranoid when they read parenting books. They tend to feel indicted or criticized in some way, thinking that, "If I don't do exactly what this author tells me, I WILL BE A BAD PARENT!"

Trust us, you won't. We are not interested in playing that good parent/bad parent game other self-help authors play. As we explained earlier, there are many ways to raise a basically healthy, normally functioning, grow-up-and-get-a-job kid. But this book is for those parents who want more from their family life, who want to practice what the Holy Father says when he encourages families to be "schools of love" in which we pursue "a respect for others, a sense of justice, cordial openness, dialogue, generous service, solidarity, and all the other values which help people live life as a gift" ("Gospel of Life").

Lisa and I are not so foolish as to think that the methods we present are the only ways to parent. But it is our opinion that the methods we describe represent an invitation to enjoy "the next level" of parenting. It is an invitation that was offered to us by caring Catholic parents who impressed us both with the compassion they expressed for their children and the loving obedience those children offered in return. Many years later, it is our pleasure to extend a similar invitation to you. Just as other Christian denominations possess some truth, but the Catholic Church has "the fullness of truth," other parents are capable of having good relationships with their children, but we believe the parents who avail themselves of the parenting style we present here are capable of entering into the "fullness of family life." Everyday Lisa and I, in cooperation with our children, are working to create that "fullness" in our lives, and God has given us a rich harvest of love as a reward for our efforts. We believe that He will do the same for you, because as the parable of the talents teaches, God richly rewards those who care for the resources He entrusts to us. And what "resources" are dearer to His heart than the children He gives to our care?

As you read through the following chapters, we ask you to keep in mind that they are incomplete. Space does not allow us to treat each stage of development in an in-depth way, although we will attempt to be as thorough as possible without overwhelming you. Finally, even if you don't have a child of a certain age, we are going to ask you to review all the chapters which follow, because even if, for example, you don't have an infant, it will be helpful to see how the type of parenting we are proposing builds from year to year and culminates in a loving, responsible adolescent. This being said, you should not be discouraged from using the methods we describe if you are coming to them later in your parenting career. Your children will benefit from this approach regardless of the age and stage you begin using it.

So, are you ready to learn how to begin perfecting your kids in love from the moment they come into the world until the time they leave your care? Let's get to it!

Chapter Five

Parenting Your Infant with Grace

"Ga Goo, Goo, Goo! Ga Ga, Ga, Ga. That's All I Want to Say to You!"

It's never to early to begin lessons in the family school of love. In this chapter we are going to look at the first stage of your child's life, infancy, with an eye toward what you can do to begin laying down a solid foundation of love and responsibility, even from your child's earliest years.

The Bun's Out of the Oven But It's Not Done Yet!

In a sense, babies are born too early. Physically speaking, they need more time in the womb to develop their neurological capacity and their ability to breathe well on their own. The problem is, if they stayed in their mommies' tummies any longer, their heads wouldn't fit through the birth canal and mom would feel like she was trying to give birth to a very large planet — instead of just a medium-sized one.

But God is a smart cookie (we're told that's how He got

Infancy

Timeframe: birth to approximately eighteen months

Major goals of this stage:
• Completing physical and neurological development, especially those mechanisms that support respiration.
• Bonding with mother.
• Developing the spiritual virtue of trust.

the job in the first place). He compensates for this need to "get the product out the door" through a process called "entrainment." Entrainment is a kind of invisible but very real umbilical cord that exists between a mother and child for about the first year after birth. When a mother — and medical research demonstrates that it is the mother's body that is most capable of producing these effects — stays close to her infant, carries the infant close to her body, and even sleeps with the baby, the baby learns — among other things — to breath in rhythm with his mother. This does two things. First, in every person's brain, there is a mechanism that regulates respiration. Because the child's brain and nervous system won't be adequately formed until approximately one year after birth, the part of the baby's brain that controls the rhythm and consistency of breathing is not yet "set." By sticking close to the mother, experiencing the wash of calming hormones that accompanies this closeness (see later in this chapter), and breathing in time with mom, the baby's respiratory mechanism is "trained" to breathe properly. In a sense, you could say that just as toddlers hold their parent's hand when learning to walk, the infant uses his mother's body to learn how to breathe and regulate other bodily systems properly.

In the pediatric and child-development communities, there is growing support for the idea that the risk of sudden infant death syndrome (SIDS) increases when the entrainment process is broken. To understand how this can be, you need to realize that everyone, infants and adults, stops breathing for short periods while they sleep. This is a normal part of the sleep cycle and for an adult, whose respiration mechanisms are mature and properly "set," this does not usually present any problem. But because the infant's brain is not fully developed, when the infant's breathing "turns off" for a time during sleep, sometimes the brain "forgets" to turn it back on — and the baby suffocates. Lending support to this theory is the interesting fact that SIDS seems to be most prevalent in Western cultures where the baby sleeps away from the parents (Small, 1998; Baumslag and Michaels, 1995). Though co-sleeping (a.k.a. the "family bed") is often frowned upon in our culture, according to Dr. Meredith Small, "Ninety percent of babies around the globe sleep with an adult," and in cultures that practice co-sleeping, SIDS is virtually unheard of.

When a child sleeps with his parents, he does not sleep as deeply, so there is less danger of the breathing mechanism being paralyzed in the first place. Likewise, if the baby's breathing is arrested, the normal jostling that occurs during co-sleeping sends a message to the infant's brain that goes something like, "Hey, brain! You forgot to breathe! Inhale!" And the respiration mechanism is jogged, not unlike thumping the side of your TV to improve reception.

The second thing entrainment does is facilitate a bond between the mother and the baby. While the father must be an involved caregiver from the very first moments of birth (and goes through a similar process of bonding as the mother), it is important that the baby form a primary bond with his mother, as this provides the launching point for future connections with the father, siblings, and eventually the world. Why, you may ask, does the baby need to bond with the mother first? This is a point of confusion for many people, who think of "bonding" and attachment as purely a warm-fuzzy psychological phenomenon, but it is not. Bonding is as much, if not more, a physiological process as it is a psychological one. The invisible umbilical cord that symbolizes entrainment is a very palpable thing to the infant. The baby needs as much consistency and security as he can possibly be given in order for his anatomy and neurology to develop in the healthiest and most efficient way possible. Before birth, the child was wrapped in the security of his mother's womb and perceived the consistent rhythms of his mother's heart and respiration rate. After birth, the infant must be wrapped in the "womb" of his mother's arms, where he can continue to set his own biological rhythms to the ones he's listened to for the past nine months. It is for this reason that many pediatricians, the most prominent example being Dr. William Sears, are teaching expectant moms to think of pregnancy as lasting for at least eighteen months, "nine months in the womb and nine months out."

For an infant, coming out of the womb, where he listened to the same "music" (his mother's voice, heart, and respiration) for nine months, and then going to another caregiver would be a bit like you or me listening to our favorite music — when all of a sudden the CD started skipping. Of course a very beautiful music can be found in the father's or other caregiver's voice, heart, and respiration, but as far as the very young infant is concerned, the rhythm is off — the music is skipping — and while he can tolerate this skipping in short bursts, if forced to listen to this less-pleasant tune for extended periods of time, it can delay the child's ability to set his own rhythms, which eventually translates from physiological stress into nervous stress.

It is no wonder, then, that babies left alone will cry. They are experiencing a trauma. Their invisible umbilical cord is being threatened. God did not design babies to be alone, and their crying is a natural God-given response to this unnatural state. Careful reading of the "Book of Nature" shows us God's plan for meeting and responding to the needs He created in our children. Wearing a child in a "sling" so that he or she can be carried close to the breast, co-sleeping, and nursing are all natural, divinely designed ways to respond to the needs of the child. Other parenting practices — well-meaning though they may be — are not so much based on science and a natural-law perspective of Scripture as they are on politics and ideologies that seem reasonable at first hearing, but fall apart on closer examination. For example, the idea that requiring a child to sleep apart from his parents, and letting babies "cry it out" promotes "independence" certainly sounds reasonable. But this thinking flies in the face of both science and reason. As Erik Erikson observes in his classic text *Childhood and Society*, a child cannot develop healthy independence unless basic trust is developed first, and this is done by attentively and generously responding to the baby's cues (that is to say, your baby's body language, for example, "rooting" for the breast, fussing for a need, and of course, mild crying). Responding to your baby's cues for feeding, sleeping, playing, cuddling, and changing is the single most important factor in laying the foundation for a proper parent-child relationship and good mental health for your baby. Regarding the latter point, several studies have shown that babies become listless and less responsive to stimuli (a serious problem for a developing brain) when their cues are not responded to within seconds! Likewise, these studies show that these same babies perk up and become more attentive to their surroundings when their mothers are subsequently trained to respond quickly to their baby's cues — as their hearts often tell them to do.

Furthermore, independence, by the very meaning of the word, cannot be given — it must be taken. This is the job of the toddler, who is beginning to understand what it is like to be a being apart from his mother, not the infant who is neither biologically or psychologically wired to understand where he ends and his mother begins. As far as the infant is concerned, they are one. As the pediatrician D.W. Winnicott was fond of saying, "There is no such thing as baby; there is a baby and someone else."

Interestingly, there is growing support for the idea that letting a baby "cry it out," rather than promoting independence, creates a condition psychologists call "learned helplessness," which can be a precursor to depression. Crying it out can create quiet babies, it is true, but since an infant is physiologically and psychologically incapable of true independence, the more likely explanation for this quiet is that they simply learn the uselessness of crying: "When I cry, nothing happens, so why bother?"

There was an old psychology experiment that illustrates the concept of learned helplessness. A dog was placed in a box, after which a technician would send a mildly painful electrical current through a metal plate in the bottom of the box. Of course, the dog would yelp and jump out. Then the experiment was repeated, but this time a lid was placed on the box so that the dog could not escape when the current was applied. Though the animal struggled at first, he couldn't get out, and eventually he stopped yelping, and instead responded to the stimuli by lying down and being quiet. Finally, the lid was removed. When the current was applied again, even though the dog could escape, he did not. He had been taught that it was useless to act, useless to cry out, and so he responded the same way he did when the box was enclosed — by lying down and being quiet.

It is not unreasonable to suggest that, in the same way, the infant who experiences the shock accompanying a disruption in entrainment eventually learns helplessness if his cries are not responded to. This serves as the first lesson in being a good member of the "Dilbert Culture" of which the Western world seems so enamored: a society where people are expected to sit in their cubicles, shut up, and accept what little they are given in the way of emotional and relational satisfaction as "enough." A society that — not surprisingly — pops Prozac and St. John's Wort like it is Pez candy. (Now there's a marketing idea for an ambitious entrepreneur: a Prozac dispenser in the shape of Freud's head!)

But Catholics are called to do better. The Church has historically taught that the needs of the child must be respected and attended to. As the prominent Catholic moral theologian Fr. Benedict Ashley has written, "The rights of the parent with respect to the child are always subordinate to the rights of the child. That is, the parents have no rights over the child except for the good of the child."

And yet, the child is not the only one who benefits from these self-donative parenting strategies. "Wearing" the baby in a sling, co-sleeping, and attending quickly to a child's cries have several benefits for parents as well. First of all, it increases the warm feelings between the parents and child. Parents who practice such a parenting style often report feeling more positively toward their children than parents who use more conventional Western parenting methods. Likewise, due to the quick response time between a baby's fussing and the parent's intervention, babies parented in this manner learn to cry less than other infants, accounting for a decreased "parent burnout rate" among those using attachment-parenting practices. This "learning to cry less" is a matter of simple "Pavlovian conditioning." You might remember Pavlov's experiments in which he taught a dog (apparently, it's bad luck to be a dog and be owned by a psychologist) to salivate when he rang a bell by pairing the sound of the bell with the animal's dinner-time. In the same way, when you wait until a child is wailing and gnashing before you respond, you teach the child that he must cry loud, hard, long, and often in order to get his needs met. (Unless, of course, you don't respond at all, and then you teach him learned helplessness). But by anticipating a child's needs by keeping him close, feeding him on request, and protecting the invisible umbilical cord that regulates bonding and neurological development, the child does not learn to cry — or at least does not learn to cry as much — in order to get his needs met. He learns trust. First in his parents, and then, as you will see later in this chapter, in God.

Thanks for the Mammaries — Breast or Bottle?

So far we've talked about the best sleeping arrangements for baby, the importance of keeping the baby as close as possible, and the importance of responding to a baby's cries quickly, but besides sleeping, cuddling, and crying, babies spend a lot of time eating. For most parents, how to respond to this need often boils down to a choice between the "romantic" idea of breast-feeding and the "more convenient but just as good" option to bottle-feed. But in our quest to develop a uniquely Catholic method of parenting the big question is this: "What manner of feeding is most respectful of the traditional teaching of the Church and most consistent with the goals of modeling love and responsibility from the earliest phases of the child's life?" Breast or bottle? Over the next few pages, we're going to take a look at this question from medical, psychological, and spiritual sides.

The One Doctors Recommend Most....

By now, most people know that medically speaking, breast-feeding has been proven beyond a shadow of a doubt to be the best way to feed a baby (See the American Academy of Pediatrics publication *Caring for your Baby and Young Child: Birth to Age Five*).

One of the most fascinating things about breast-milk is its ability to adapt to the needs of each baby and circumstance. A baby will suckle to get exactly what he needs. When he is merely thirsty, he will nurse for a shorter time, taking advantage of the more watery foremilk. When he is hungry, he will nurse longer, enjoying the hind-milk, which is higher in the fat content he needs to support his brain development. Incidentally, this is why the common mis-advice that mothers should nurse for "ten minutes on each side" often results in undernourished babies. Nursed in this way, the baby is only getting a drink, not a meal.

Breast-milk is also easier for the baby to digest than formula, which leads to a decreased incidence of colic. Since breast-milk is easier to digest, breast-fed babies tend to be more alert than their bottle-fed counterparts, since they don't have to exhaust themselves working so hard to digest formula. The ease with which breast-milk is digested also accounts for the fact that you cannot nurse a baby on a two-hour formula schedule without the danger of under-nourishing him. Because he processes the milk more easily, he becomes hungry more often. "Normal" nursing frequency is dependent entirely on the cues your baby gives you, but averages range from every twenty minutes to every two hours. Likewise, if the baby has been exposed to an illness, the mother's milk will automatically produce the antibodies necessary to combat the infection, giving the child a stronger immuno-response than a formula-fed baby. As evidence of this last fact, take a look at the following:

- Breast-fed children are sixty percent less likely to develop ear infections than formula-fed children (Cunningham, 1981).
- Breast-fed infants are three to four times less likely to have diarrheal diseases than formula-fed infants (Duffy, Riepenhoff-Talty, Ogra, et al., 1984). Incidentally, each treatment for diarrhea costs $50-$70 for mild cases and $1,500-$3,000 for severe cases requiring hospitalization.
- Breast-fed children have an eighty percent decreased risk of lower respiratory infection (Cunningham, 1981). Each treatment for bronchitis or pneumonia costs $60-$80 for simple cases and $4,600-$5,000 for cases requiring hospitalization.
- Breast-fed children are four hundred percent less likely to contract

infections leading to meningitis than formula-fed infants. Treatments for these diseases cost between $4,500 and $32,000.

- Recent studies indicate that breast-milk, when combined with digestive enzymes in the baby's stomach, creates a chemical that actually kills cancer cells. This effect, which pharmaceutical companies are seeking to reproduce in the lab, would seem to account for the fact that breast-fed children are *nine times less likely to contract childhood lymphoma* than bottle-fed children (Radetsky, 1999).

But baby isn't the only one to benefit. In gratitude to the mother for feeding His little one with the food He created, God honors the mother with special blessings as well. Nursing returns the uterus to its pre-pregnancy state more quickly and helps the mother lose the weight gained during the pregnancy by burning upwards of eight hundred calories per day. He gives her an increase in hormones like prolactin, which — besides aiding in milk production — gives the mother a feeling of relaxation and well-being. Likewise, the breast-feeding mother's risk of breast cancer is dramatically less than mothers who do not. Nursing improves bone strength (apparently nursing works for bones the way that exercise works for muscles, in that bone strength decreases initially during nursing but is replaced by the body in greater amounts than was used), and is a natural method of family planning insofar as it stops ovulation — sometimes for years. And this is just the short list of physical benefits to the mother and child. Beyond this there are spiritual, social, and even moral benefits which can be gained from nursing.

Wiring for Love

Here's where it gets really interesting. The results of recent studies are making it possible to suggest that breast-feeding may have a role in a child's ability to maintain long-term relationships in adulthood. "Oh, get real!" you say. Let us assure you we are very "real." To understand this, perhaps it would be helpful to think of the brain as a computer. Computers are only as useful as their capacity for running powerful software. To do this they need to be wired properly. The same is true for human beings' capacity for long-term, intimate relationships. That is, the brain needs to be "wired" properly in order to handle the "software" it takes to have a deeply intimate, loving, and responsible relationship. The "wiring" for this process is done by the hormone oxytocin.

In his profound work *Mother and Infant*, Fr. William Virtue (Virtue — what a cool name for a moral theologian!) cites an article in the science journal *Nature* which calls oxytocin the "hormone of love" because "wherever there is love there is oxytocin." Fr. Virtue goes on to note that oxytocin "is involved in male and female orgasm, as well as initiating the 'placental-ejection reflex' and the 'milk-ejection reflex.' " Also, "The *baby absorbs [oxytocin] from the mother's milk* [italics mine]." Now, flash forward to adulthood.

In study after study, neurobiologists are discovering that oxytocin plays an extremely important role in creating the feelings of caring and warmth that are essential to a long-lived and fulfilling marriage. Other hormones are responsible for the warm-fuzzy feeling of new love, but once these levels drop off, it is oxytocin that helps the couple hold on for the long haul. (For those who would like an easy-to-read summary of the role oxytocin plays in long-term relationships, I highly recommend the article "The Science of Love" in the February 1999 issue of *Life* magazine.)

Considering these facts, it would not be unreasonable to suggest that through nursing, God is giving the mother the means to hardwire her baby to have the kind of deeply intimate, long-lasting, sacramental relationship He wants His children to have in later life. In general, people tend to think of the soul and body as two separate entities, but God did not create us to be this way. The soul and the body are intimately entwined (theologians refer to this union as "ensoulment"). Considering this "God's-eye view" of humanity — that is, human beings as an intimately connected union of body and soul — it would seem perfectly reasonable for God to not only give us the spiritual command to love, but also to hard-wire the potential to fulfill that command in the bodies He has given us.

Even if the more skeptical reader were to consider this association to be a stretch, there is a venerable history of support in the Church for this concept. In fact, Fr. Virtue notes that "a typical expression found in the lives of the saints is, 'Along with milk, *he suckled virtue from his mother's breasts*' " [italics ours].

Nursing is one of the first lessons in love for the child. As the Catholic physician and philosopher Dr. Herbert Ratner wrote in *The Natural Institution of the Family*, "… the chief need of the child is to experience love. But because love is to be taught essentially through a one-to-one relationship, … each child has his or her own private tutor of love [the mother]." Fr. Virtue picks up where Dr. Ratner leaves off, adding that "Through the relationship with her, the mother teaches the child how to be a social being."

Dr. Ratner was part of a long line of Catholic medical professionals, including Dr. Maria Montessori (who spoke of the "child's right to nurse"), who were strong supporters of breast-feeding. Perhaps the following quote from *The Natural Institution of the Family* best summarizes the opinion of faithfully Catholic philosophers and theologians who have examined the question of infant feeding:

> Jesus, for instance, tells us to love our neighbor. But Jesus does not instruct the mother how to love her nearest and dearest neighbor, the newborn. Thus the mother is not told to nurse ... her baby [because] the Son, respectful of the Father [who wrote the Book of Nature] assumes that with eyes to see, with milk dripping from postpartum breasts, with hungry suckling lips rooting in search of the mother's teats, the woman can figure this out for herself.

It would be easy to dismiss these ideas about parenting as hopelessly romantic and anachronistic, if the claims of these moral theologians were not supported time and again by hard scientific data. But they are. In fact, in preparing to write this chapter, it was stunningly amazing to lay the writings of moral theologian Fr. Virtue alongside of the writings of physician Dr. Ratner alongside of the work of secular anthropologist Dr. Meredith Small alongside of the body of work of Christian pediatrician Dr. Willam Sears and see how they match practically point-for-point. Of course, this is good news for the longstanding tradition of support in the Church for mother-child nursing and other attachment-parenting practices. In the first place, according to a Hebrew tradition that goes back two thousand years before the birth of Christ, the Blessed Mother would have nursed Jesus for at least three years. Beyond this, Fathers of the Church, several popes (From Benedict XIV to Pius XII to John Paul II, who wrote: "The overwhelming body of research is in favor of natural feeding rather than its substitutes.... This natural way of feeding can create a bond of love and security between mother and child, and enable the child to assert its presence as a person through interaction with the mother.") and saints ranging from St. Frances of Rome to St. Bernadine to St. Albert the Great, among others, all taught the preference of mother's nursing their babies as opposed to other options, including using a wet nurse (the ancient equivalent of bottle-feeding).

Another powerful spiritual benefit to the nursing mother is that she is empowered to identify with Jesus in the Eucharist as no other mother could. When a mother nurses, she feeds the baby her own flesh, just as we are nursed at the breasts of our Mother the Church when we receive her milk; the Precious Body and Blood of our Lord and Savior, Jesus Christ. Incidentally, this metaphor was a popular image among the Church Fathers. Understanding nursing in this way can allow it to become a physical prayer that not only allows the mother to identify with the Blessed Mother who nursed Jesus (and is honored by Catholics with the title *La Señora de la Leche* — Our Lady of the Milk), but also to identify in a unique and beautifully personal way with the self-gift of Jesus Christ and the saving and nourishing power of the Blessed Sacrament

Nursing a child promptly on request also has benefits to that child's faith development and ability to trust God's providence later in life. As Dr. James Fowler notes in his book *Stages of Faith* (in which he examines faith development as a psychological phenomenon) the seeds of faith (or, for that matter, doubt) are sown even in the earliest experience of the infant. When a mother responds to her baby's cues promptly:

> ... The baby is reconfirmed in ... well-being.... In such a way does trust take form — trust in the caregivers and the environment they provide; trust in the self, its worthiness and its being at home; trust in the larger world of meaning.... Those observers are correct, I believe, who tell us that our first pre-images of God have their origins here.

In other words, the trust that a baby develops as a result of his mother responding promptly to his cries plants the seeds for his later ability to trust God to respond to his cries. Though parents do not often think of it in such a way, there is clearly more at stake than convenience when it comes to choosing a method of parenting.

Hey Dad, It's Your Turn

There are probably many fathers reading this who are thinking, "Excellent! My wife gets to do all the work and I get to sit on my paternal arse watching the game and drinking a cold one." Well, before you get your "clicker finger" all warmed up, you might want to read the following.

As your child grows and develops, he or she will be drawing closer and closer to you as a matter of course. In the meantime, you have several contributions you need to make in order for your wife, your marriage, your child, and your home to actually flourish, instead of merely struggle though.

1. Take the initiative in baby care you can *do.*

It is essential for you to begin developing your relationship with your child from the very first moments of birth. The best way to do this is to be available to meet all the needs of your child that your wife is not biologically equipped to handle better (i.e., feeding).

In our home, that usually translates into several duties for me. First, since my wife does all the nursing (try as I might, I haven't yet learned to lactate), I get the diapers. Yes, it's stinky. But it can be fun, too. Having the chance to rub my baby's feet on my beard, watching the baby giggle and wiggle when I "zerbert" (make a "raspberry" sound against the baby's skin) her bellybutton, making goo-goo faces with my baby, and meeting her eyes with mine are all experiences that are worth the price I pay by undergoing thirty seconds of "P. U.!"

Likewise, it is important for me to spend as much time as my baby will allow me to spend cuddling, "wearing" the baby in a sling, bathing the baby, and playing with him or her. Some fathers are content to play with the baby as long as he is quiet, but as soon as the child begins to fuss, dad immediately passes him off to mom. Some moms are just as bad, taking the baby away as soon as the child begins fussing — making the father feel like an incompetent boob in the process. It is better to let dads struggle with finding their own ways to comfort baby so that both the child and the father can get used to their rhythms and their own unique music. Of course if the child begins wailing, or it is obvious that he is hungry, mom should be given her shot at comforting the child. But take care not to do this at the expense of the father's feelings of competence surrounding his ability to bond with his child. Dads, I'm going to let you in on a secret. Besides nursing, women don't know any more about comforting babies than you do. There are no secret "girl meetings" about infant care any more than there are secret "boy meetings" about child care. Your wives learn their baby-comforting repertoire the same way you do, through trial and error. And they have to learn a new repertoire with each new baby. Take the time you need to learn your baby's cues and develop your own unique ways to fulfill the needs those cues represent. In this way, you will be able to provide exceptional care to your wife and your child, giving the former a much-needed break and giving the latter a rewarding experience as he begins to venture out of the world of his mother's arms, and learn about the world in yours.

Beyond this, I consider it my job to help my wife feel put together every day. Moms who do this kind of "attachment" parenting without the proper support from their husbands can get burned out. They can feel guilty taking a shower or going to the bathroom alone because the baby is crying while they do it. Of course, the creative mom can work around some of this (for example, by playing peek-a-boo with the shower curtain while she is bathing) but nothing takes the place of a present father to help mom maintain some sense of herself and her sanity. When our children are infants, besides diaper duty, I take advantage of this very special time to cuddle and play with the baby while my wife does what she needs to do to make herself feel somewhat "pulled together."

2. Take charge of your relationship while protecting the bond with baby.

Your child will be a constant reminder to your wife of her motherhood. You must be an equally devoted reminder to your wife of her youthfulness, sexiness, intelligence, and femininity. Some men try to do this by nagging, "When are you going to spend some time with meeeee?" Or by constantly nagging the wife, saying, "Don't forget about me! Why don't you leave the baby with a sitter so we can get some time?"

This never works. It only makes the woman feel like she has even more demands to meet. The only way to successfully solve this problem is for you to be as giving to your wife as she is to your child. First, try to keep in mind that your wife might be feeling somewhat guilty that she can't be there for you the way she would like to be. Let her know that the most important way she can love you is by being a good mom to your child and in the meantime, you are going to take care of her.

This might seem paradoxical to you. After all, you want more time with your wife, not less. The only way to get this is not to demand her attention, but to invite it as a loving response to your loving response. In plain English, when you are stressed, to whom are you more likely to show affection, a person who gives you a "things-to-do" list, or a person who cleans your house, cooks you dinner, buys you a rose, and gives you a neck massage? You get my point.

Make it your business to be present to your wife as much as possible. Cut back on some of your commitments. You need to be as available to her as she is to your baby. Your wife may be struggling with feelings of "losing herself" to her motherhood. This is a natural concern, and with time and husbandly support, it will evolve into your wife's ability to integrate her motherhood with her personhood. For the time being, the best way for you to support her in this is to join her as intimately as you can in the parenting role. It will be difficult for your wife to get through this phase without resenting your baby or you if you are out golfing, playing, socializing, traveling, or even working too much instead of being home to support her and your child. Your presence is the best indicator of the value you place on her motherhood and the worth of your children. For a while, you may need to back off some of your hobbies and other acquaintances in order to take the time you need to nurture your wife and your marriage through this transition.

I believe it is also important for husbands to increase their capacity for non-sexual expressions of romance during this phase. Some men are used to their wives maintaining the relationship in general, and experience resentment when their children prevent their wives from doing their "job" of nurturing the marriage. Guess what, dads? If you've been hanging back, it's your turn now. God is giving you the opportunity to practice self-donation by developing all those relationship skills you were able to coast through before because your wife's efforts were letting you off the hook. You can either accept God's challenge and reap the rewards of the exceptional intimacy in your marriage that results (imagine that, marital intimacy that thrives because of having kids). Or, you may refuse God's challenge and devolve into that quiet resentment experienced by so many husbands and wives who say, "It just isn't the same once you have kids." Your marriage, your choice. Choose well.

For those dads who are up to the challenge, this is your time to shine. Communicate your love for your bride through all of her senses. Tell her how much you love her, one hundred times a day — even if it seems redundant. She needs to know it and you need to tell her. Stimulate her intellectually (by reading aloud together or conversation or some other creative venue). Many people will be treating your wife as if she has contracted maternal brain-rot. She needs to know that you do not agree with those people.

Show her that you love her. Make eye contact with her when she speaks. She needs to know that she is still interesting to you. Look at her when she's nursing your baby and let her know how beautiful it is to you. She needs to know that you like this new role she has. Write her a love note. Buy her the traditional cards and flowers and seek out other, even more creative ways to show your love for her, all the while — and this can be the tricky part — resisting the evil temptation to imply by your attitude that you expect to be "paid" for your efforts with sex.

Touch her. Often you hear that new and nursing mothers feel "all touched out." Of course, you will have to get your wife's feedback on this, but many times I find that new and nursing moms don't mind being touched, unless that touch implies that they must perform sexually in some way. The transition from new, physically sore, breast-feeding mom to seductive vixen is a difficult one that often takes more energy than most new moms feel they have. If she tenses up when you touch her, let her know that you expect nothing from her except to lie back and let you give her a neck, shoulder, whatever, rub. Take care of her and follow her lead. Your gentle, patient, and mature response will be rewarded with her own loving response when she feels enabled by your caring for her needs. You may soon find yourself in the enviable position of having a better postpartum love life than a pre-partum one. It is possible with some loving attention on your part.

Don't hide behind that pseudo-macho excuse that "mushy stuff" isn't for you. If romance and affection don't come naturally to you, it is time to learn. I recommend the books *For Better ... FOREVER!*, *Isn't it Romantic*, and *Creative Dating* for starters. Of course, there are many other titles like this in your local bookstore. Make the investment in your marriage by learning how to give more of yourself.

3. Cheerfully pick up any slack around the house.

The primary job of a new mother is to nurture her baby. You can hire someone to clean your toilets, and dust your furniture, or better yet, a dad can jump in and do those things himself, but you cannot hire someone else to nurture your baby. Admittedly, you may be able to find someone to supervise your child, change his diapers, and make sure he doesn't stick his tongue in a light socket, but no one will nurture a baby like a new mom.

If your wife has been primarily responsible for maintaining the home, it is time for you to do more than "help" around the house. You will need to learn to be a cheerful partner when it comes to identifying and completing household chores. For a clearer understanding of how these efforts lead to a stronger marriage and greater personal satisfaction, I strongly recommend *For Better ... FOREVER!* (especially the sections on the complementarity of roles) and my book *The Exceptional Seven Percent: Nine Secrets of the World's Happiest Couples* (especially the sections on the "Dance of Competence").

For additional help in learning how to be an exceptional father, I highly recommend Dr. Bill Sears's *The Baby Book* and *Becoming a Father*. If you don't have these books, get them. They are an invaluable resource to all fathers.

HEEYYYYY YEAH-BUT!

Many times parents will tell us that they think these parenting ideas are sound, but then go on to give us reasons for why these ideas won't work for them, asking those questions we call the "Yeah, buts." These questions range from technical questions about co-sleeping to medical questions on nursing to further questions about the psychological and spiritual aspects of attachment parenting and so on. Addressing the medical and technical aspects is beyond the scope of this book. These questions have already been answered very thoroughly by other parenting authors, whose books and organizations I refer you to at the end of this chapter.

We would, however, like to spend a little time addressing some of the most popular psychological and spiritual questions.

1. Won't we spoil our kids if we raise them this way?

Children are like fruit. They spoil when they are left to sit. Children are not spoiled by giving them all God wants them to have. How can we know what God wants them to have? Because God is the one who created the infant to be wholly dependent upon his parents. And God is the one who gives parents the resources to respond to those needs. For example, God creates a perfect food for His babies, breastmilk, and He gives it to the mother to — in effect — hold it "in trust" for the infant. (After all, even though it's in her body, God isn't making the milk for mom's sake! It "belongs" to the baby.) In other words, God created our bodies to work for the good of each other. Bottlefeeding willfully inhibits the mother's body from doing the good work God created it to do.

Likewise, through their research on infants who develop the condition known as "failure to thrive," scientists know that touch is even more important than food to infants. When babies are not touched enough, they will refuse to eat and they become lethargic and depressed. In the most extreme cases, when a baby is not touched enough, he or she will simply die. God created babies to be dependent, to be touched, to be fed the food He creates for them. Western culture is not supportive of God's plan for caring for His children and we are paying the price for this neglect in the form of what the Holy Father refers to as our "culture of death."

2. Won't attachment-parenting practices inhibit our children's independence?

Parents are often reluctant to use attachment parenting because "it will inhibit our child's independence." In fact, it is traditional Western parenting practices like crib sleeping and leaving children with sitters and other caregivers from the earliest ages that is more likely to create whiny, clingy kids. Why? Because children naturally want to be with their parents. When children feel as if their parents are constantly pushing them out the door, they tend to hold on that much harder. It is a secure attachment that allows a child to have the solid platform they need in order to spring into the world. A child cannot achieve independence until he learns basic trust, the foundation for which, according to developmental psychologists, is not set until at least age two or three. It is the two- to three-year-old child who has a solid sense of trust that his parents will be there no matter what who is then empowered to take his independence. Remember, true independence cannot be given, it must be taken, and taking it is the job of the toddler, not the infant.

3. We don't want to be manipulated by our baby.

Certain so-called Christian parenting authors warn parents against being manipulated by their infants. There are two problems with this. First, infants are not capable of manipulating anybody. The ability to manipulate requires intellect and conscious will, and the completely dependent infant has little of either. What the infant does have are strong drives for hunger and physical affection — drives which God gave him. He also has a voice to cry out — a voice which is also given to him by God. Scripture tells us that in order to enter the Kingdom of Heaven, we must be like little children, presumably in our ability to be dependent entirely upon God and to freely cry out to Him in our need. But many Christian parents are being encouraged to teach their children exactly the opposite lesson. They are being encouraged to teach their children to "grow up," to rely on themselves, to stop crying out, to ignore their God-given desire for community and instead rely on things (like pacifiers and toys) to pacify them, providing the first lesson of the culture of materialism: "Things, not people."

The second problem with this concern about "manipulative babies" is that is springs more from an acknowledged heresy known as Jansenism than it does from Christianity. Jansenism is a heresy that manifests itself as a super-scrupulous kind of "Christianity" that subscribes to the complete corruption of the human person and believes that in order to be saved, people have to be constantly involved in some kind of penitential practice. (Modern-day Jansenists also tend to drool over the end of the world and spend a great deal of time obsessing over whom God is going to strike dead next.) As Msgr. Ronald Knox wrote in his book *Enthusiasm*, "Jansenism [unlike Christianity] never learned to smile. Its adherents forget, after all, to believe in grace, so hag-ridden are they by their sense of need for it."

Jansenist-parenting authors, most notably the Ezzos of *Babywise* and *Growing Kids God's Way* infamy, seek to perpetuate Jansenist traditions by forcing "penitential" practices on the infant (like deprivation and corporal punishment from infancy) in an effort to correct what they consider to be the manipulative, evil-oppressed nature of even the smallest members of the human community. This depraved, joyless view of the human person is not at all consistent with Catholicism — as we said, the Church has repeatedly and formally condemned it in its many forms throughout many centuries. Considering our earlier assertion that parenting style is the most powerful form of catechesis, unless a parent is interested in raising a child to be a self-hating, joyless, super-scrupulous heretic, the unscientific, uncharitable, un-Christian recommendations of the Ezzos and their tragically warped ilk are to be avoided.

For a point-by-point defense of attachment parenting and rebuttal of the Ezzos' methods from a medical and theological perspective, please see the article by The Pastoral Solutions Institute advisory board member Thomas Mezzetti, M.D., entitled "An Alien Gospel" (available on-line at http://members.aol.com/ncp2000/). It is a truly profound piece of writing and summarizes what we believe are the foundational thoughts behind the integration of Catholicism and attachment parenting.

4. "We believe that the marriage bed is sacred. Besides, we don't want to have sex with the kids in our bed."

Well, of course you don't. Who asked you to? But one thing at a time....

There are two questions here. The first is about "the sacredness of the marriage bed." The second is about discretion and lovemaking. Let's briefly touch on both of these.

First of all, just like marriage, what makes a marriage bed "sacred" is its openness to life. It is the place where you celebrate your love for one another and bring new life into the world. But if your bed is only open to the "celebrating love" (i.e., lovemaking) part of that equation and not open to the life that lovemaking creates (by being open to having your child share that bed with you), then that bed is not so much sacred as it is contraceptive in that it squeezes children out of the picture simply for the sake of pleasure and convenience.

Now to the issue of privacy. Of course, you need to exercise some discretion and creativity when pursuing your sex life while practicing co-sleeping. One very practical suggestion is to get the child down elsewhere and bring him to bed after you and your mate have had your time together. But one thing that many people don't appreciate when they first hear about co-sleeping is that there are lots of other places in a home in which to be intimate. When you're a co-sleeping parent, lovemaking is always creative, especially because — how shall we put this? — you begin viewing all the horizontal surfaces (and perhaps a few vertical ones) in your home in a new, much more interesting light. In a sense, you could say that the sexual creativity that results from co-sleeping empowers a couple to make their whole house — from the stairways to the kitchen counter and everywhere in between — a sacred space, overflowing with the couple's love for each other.

5. What if we squish the baby?

This is the stuff of urban legend. Just like everybody knows some old lady who put her cat in the microwave to dry it off, everybody seems to have some friend whose third cousin's hairdresser's astrologer rolled over on their baby in the middle of the night. The problem is, there is precious little public-health data that supports this claim.

On the other hand, there is a great deal of data indicating the dangers of crib sleeping, which range from a baby getting her head stuck between the bars of an older crib, to the child hanging herself by getting her clothing tag or collar caught on crib latch, to the crib collapsing because it was defective or not properly assembled, to the child suffering head trauma after a fall from trying to climb out of the crib. It is not our intention to be sensationalistic; we are simply asking you to consider the facts, and the most glaring fact is that cribs come with warning labels for a reason.

However, because it is better to be safe than sorry, attachment-parenting experts always state that you should not co-sleep if you are grossly obese, are a heavy drinker/drug user, or are on any medications which cause drowsiness. All of these conditions could theoretically increase the likelihood that you could harm your child by co-sleeping. In these cases, attachment-parenting experts recommend letting the baby sleep on a mattress next to the adult bed, so that the parents can respond quickly to any needs. Such concerns aside, anthropologists tell us that ninety percent of the world's parents agree that co-sleeping is a safe and beneficial experience for both parent and child. And nothing attests to this fact better than waking up to the smiling, joyful face of your baby, who is thriving because you are using your body for what God designed it to do — giving love to another.

6. What if both of us have to work?

Two parents working is a reality. But this does not necessarily prevent a couple from attachment parenting their infant; in fact, the more a couple is away from their child during the day, the more that couple should practice night-time parenting (co-sleeping and associated activities) as a way of compensating for the extended daylight absences.

Besides this, we encourage working moms to pump breast-milk. While not giving the baby all the benefits of the cuddling involved in nursing, the nutrition is still far superior to formula. The Le Leche League or a skilled lactation consultant can advise you on the best methods for this. When two parents are away from their child all day, attachment-parenting practices are that much more important for supporting the healthy development of the child. Many working parents practice co-sleeping as a way to get more cherished time with their child. And babies sure appreciate it.

7. I don't have enough milk/I can't nurse.

Insufficient milk syndrome (IMS) does exist, but except in extremely rare cases (about five percent of all women) it is not a medical problem (see Gussler and Briesemeister, 1980). Interestingly, medical and anthropological studies indicate that IMS exists only in Western cultures — where the most well-nourished women in the world live. Even in the most impoverished, undernourished Third World countries, mothers are producing milk with ease! (Gussler and Briesemeister, 1980; Khin et al., 1980) The problem in the West boils down to poor education, poor support, and certain psychological factors (like believing that nursing is "gross," "immodest," "vulgar," or "draining," or anxiety that results from the belief that "I don't know how to do it right," etc.). Beyond this, the medical profession as a whole is chock-full of patently stupid nursing advice. For example, most American hospitals do not meet the standards set by the World Health Organization's Baby Friendly Hospital Initiative, which strongly endorses attachment-parenting practices as best for baby. Sadly, most U.S. hospitals aren't even trying. Out of fourteen thousand hospitals participating in this worldwide initiative, only seventeen are located in the U.S. Why? Essentially because formula companies pay U.S. hospitals not to participate by making the hefty contributions needed to build those spiffy-looking "birthing centers." Most U.S. hospitals practice the philosophy that it wouldn't do to bite the hand that feeds them. Likewise, most doctors know nothing about good breast-feeding practices (though many would be loathe to admit it). This includes pediatricians and ob/gyns, most of whom receive no training on the anatomy of the human breast or the biochemistry of breast-milk. (Before talking to your physician about nursing, ask him or her if (s)he has had such training.) Until a few years ago, such courses were not even offered in medical school! To nurse well, you need to have the support of others who know what they are doing from personal experience, preferably another mother who has nursed successfully or a trained, certified lactation consultant. Contact the La Leche League (1-800-La-Leche), or the Pastoral Solutions Institute for information before you decide you can't nurse.

8. We're adopting.

The ministry of an adoptive parent is a beautiful and powerful charism, but it requires special skills and the willingness to do what must be done to re-attach the child to you. This process of "reattachment" is as delicate and serious a procedure as grafting a new limb onto a child who has had one severed in a tragic accident. In fact, this is exactly what is being done. The "invisible umbilical cord" that existed between the birth mother and the infant was severed, and the adoptive mother must graft a new one between herself and the child. If attachment parenting is essential for every biological parent to aid in bonding and provide for healthy development of the child, it can be critical for the adopted child.

In all likelihood you will not be able to nurse your adopted child. (Although you might be surprised to know that some women are able to produce breast-milk for their adopted babies. Not every woman can, but for some women it is worth knowing that such a thing is possible. Contact the La Leche League to learn more about stimulating milk production if you are interested in trying to nurse your adopted child.) However, we strongly encourage you to practice the other elements of attachment parenting (co-sleeping, baby-wearing, and loving-guidance discipline) because one problem that occurs with greater frequency among adopted children than others (except in abused/neglected children) is a clinical syndrome known as attachment disorder. In its mildest forms, attachment disorder seriously impairs the child's ability to experience healthy identity-strength, and intimate relationships in adulthood. It has also been positively correlated with high-risk sexual behaviors, drug/alcohol abuse, depression, and suicidal tendencies. In its most severe forms, it creates children who have no conscience. (For a more thorough examination of the effect attachment disorder has on children, see Dr. Ken Magid's book *High Risk*.) As an aside, it is worth noting that as both parents in general (both adoptive and birth parents) rely on more and more detached styles of parenting, we are seeing a dramatic increase in the number of kids with attachment disorder. You see this in the form of children from "normal American families" who are becoming killers at disturbingly early ages.

Attachment disorder is notoriously resistant to talk therapy. Not surprisingly (considering the attachment-parenting thesis), the most effective form of treatment for this disorder is called "holding therapy" in which the parents, assisted by the therapist, break through the child's agonizingly thick layers of pure rage — a rage that resulted from early, extreme detachment and lives not in the child's consciousness, but in the muscle memory of infancy — while holding the child still in their arms for hours on end (often while the child kicks and screams and tantrums in response to the love he is being given). It can be an extremely effective therapy (though it is far from one hundred percent effective and not used with children older than seven), but it is also an excruciatingly painful process to go through for the parent and the child.

Fortunately, you can avoid attachment disorder with your children (adopted or otherwise) by using a kinder, gentler form of "holding therapy." That is, holding the baby in your arms as much as possible, and sleeping with the child from the first day you get him or her, and letting your child slowly marinate in a constant bath of love over a period of years. This loving attention will help you have the kind of relationship you dream of having with your child, adopted or otherwise.

9. So, are you saying that I am/was a bad parent if I don't/didn't parent this way?

No. Of course not. The reality is that a caring, attentive, loving parent who uses traditional Western parenting practices is still doing a better job than a parent who does "attachment parenting" grudgingly and resentfully. But if you are a caring, attentive, and loving parent to begin with, then why stop yourself from giving your child all your heart longs to give? Co-sleeping, nursing, and "baby-wearing" (i.e., when a mother or father carries the baby close to the body in a sling) enable parents to fully experience the self-donative nature of their bodies and model love and responsibility to their children from the earliest ages. Such practices allow you to experience parenting — from the earliest stages — as a spiritual exercise in which you configure yourself to Christ, even to the point of sharing your precious body with your child. The Church teaches that our bodies were made to give and receive love, and the grace of marriage exists to help Christians learn to use their whole selves, bodies and souls, as instruments of Christ's love.

We are told that we are made in the image and likeness of God. Well, God is generous beyond all reason. As the ancient Jewish Passover prayer says, "It would have been enough" had He delivered our ancestors from slavery in Egypt. "It would have been enough" had He given us His Commandments. "It would have been enough" had He saved our forefathers again and again throughout salvation history. And yet, Christians believe that God said it wasn't enough. Beyond these many good gifts, He gave us Himself, His Son. He lived among us, and then He suffered, died, and rose again for us. And then He made us to be His own sons and daughters, allowing us to join the "firstborn among many brothers" (Rom 8:29 NAB), Jesus Christ.

As the parable of the ungrateful servant teaches, God calls us to model the same generosity He shows to us. Yes, it would be enough to be a good, loving conventional parent. But by God's own example, Catholic Christians are called to be more than "enough." We are called to be "perfect, as your heavenly Father is perfect" (Mt 5:48). That is, perfect in love. Though it is true that the Church has not formally proclaimed the parenting practices we described to be the "one right way" to parent, the Church has given Catholic Christian mental-health professionals the authority (cf. "Gospel of Life") to extend to you an invitation to practice those parenting methods which research indicates are most consistent with the mission and identity of Catholic Christians, and are most likely to enable families to live life as a gift. Consider this book to be your most cordial invitation.

Seeking Support

Should you choose to accept your invitation, we would also encourage you to seek the support and counsel of other like-minded Catholic parents. The best source of support for Catholics who decide to practice attachment-parenting methods is The Couple to Couple League (513-471-2000), which in addition to promoting Natural Family Planning, is also highly supportive of attachment-parenting practices such as co-sleeping, child-led nursing, and "baby-wearing." The co-director of the Couple to Couple League, Shiela Kippley, has an excellent pamphlet entitled "The Critical First Three Years." Contact CCL for more information. Another good source of information is the La Leche League International (1-800-LA-LECHE). Most people are familiar with this organization, but what many do not know is that all of the founding mothers were Catholic, the first medical consultant was the pre-eminent Catholic physician and philosopher Dr. Herbert Ratner, and that the group gets its name from *La Señora De La Leche* (Our Lady of the Milk). There is a shrine to the Nursing Madonna under this name in St. Augustine, Florida. Besides supporting healthy breast-feeding practices, the La Leche League publishes a great catalog filled with books and products to support parents in attachment parenting and loving-guidance discipline techniques.

We would also encourage parents who would like more information about purchasing or how to use a baby sling — by far the most comfortable, versatile, and practical way to keep a baby close to you while still being able to get things done — to call the Over the Shoulder Baby Holder Company (1-800-637-9426). They sell an excellent product, and all their slings come with a short instructional video on how mothers and fathers can maximize their sling-wearing experience.

Of course, parents with specific questions or concerns are always welcome to call The Pastoral Solutions Institute at (740) 266-6461 for assistance. Likewise, we highly recommend Dr. William Sears's books on infant and child care including *Christian Parenting and Child Care*, *The Baby Book*, *The Birth Book*, and *Becoming a Father*.

In the next chapter, we're going to take a look at how to turn the terrible two's into the terrific two's, a time of adventure and challenge for both you and your child.

References

Baumslag, N., Michels, D., and Jolly, R. *Milk, Money and Madness: The Culture and Politics of Breastfeeding*. Westport: Bergen and Garvey, 1995.

Cunningham, A.S. "Breastfeeding and morbidity in industrialized countries." *Advances in International Maternal and Child Health*, Volume 1. Oxford University Press, 1981.

Gussler, J.D. and Briesemeister, L.H. "The Insufficient Milk Syndrome: A Biocultural Explanation." *Medical Anthropology*, 4:145-174, 1980.

Khin, M. N., et al. "Study on lactation performance of Burmese mothers." *American Journal of Clinical Nutrition*, 33:2665-2668, 1980.

Radetsky, P. "Got Cancer Killers?" *Discover*, June, 1999.

Small, M. *Our Babies, Ourselves*. Anchor Books, 1998.

Chapter Six

Parenting Your Toddler with Grace

All Four Seasons in One Day

Toddlerhood can be one of the most exciting and, at the same time, frustrating stages of both your child's life and your parenting career. More than any other stage — except perhaps adolescence — toddlerhood allows parents to experience more intensely positive and negative feelings toward their children in the first five minutes of the day than they previously ever thought possible.

It will be the goal of this chapter to help you hone your skills so that you can negotiate the problems and pitfalls of this stage with grace, turning what others call "the terrible twos" into a time you can experience as mostly terrific.

Trust Me, Baby!

By using attachment-parenting strategies in infancy (see last chapter), you "poured" a solid foundation of trust on which to build a future of love and responsibility in your child's life. Toddlerhood is the time when that foundation must be allowed to "set up."

In a sense, toddlerhood is a sub-stage of infancy. While

Toddlerhood
Timeframe: approximately eighteen months to three years

Major goals of this stage:
- Continuing to lay the foundations of basic trust.
- Beginning to take independence.
- Developing physical competence (mobility and toilet habits).
- Exercising the will.

toddlers have their own unique issues — and we will deal with those in a moment — they are also continuing to build a sense of trust, first in their parents, then in the world at large. Sheila Kippley of the Couple-to-Couple League agrees with child-development experts in her publication *The Critical First Three Years*, when she explains how extending attachment-parenting practices, such as child-led nursing and co-sleeping, to encompass the first three years of life are absolutely essential to the solid development of trust. As parents and professionals, Lisa and I were aware of the studies supporting this idea, but it was not until our daughter turned two that we came to appreciate their practical significance.

Generally speaking, children who are attachment parented have a certain peace about them — even in toddlerhood — that other children simply don't have. That's not to say they are perfectly well-behaved all of the time, just that they are somehow less belligerent and more peaceful than "the av-er-age bear" (as Yogi Bear might say). However, when our daughter was approaching two, she did not have this peaceful spirit, and we were concerned.

Though we co-slept, nursed on request, and carried her as much as we could throughout her first year, two factors inhibited her ability to bond as well as she could have. The first was that as an infant, she had terrible eczema and allergies that caused her skin to be in an almost perpetual rash. Worse still, when she was around animals and certain other allergens, her skin would become so irritated that it would crack and bleed. All this meant that she was not too fond of being touched. Unlike our son, who loved to be carried and cuddled, her allergies caused her to be happiest when she could simply sit on the floor and play in our presence, and so we concentrated on giving her focused attention in the way she seemed to prefer.

The second issue was that while Rachael was between the ages of twelve and eighteen months, we were building our home. While we had a contractor, we did much of the work — and all of the clean-up — ourselves. Our children were with us at all times, dividing their time between "helping," exploring the woods around our home, and finger-painting on the exposed sub-floor, but we were not able to hold our daughter as much as we had held our son at this stage of his life.

While she was far from unattached, after seriously considering the lack of peace our daughter was exhibiting, we decided that her attachment could benefit from some strengthening. Because her allergies were clearing up, we were able to spend a good deal of her second year carrying her in a sling, nursing her, and cuddling her as much as we had wanted to — but were unable to because of her discomfort — in her first year. She ate it up, and the change was remarkable. Within a few weeks, the daughter who was fighting us at every turn became more compliant and more peaceful. Even we were surprised at the remarkable difference that allowed us, in many ways, to enjoy the period from two to three much more than the time between birth to eighteen months with our daughter.

As you can see, bonding is not something that is limited to the first six weeks or the first six months of childhood. It is a process that extends for at least the first three years and then is continued by pursuing both an ongoing relationship with the child and discipline which respects the rapport developed during those early years. We often wonder what our daughter would have been like had we stopped nursing and co-sleeping earlier "because it was time," rather than focusing on what her unique needs were. While we quite sure that she would not have become some kind of axe-murderer ("It's all because you didn't practice extended breast-feeding! Aaaaaarggg!" Chop!) we are just as sure that she would not have been as peaceful a two-year-old as she was and as charming a young lady as she is now. Letting her know that we would attend to her needs — when she needed it, as opposed to when some chart said she should need it — allowed us to build a trust that enabled her to offer more obedience than she had been capable of previously.

But even the child who attaches without complications early in life benefits from the extended attention and love given to him through extended attachment-parenting practices. For some of you reading this, it may be unnerving to think of nursing a child who is two, or three, or even older, but according to the World Health Organization, the majority of the world's children are nursed for an average of five years. That is not to say they are nursed exclusively for five (or more) years, but rather, that the comfort of the breast can be reasonably offered for this period of time. Remember, according to ancient Hebrew tradition, Jesus would have been nursed for at least the first three years of his life, and Scripture pays homage to the Blessed Mother for doing so, "Blessed is the womb that bore you, and the breasts that you sucked!" (Lk 11:27).

If God the Father saw to it that His only-begotten Son was reared in this way, would it not please Him to see all of His other children raised similarly? Of course, the added benefit to extended breast-feeding is that nursing encourages toddlers to sit still for periods of time that other toddlers simply will not, giving the young child time to calm down, and giving the parents five minutes where they can stop chasing after their little demolition derby. And, as an important aside, the toddler who is read to while he is nursed is on the way to developing a life-long love of reading due the powerful association that is fostered.

By respecting the self-donative nature of the body, God empowers infants and toddlers to experience greater trust, first of their parents, and then of God Himself. And He empowers parents to experience greater warmth and trust toward their child, setting the stage for the loving-guidance discipline which flows logically from this type of parenting.

Independence Day

Having the beginnings of trust, the child begins to spontaneously take some of that independence we Americans are so concerned about. The child first begins to think of himself as separate from the parent (developing, as Erikson put it, "autonomy"), and later in toddlerhood, starts to explore his world on his own initiative. These early efforts to explore provide the foundation for future feelings of competence as well as the child's ability to feel creative and effective.

Occasionally a child will try to express his or her will and initiative in inappropriate ways, and parents will need to stop the child. Gentle interruptions of the toddler's efforts will enable him or her to eventually develop a healthy sense of guilt (as opposed to an unhealthy sense of guilt), which sets the stage for the beginnings of a healthy conscience. It may surprise some readers to hear us speak of a healthy sense of guilt, but guilt can be healthy as long as it is proportional to the offense and helps motivate the person to seek more appropriate options. Guilt is similar in function to physical pain. While no one wants to experience physical pain, it does let us know when an injury needs to be attended to. For example, we are told that Hansen's Disease (formerly known as leprosy) is not so much a disease of the skin as it is a deadening of the person's pain receptors. Because the person is less sensitive to injury, he is less likely to care for his wounds, resulting in the infections (and subsequent decay) that are most often associated with leprosy. In the same way, guilt — in rational measure — can allow us to attend to the wounds to our soul, preventing us from rotting from the inside out. While punishment-oriented strategies have been strongly associated with the kind of unhealthy, Jansenistic guilt we spoke of in the last chapter, true loving-guidance forms of discipline are just as strongly associated with healthy moral development and strong consciences.

The chief tasks of loving discipline at the toddler stage are finding ways to:

1. Respect that the child's initiatives (even the inappropriate ones) are not motivated out of destructive or evil impulses, but by God-given curiosity.
2. Nurture a healthy sense of will by finding ways to stop inappropriate initiatives without overdoing it (for example: redirection), thus allowing the child to learn healthy boundaries without feeling completely foiled and frustrated.
3. Discover respectful ways to deal with the increased tantrums which result from the fact that, at this stage, a child's sense of will and initiative is greater than his ability to communicate his intentions or express emotional control.

Will and Grace

The biggest struggle for parents in this stage is dealing with their child's "willfulness." In the introduction, we explained how the Catholic understanding of the human will is different from most Protestant theories. Protestants, like Dr. James Dobson (who has argued that infants are "inherently evil" — cf. "Focus on the Family," December 1998), and to a much greater extent, Jansenists like the Ezzos, tend to view the human person as completely corrupted and bent toward evil. This leads many — while certainly not all — Protestant (and especially Jansenist) parenting experts to be highly supportive of those parenting strategies that will suppress the child's will (corporal punishment being a chief example).

In the short run, such will-suppressing strategies lead to a very compliant child. But parents would do well to remember that same "No!" their toddler screams at them, when properly cultivated rather than subverted, evolves into the same "No!" that the older child needs to assert to others who try to lead him or her into drugs, alcohol, promiscuity, and a host of other sinful behaviors later in life.

This is why Catholics believe that the human will must be respected. We do not, like so many of our Protestant brothers and sisters, believe that the human will is naturally "oppressed" by the devil.

In fact, by becoming man, Jesus Christ raised all aspects of humanity to a new dignity, including the will which must be channeled and trained, but never disparaged or broken. As evidence of this, in the "Gospel of Life," John Paul II lists "attempts to coerce the will" among the "torments of the body and mind" which he condemns in no uncertain terms. You may ask, "Well, if the will is so good, why is it so ... willful? The answer can be found in one little word — concupiscence (con-CUE-pih-sense).

Lying in the Driveway Again

Simply put, concupiscence is the "longing for the mud" that remains after the waters of baptism have washed us clean. In a sense, concupiscence does not represent who we are so much as it is a powerful memory of what we once were. An analogy might help.

Imagine that you left your garden hose lying every which way in the driveway for several weeks on end before you got around to coiling it back up again. Lying around for this amount of time, the hose would not only be filthy, but it would be a tangled mess. Now, when you finally got around to putting it away, chances are that it would clean up just fine — all the mud would wash off — but when you went to wind it up again, it would fight you. It is a matter of simple physics. Even though the hose has been washed clean, and is a perfectly good hose, it retains the "memory" of lying in the driveway, and tends to want to return to that distorted shape. In a similar way, even though we were washed clean in the waters of baptism, we retain the "memory" of what we once were (from the fall to the resurrection was a long time to lie in the driveway). This being the case, we tend to fight what God wants us to be when we "grow up," but we are far from hopeless — God can still use us to water His garden — thanks to the saving power of Jesus Christ and the grace He gives us through the sacraments.

It is important to remember that this tendency to fight against our own good is not sinful in and of itself, but it accounts for our ability to be tempted, and the difficulties we face in living the Christian life. As such, Catholic parents are called to teach their children how to use their wills in a healthy way. But we must also be careful to do this in a manner that allows our children to experience "a respect for others, a sense of justice, cordial openness, dialogue, generous service, solidarity, and all the other values which help people live life as a gift" ("Gospel of Life").

170

Considering this more gentle attitude Catholics have toward the human will, it simply does not do to use punitive methods — like some Protestants and Jansenists suggest —to "beat the devil" out of our children. As far as Catholics are concerned, the devil isn't in there in the first place (although some days you may wonder ...). In the following section, we'll examine the most effective and yet gentle ways we know to help children begin to learn the first lessons of exhibiting love and responsibility in their own lives by developing healthy autonomy, appropriate initiative, and the beginnings of self-control.

Do Bee, Do Bee, Do —
The Buzz on Parenting Your Toddler with Grace

Some readers may remember the television show "Romper Room" from their youth. (For those of you who don't remember it, think Teletubbies — but with a preschool teacher and a giant bee.) On it, the host would instruct young viewers in good behavior by listing "Do-Bee's" (like, "Do Bee ... Gentle") and "Don't Bee's" (like, "Don't Bee ... a Jansenist") on a bee-decorated felt-board. (Real low tech. But hey, it was the '60s). Well, in the same way, there are several "Do-Bee's" every parent should know so that both they and their children will emerge more or less unscathed from the toddler years. They are:

1. Do-Bee aware of the primary mission of toddlers.
2. Do-Bee a child-proofer.
3. Do-Bee a good model by saying, "No, thank you."
4. Do-Bee a parent who gives their children healthy ways to express autonomy and initiative.
5. Do-Bee willing to use redirection as much as possible.
6. Do-Bee comfortable using "do-overs."
7. Do-Bee educated about gentle tantrum interventions.

Let's take a brief look at each of these:

1. Do-Bee aware of the primary mission of toddlers.
The primary mission of toddlers is to learn how to use their bodies to meet their needs. First, this means acquiring mastery over one's limbs, then over one's bowels, and finally, over language as well. Your goal as a parent will be to help your child gain mastery over his body in healthy ways. All the other skills you want your child to have, like emotional control, respect, obedience, and plenty of other good things

can come only to the degree that the child has mastered the use of his body and language. It will be your primary mission to help your child accomplish these tasks by removing unnecessary temptations (see number two, below), teaching your child respectful ways to express himself (see number seven, below), and of course, through toilet training.

There really doesn't have to be a lot to toilet training. The first thing you need to do is be patient, and keep reminding yourself that your child will go to the bathroom ... eventually. Children are not usually considered to have a problem training their bowels unless they are still struggling past the age of four (if your child is older than four and struggling, contact your pediatrician). Even at this, children can reasonably be expected to experience night-time bed-wetting as late as six or seven, though the occurrence should definitely taper off as the child is maturing (again, if you have concerns, contact your pediatrician).

Many children will teach themselves to use the potty. Some need a little extra encouragement. The best time to toilet train is the summer. Simply take off the child's diaper so that he or she can feel the wetness beginning to come. This will be their cue to use the restroom. Be encouraging. Regularly have the child sit on the potty to "try." Be forgiving of accidents. The most common problem with toilet training presently is that new diapers are so absorbent children don't feel the wetness, and so they have little motivation (i.e., the discomfort of a wet diaper) to train themselves. Removing the diaper helps the child be more attuned to the signals that accompany the need to use the toilet.

There are many books and videos on good toilet-training strategies. Dr. Sears offers suggestions in his many parenting books. Besides this, *Toilet Training Without Tears* by Dr. Harles Schaefer is also worth examining. Likewise, the "Once Upon a Potty" videos are cute and effective resources for parents and children. Check out your local library or bookstore for other resources. Or, ask your pediatrician.

2. Do-Bee a child-proofer.

Child-proofing — both eliminating potential dangers (e.g., covering electrical outlets, etc.) and removing temptations (e.g., breakable decorating accents, etc.) — is an important part of gentle discipline. In the first place, it prevents you from leading your children into temptation they are not developmentally ready to negotiate. It is simply unjust to take a child who — because of his age — has poor impulse control to begin with, and then set him up for failure and punishment by dangling fascinating, but dangerous and forbidden things in front of him. Second, it keeps your children safe from accidental injury. Third, it eliminates the struggle some parents have trying to decide whether or not to smack their child's hand for playing with something they shouldn't. (They shouldn't. Studies have shown that such ill-advised interventions can inhibit toddler exploratory behavior for months after, thus negatively affecting intelligence.) And finally, it gives you fewer things to clean and more time to enjoy your child.

We also believe that the "hold hands or hold you" rule we described in an earlier chapter is an important and effective way to "child-proof" the outside world. You will recall that this rule requires the child to chose to hold the hand of a parent or be held when he or she is out-doors. Some parents tell us, "My child refuses to hold my hand. He fights me all the way." So did our children, but this objection misses the point. The average parent is at least three times stronger and (God willing) at least three times more intelligent than the average toddler. When our children would refuse to hold hands, they were told "then you are choosing to be held." (It was, after all, their choice to walk holding hands or be held.) While we did not hold them in any kind of punitive way, taking care to be gentle even though we weren't about to let them escape from our arms, they kicked and fussed at this intervention at first. But soon, they learned we were serious and got to the point where they would willingly and consistently offer their hands before we even asked for them. Frankly, we would rather our children learn to hold our hands as they are learning the respon-sible use of their mobility in the first place, than allow them to run about pell-mell, risking the danger of being run over, stolen, or in-jured. While you certainly cannot plan for every problem, we believe that it is a parent's job to reduce at least the most obvious dangers. Practicing the "hold hands or hold you" rule is a much more gentle, effective, and charitable way to teach children to take responsibility for their mobility. It certainly is better than allowing your child to run around unshepherded and then spank them for — well — running around unshepherded.

As your little one matures, you can bring out more knick-knacks and give your child more responsibility for maintaining himself — in and out if the house. However, it is our belief that before doing this, charitable parents must first teach their children the skills needed to handle such tempting circumstances by liberally using both redirection and "do-overs" (see numbers five and six, below).

3. Do-Bee a good model by saying, "No, thank you."

A major preoccupation of toddlerhood is saying, "NO!" and throwing tantrums. Wouldn't it be nice if there was a way to allow the child to disagree with the parents — to express his or her emerging self — while still being respectful? Believe it or not, there is. The method for achieving this miracle of modern science is modeling.

From the day your child is born, when he or she does something inappropriate — anything from grabbing your nose too hard, to biting you while nursing, to trying to feed the cat to the heating duct, respond with a firm but loving, "No, thank you!" while you gently interrupt the action. If you are consistent with this, your child will come to both hear and say that phrase as one word ("NoFANKyoo!"). Sometimes parents say, "Why should I say 'No, thank you'? It isn't as if my child is trying to give me an extra piece of pie. He's bopping me in the nose!"

Point taken. Nevertheless, you are modeling respect to a child who simply doesn't know any better ("Father, forgive them....") and your efforts will be rewarded. Several times, when our children were toddlers, we have had to correct them in public, which resulted in the predictable, developmentally appropriate but nonetheless humiliating, tantrum. As mortifying as this experience can be (and every parent of a toddler can relate), we cannot tell you how rewarding it is to have a stranger hear our children screaming, "NoFANKyou!" over and over and have them come up to us — mid-tantrum — and say, "How do you get him/her to be so polite!?" Somehow, hearing "NoFANKyou" is just a whole lot easier on the ear, and makes us a little less crazier than the other possibilities. Granted, the child is still being inappropriately willful, but it sounds so much nicer, and we find that we are able to respond to this willfulness in a much more compassionate way, helping our children eventually find the strength to express their frustrations without having a tantrum.

Tantrums aside, it is excruciatingly important to model politeness to your children in every area of their lives if you hope to have politeness returned to you. As Scripture tells us, "the measure you give will be the measure you get (Mt 7:2).

4. Do-Bee a parent who gives their child healthy ways to express autonomy and initiative.

Children at this age need to feel like they can be effective. "Do by-SELF!" is a kind of mantra. Unfortunately, they often choose inappropriate ways to exhibit this effectiveness, which leads to you having to stop them, which leads to a tantrum, which leads to parental insanity.

To maintain rapport in spite of having to interrupt your toddler so often, you need to give your child some appropriate ways to express initiative. This represents the beginning of responsibility. "Help daddy carry this," "Help mommy dust the table," are all ways to let the child feel effective. When our children are about two-and-a-half to three, they are allowed to use the hand vacuum to clean the stair carpet (with parental supervision to prevent falls). All that power and noise at their fingertips makes them positively giddy, as if we promised them a lifetime of chocolate for dinner.

One caution, however. You should not expect perfect follow-through on these tasks. Follow-through (what Erikson refereed to as "industry") comes later (between ages seven to twelve years). It is enough that your toddler is being given tasks which he or she can "play at" completing. Through this kind of helpful play, a child learns to (a) enhance his or her sense of autonomy and (b) meet his or her desire to find healthy outlets for initiative. At this stage of the game, your focus should not be on the perfect completion of a task so much as it should be inviting the child to help as much as he or she is able, for as long as he or she is willing (plus a minute or two).

5. Do-Bee willing to use redirection as much as possible.

Toddlers have the ability to turn any house into the "House of No!" Parents are yelling "No!" at their children, children are yelling "No!" at their parents, and everyone wants to crawl under a very big rock.

While there will be times when a firm, "No! Thank you!" is the only thing you can say, it is helpful to use redirection whenever possible instead. In this way you won't spoil the effectiveness of your "No! Thank you!" when using it to shepherd your child away from the most serious dangers.

The secret to good redirection is asking yourself the following question: "What will my child be more interested in than the thing he or she is heading toward?" The answer to this question is: "Almost anything, so long as it is presented well." As in life, the sales pitch is everything. When your child is heading toward that beloved Tiffany lamp you have out (although you might want to think about putting it away after this...), crisis might be averting by doing something as simple as casting a glance under the couch and saying enthusiastically "Look at those WONDERFUL dust bunnies. Come help mommy/daddy catch them." (Ahem. Not that your house has dust bunnies, mind you. Just an example....)

But even when you must say "No! Thank you," always pair it with suggestions for what the child might do instead, otherwise you will run into the problem of having a child repeatedly and immediately go back to that undesirable thing. Believe it or not, the tendency your toddler has to do what you just told him not to do is not an act of disobedience at this stage. Rather, it is a manifestation of your child's developmental inability to redirect himself or herself. God is relying on you to teach your child healthy things to be interested in. He did not give your toddler the ability to figure this out for himself. Redirection is the chief means by which these important lessons are taught.

The chief complaint parents offer to using redirection is, "I'll have to stay on top of him all the time. I'll never get anything else done." This is an overstatement. You may get less done, but try to remember that there is no work more important than teaching life lessons to God's children when they need to be taught.

6. Do-Bee comfortable using "do-overs."

Do-overs are very important for teaching the first lessons in self-control. For example, toddlers often have a hard time with the concept of "being gentle," and so it can be useful to have them do a particular activity over in a more gentle way — even if it requires you taking their hand and gently helping them do it. "Please hand the toy to me gently." "Please touch the picture frame gently." "Please touch your baby brother's cheek gently." Are all more charitable and effective ways to redirect a clumsy first effort on your child's part than slapping her hand or simply yelling, "NO!" And if your child has a hard time fulfilling these requests to your satisfaction, show the child exactly what you expect by gently taking their hand and leading them through the action while saying "See, honey? Gen-tle."

We have found that teaching gentility to children eventually aids in their ability to express emotions in respectful ways. Although this process will not be complete for several years, encouraging gentle activity from your children allows you to cultivate a gentle spirit in your children. Do-overs and gentle, physical redirection play an important role in giving your child concrete ways to relate to what can be, for them, a very abstract concept.

7. Do-Bee educated about gentle tantrum interventions.

Tantrums result when a child's resources are outmatched by the child's circumstances. It is true that older children engage in more manipulative tantrums as power-plays, but this behavior is more consistent with six- and seven-year-olds, not with toddlers, who are simply overwhelmed by the frustration of knowing what they want to say but not being able to get their brain and mouth to use the right words, of knowing what they want to do, but not having the coordination to do it well enough to succeed.

To get of a sense of the world of the toddler, imagine what it would be like to suffer a disability (like a stoke) that impaired your brain's ability to communicate with your body and vice-versa. Imagine wanting to talk to someone and being able to hear the words you wanted to say in your head, but not being able to adequately choose or form those words in your mouth. Imagine a disability that allowed you to visualize yourself doing certain activities with a high degree of competence, but did not permit you to actually do those activities with the same degree of competence. Then, imagine a nurse who is always standing over you saying, "Please stop that. Don't do that." If you can imagine all this, then you can have pretty good insight into the interior world of the toddler. And, you probably understand how tantrums result from such frustrations.

The good news is that tantrums tend to decrease as a child's facility with language and coordination increase. How firmly you respond to a tantrum should be guided by the level of your child's ability to put emotions into words and communicate needs respectfully. As you deal with your child's tantrums, the two things you need to do constantly is remind him or her to is "use your words" (instead of kicking, hitting, or biting) and teach him or her how to say things more respectfully. For example: If your child says, "I HATE you!" you should firmly respond, "No, thank you, Johnny. Say, 'I'm angry,' " (and require your child to repeat the phrase).

The first step in any tantrum is to remove your child from the immediate environment you are in and try to comfort him. You should feel free to hold your child, and talk him through the strong feelings. Remind him to "use your words," tell him to take a deep breath, and then breathe with him to show him what you mean. Tell him to relax his legs and arms; rub them if he'll let you. Tell him you understand that he is angry, ask him to say "I'm angry," and compliment/validate him if he says it. ("I know you are, sweetheart. Thank you for telling me. It'll be okay, etc....")

If holding the child is simply making matters worse, then a time-out or cool-down time is appropriate. Let the child know that he or she is welcome to rejoin the family when he or she is calmer, and stick close to the place where you put your toddler. One of two things will happen. The child will either emerge after a few minutes in a semi-pouty, "humble-Tigger" mode, at which time you can cuddle the child and in a simple fashion, talk him through the problem, offering better ways to handle similar circumstances in the future. The second possibility is that the child will escalate. When this happens, it is usually because the child has worked himself into such a state, with so much adrenaline running through his system, he could not get a grip on himself even if he wanted to. He needs your help. Take the child to a quiet, darker place. Hold him as still as he will let you. Talk to him, cuddle him. Nurse him (works nine out of ten times) or give him a bath. Baths have a magical effect on even the most severe toddler tantrums. Help him calm down. Chances are he'll fall asleep after such a display, but if he doesn't, use the quiet time to talk him through your expectations for the next time and ask him to apologize.

Asking a child to apologize to all the people a tantrum affects (parents, siblings, guests) can be an important part of teaching a child to ultimately take responsibility for his emotions. But you'll want to use your judgment on this. Require the child to apologize to you. Ask the child to apologize to anyone else you think you can get him to apologize to without starting another battle of wills.

To recap, the five steps to dealing with tantrums are (a) remove the child from the immediate environment; (b) tell the child what he needs to do to get through the immediate crisis; (c) do what is necessary to help the child calm down (including the use of cuddling and time-outs); (d) tell the child how to handle similar problems in the future; and (e) encourage him to take responsibility for his emotions by apologizing.

While these steps will not eliminate tantrums immediately (only maturity will do that), they will begin helping a child get control of himself until he has developed more communicative abilities. We will revisit the subject of tantrums over the next two sections (early childhood and the school-age child).

Love and Responsibility

We would like to take a few moments to address the need to lay down a good foundation for the child's future sexuality in toddlerhood.

At this stage of the game, getting a child's sexuality off to a good start involves three things: (1) extended nursing and cuddling that illustrates the self-donative nature of the body; (2) encouraging the toddler's natural love for "little babies;" and (3) gently redirecting the toddler's innocent attempts to comfort him or herself by means of genital self-touching.

Extended Nursing

The Church contends that the root of most sexual evil is the idea that "my body belongs to me, pleasuring it is the greatest virtue, and I can choose the best way to meet that end."

Extended breast-feeding challenges this notion, showing children from the earliest ages of conscious awareness that God made the body as a gift to be used to work for the good of others.

A mother once told us of the following interaction between herself and her three-year-old son, who still nursed occasionally (about ten minutes right before bed).

Child: "Mommy, Eric's mommy doesn't na-na [nurse]. How come you let me?"
Mom: "Well, would you like to stop? Because you may if you like."
Child: [Shook head "no."]
Mom: "How come you like to na-na?"
Child: "I get all cuddly and warmy!"
Mom: (smiling) "That's why I do it. Even though I have lots of work to do, there's no work more important than loving you."
Child: (Giggled and latched on.)

If such lessons are expounded upon consistently throughout a child's life, he or she will come to understand — on an experiential level — that there is no more important work than the work of love. Also, the child will come to understand the self-donative meaning of the body, which can decrease the likelihood of being involved inappropriate romantic relationships later on.

Regarding this second point, there is strong anecdotal evidence to suggest that attachment-parented children are more sexually chaste than their traditionally parented counterparts. As one sixteen-year-old girl told us, "All my friends are dying to have some boy hold them and make them feel loved and special. I got all my holding needs met at home. I don't feel the same desperation to have some boy, any boy, hold me and make me feel special, because I know I am loved. My mom and dad made me feel special my whole life."

Further, such anecdotal reports would seem to be supported by psychologist Dr. Ken Magid's research, which suggests a strong correlation between promiscuity and poor and weakened attachment. In light of all this, we strongly believe that fostering solid attachment and rapport through toddlerhood and beyond plays a huge role in the child learning appropriate ways to get his or her needs for love met later in life.

Encourage a Toddler's Love for "Little Babies"

Toddlers seem fascinated with "little babies." Catholic parents should encourage this fascination by making a fuss over the babies they see, helping their children learn to touch babies gently, getting dolls for their girl and boy toddlers so that they can play mommy and daddy (they now make more "manly" dolls for boys — in case you were concerned), and telling their children, "Aren't babies wonderful! They are such special gifts from God. Thank you, God, for babies."

This begins your child's early "pro-life" catechesis, and also reinforces the lesson that God calls both girls and boys to be as nurturing as He, Himself, is.

Gently Redirect Your Toddler's Innocent Genital Touching

We prefer not to use the word "masturbation" at this age because of the connotations, but call it what you like. Toddlers are engaged in the work of seeking independence, but sometimes independence is scary, so they need to hold something that makes them feel good. Let's face it — genital touching feels good.

Even so, it is inappropriate. But it is up to the parent to gently redirect the child engaged in this behavior and not come across like the child is engaging in some kind of ritual satanic sacrifice ("Be gone from my child, demon spirits of masturbation! Be gone I say!")

If you see your toddler touching himself or herself, it is enough to say "No, thank you, honey, we don't touch ourselves that way," and then offer another way for the child to feel comforted. For example: scooping him up in your arms, tickling him and telling him that you love him, or encouraging him to play a particular game he enjoys, or asking him to find his favorite stuffed animal to cuddle. Incidentally, these same recommendations work for girls as well as boys.

As we said above, there is no need to become apoplectic about toddler genital touching, but it is a concern for Catholics, and as the Church says in *The Truth and Meaning of Human Sexuality*: "From the earliest age, parents may observe the beginning of genital sexual activity in their child. It should not be considered repressive to correct such habits *gently* that could become sinful later, and, when necessary, to teach modesty as the child grows [italics ours]."

A child's sexuality is present from the earliest stages of life, and this is a good and beautiful thing. However, it is up to Catholic parents to train their child's sexuality the same way they train their child's will. Gently, lovingly, and consistently.

Toddlerhood can be a challenging time for both parents and children, whose drive for autonomy and purposeful action outweighs their skill level and expressive abilities. By responding patiently to the intentions of their behaviors rather than just the clumsy or irritating behaviors themselves, you can help your toddler build a solid framework of love and responsibility on top of the foundation of trust you laid in the first three years.

In the next chapter, we are going to take a look at the early childhood years, where initiative really takes off, faith development explodes, and the child begins to learn the skills necessary for good emotional control.

Chapter Seven

Parenting Through Early Childhood with Grace

The Magical Mystery Tour

Early childhood is a magical time where imagination takes off, a more formal spirituality begins to develop, conscience begins taking shape, and the child is able to use both his body and his emotions in a more purposeful way.

As the child approaches age four, the experience of what C.S. Lewis called "joy" — experiencing the wonder, beauty, and power of God in the created world — is very present. The child's sense of mystery and greater capacity for spirituality is also fostered by her strong and quickly developing imagination. While this imagination can be a powerful friend to children, parents need to be sensitive to it, because sometimes imaginative play can be so intense that it gets away from them. For example, one time when our son was four, he was acting out "The Legend of Sleepy Hollow" and came screaming into our bedroom convinced that he really was being chased by the Headless

Early Childhood

Timeframe: Approximately three to six years

Major goals of the stage:
- Furthering initiative and competence.
- The beginnings of emotional control.
- Fostering spirituality and conscience.
- Getting ready for first school experience.

Horseman. As can be expected with four-year-olds, he started out knowing it was a game, but somehow lost sight of that in the middle of play.

Additionally, the typical four-year-old begins to look for rules that guide the way the world works, including moral rules. He or she tends to think in terms of "always and never." Likewise, the awareness of good and bad begins to dawn, and the child starts being capable of consistently matching causes with their effects. (e.g., "If I run with a glass then it could drop and break.") Of course, this doesn't mitigate the fact that children of this age love a good adventure and fairly regularly bite off more than they can chew.

By contrast, five tends to be an age of introspection. The five-year-old may begin asking more complicated questions of right and wrong. For example, one five-year-old I know asked his pastor after Mass: "When Robin Hood robbed from the rich and gave it to the poor, was that a sin, or was he doing a good thing?" Likewise, the child of five is increasingly more capable of emotional management — though he or she may still struggle with tantrums from time to time. The best way to respond to tantrums at this stage is to follow all the steps we suggested in the last chapter, but move to the time-out stage more quickly. In this way, you give the child increased opportunities to practice self-control. However, keep in mind that children at this age have not yet completely mastered their emotions. Be prepared to offer support in a debriefing after he or she emerges from time-out.

Spiritually speaking, five-year-olds love morality stories including Bible stories, lives of the saints, fables, even tales of your own life as a child when you had struggles to face and how you overcame them.

One struggle common to fives is that sometimes they will choose not to do things that they have shown themselves to be perfectly capable of doing in the past (for example, dressing themselves, doing simple chores). Gentle reminders backed up by logical consequences, practicing, and occasional physical redirection (see chapters two and three) are all acceptable ways of dealing with these momentary lapses.

Finally, six is an age of indecision and limit-testing. According to Dr. Louise Bates-Ames of Yale University's Gesel Institute of Child Development, "What [the six-year-old] needs most is parents who understand him." This age is characterized by "bi-polarity," that is, the child may want two opposite things at the same time and find it next to impossible to choose which option is the best. The result is often very frustrating to parents. For example, when one six-year-old boy was asked if he wanted a cookie, he responded, "Maybe I do. I think so ... well, maybe not ... I'm not sure ... well, okay." Such responses, though frustrating to parents, are typical for the age.

Similarly, some children around this time go through a super-scrupulous phase, where they wonder if every little thing they do is a sin. They often have a tough time telling the difference between mistakes and sins. A child of this age will often say that a person who dropped a glass by accident is equally guilty of wrongdoing as a person who smashes a glass against a wall on purpose, because both things involve breaking something, and "You shouldn't break things." It can be important at this time to begin explaining the difference between accidents and sins (sin requires intention and full knowledge) although, chances are, you will have to explain this several times until your child is developmentally ready to understand what you are trying to tell him.

As you might guess, this emerging and undiscriminating sense of right and wrong can cause some children will be very sensitive to criticism. It common for sixes to feel "picked on" by their parents and often wonder, "Do you love me anymore?" It is best to respond sensitively to the gaffes a six-year-old makes. You should also expect that when more serious forms of correction are necessary, you will have to spend some extra time cuddling, affirming, and re-establishing rapport after the discipline has been administered.

Furthering Initiative and Competence

Early childhood is marked by a child's desire to take on new challenges and have new adventures. Parents should channel this desire in such a way as to encourage responsibility and family solidarity by giving the child simple ways to help with housekeeping chores. Dr. Maria Montessori encouraged children to do all that they were capable of around the house, and she believed that they were capable of a great deal. Indeed they are. However, parents should be careful to not expect a child to complete tasks perfectly without supervision. Parents would do well to think of themselves as coaches at this stage. Think about it: If a coach said, "Okay, you guys run some drills, I'm going out to play golf/get a drink/do some paperwork/clip my toenails/ etc." do you really think that the team would follow through? Of course not. Just as the coach needs to keep on top of the assignments he gives his team, a parent needs to stay on top of the chores he or she gives to his or her children. It is unreasonable to expect perfect, self-motivated follow-through from a child younger than twelve or so, and even then, some supervision is a good idea.

Some parents become frustrated with the idea of having their small children do simple chores like cleaning up their toys, straightening their rooms, clearing the table, dusting, and the like, so they say, "It's just easier to do it myself. I have to stand around making sure it gets done correctly anyway, and I could do it in half the time." The problems with this sentiment are two-fold. First, it misses the point of parenting, which is to teach kids to be able to take care of themselves and have healthy adult relationships. It should be fairly obvious that exhibiting competence with and responsibility for household chores is an important step toward meeting both of these goals.

The second problem with a parent's "I can do it myself in half the time" philosophy is that later on, when your children are more capable of doing things, you are going to want their help, but because they are not used to offering it, you will have an uphill battle extracting help from them. An important rule of family life is that each member of the family must contribute all that they can for the good of the others. It is a parent's job to model this rule, and to make sure that from the earliest ages, children are doing all that they can to be productive members of the family.

Throughout this book, we have talked about the importance of maintaining rapport with your children. Often, parents make the mistake of thinking that we mean that family life must be one long carnival — filled with fun and games. While fun is absolutely an essential part of family of life (without it the emotional bank-account can run dry fairly quickly), working together is just as important an aspect of family rapport. It builds team spirit, responsibility, stewardship, and many other virtues that help families live life as a gift. And the competence that comes from knowing how to be a productive member of the family is an essential building block of good self-esteem.

The Beginnings of Emotional Control

In early childhood, children are gaining greater and greater competence with speech as well as both gross and fine motor-skills. With this increase in physical and verbal, parents should see a decrease in the normal tantrums of the toddler stage. Children at early childhood still get frustrated, though, and need a parent to help them continue to find appropriate ways to express those strong emotions.

The best way to teach healthy emotional control is to consistently use the following steps:

1. Be respectful of their feelings.

Whether a feeling is expressed appropriately or not, a parent must try to be understand of the intention behind the emotion. This can be difficult, but it is essential. While a parent cannot and should not tolerate disrespectful behavior from their child (see number two below), before you can address the inappropriate display of emotion, you must be willing to understand what the child is trying to communicate through the emotion. If you do not, you will give the child the impression that you are disciplining him for his feelings and not merely for his clumsy effort at expressing them. Over the years, this will create a child who is sullen and secretive — a parent's worst nightmare.

While the next few pages will show you where to go from here, the following are examples of some things you can say to initiate a discussion about healthier, more respectful ways to express emotions:

— Wow. Those are really strong feelings.

— You seem really sad/angry/frustrated/disappointed about that.

— I understand that you are very upset right now. Take a breath and think about what you are really trying to tell me.

— I know that you feel like hitting. Please use your words.

— I know you are angry, but you may not speak to me that way. Please say "[fill in the blank]" instead.

— You obviously need to tell me something that's very important to you, but you're too upset to tell me the way you need to. Please go to your room and when you're ready to speak respectfully, I will be ready to listen.

As we said, these are ways to initiate a discussion about emotional outbursts. The following describes the next step in the process:

2. Offer acceptable alternatives.

When a child demonstrates inappropriate speech or action, the first line of defense is to give an alternative way to express that emotion. Look at the following for some suggestions on how to redirect your child when he or she expresses emotions disrespectfully.

The chart on page 188 represent the front-line, first-aid tips for teaching your child more respectful ways to communicate their emotions. We use them successfully both at home and in the practice, and we invite you to try them in your home. Feel free to add your own statements to the list, or to word our suggestions in a manner that is

When Your Child Says/Does:	Respond with:
"I HATE you."	"Please say, 'I'm so angry!'" Have child repeat. Say, "I know you are, honey, what do you need to do to feel better?"
"You don't love me!"	"Please say, 'Do you love me?'" Or, "Could you hold me?" After child repeats, respond to request.
Child calls you a name.	Have child apologize, and then say, "Please say, 'I'm so [insert emotion].'"
Child tries to hit, kick, or bite.	"Stop! Use your words!" If child cannot, see step three on page 189.
Child rolls eyes at you or offers other gesture of contempt.	"Please don't make faces at me. If you have something to say, please say it. I will listen." (Ask for an apology if you feel it is warranted.)
Child grunts and disgustedly says, "Okay, okay already" (or something to the effect).	"Please say, 'Yes, mom/dad.'"
Child stomps away angrily and/or slams door.	Have child come back to you. Firmly, calmly say, "I know you are angry, but you must still be respectful. Please say, 'I would like to be alone for a few minutes.'" Child repeats. Then say, "That would be fine. You may go — without the attitude this time — but if you need to talk more later, let me know."

more consistent with your own style, but always remember that regardless of how disrespectfully a child expresses emotion, you must model respect by showing sensitivity to the intention behind the emotion and giving your child a more acceptable way to express that intention.

Most of the time, when used consistently, these simple redirections work. Sometimes they don't. This is especially true when a child's emotional temperature is too high. When this happens, use step three below.

3. Use cool-down time or a time-out to teach the need for respectful breaks.

When your child's emotions are getting out of hand and efforts to reason with him or talk him through the problem are proving fruitless or downright infuriating, take a break. Tell your child that in order to be around others, he must be capable of maintaining a certain level of respect and self-control, and that until he can show you that, he must be away from you. Send the child to cool-down time or a time-out. Tell the child that when he is calm and ready to speak respectfully he may come out. Follow the tips on working through a time out that we enumerated in the corrective-discipline chapter.

4. When absolutely necessary, use logical consequences.

A five-year-old girl decided to have a tantrum on her way out the door to a carnival with her parents. The girl wanted a drink. When the parents offered her water, she screamed, "I want soda!" The parents rightly refused the obnoxiously stated request, at which point their daughter's behavior escalated. After several attempts to calm her failed, including a time-out, the parents told her that she lost the privilege of going to the carnival. This was absolutely the right thing to do, but of course the daughter acted as if the parents were trying to cut off her head with a spoon. Nonetheless, the parents stayed home. The daughter was sent to her room, where she stayed until she was calmer. After this, her parents talked her through the situation and told her exactly what they expected from her the next time. She asked if they could still go and she was told that it was now too late to go to the carnival. She began crying — but not in a tantrum-y sort of way. The parents comforted her and worked out a way for the child to save face, taking care not to undermine their own intervention. They told her that if she behaved herself that night and the following day, they would be willing to take her to the carnival for an hour after dinner "tomorrow." This was a shorter time than the family would have originally spent there, but it would be better than nothing. The child agreed and managed to behave exceptionally well during the specified time. The next day, she was rewarded with praise for her self-control and was taken to the carnival as promised. Later, the parents told me in session, "She did really well. Even when we told her it was time to leave the fair after only an hour, she just said, 'Okay, mommy.' We were thrilled."

If you are going to use a logical consequence, it is important to also give the child a way to earn back the privilege by demonstrating some kind of change. Note we do not say it is important to simply give back a privilege after the child has simply served his time. Rather, a child must be given the chance to earn back the privilege by behaving appropriately for a reasonable amount of time. The time it takes to earn his or her way out of a logical consequence is entirely up to the child, but it should be at least a significant enough period of time (for example, a day with a younger child, a week or two with an older child) for the parents to know that the child is making a sincere and consistent effort to change. After such a period of time has passed to the parent's satisfaction, the child may be given another chance. This gives the parents a way to set a firm limit while not causing the child to lose heart.

The above four steps, used consistently and firmly, combined with the modeling of an emotionally astute parent, are often all a child needs to master his or her emotions throughout early childhood and beyond. We would encourage parents who are less confident of their own abilities to manage their emotions well and respectfully to seek competent professional assistance.

Fostering Spirituality and Conscience

The ages of three through six are a critical time for the spiritual development and conscience formation of your child.

Spiritually speaking, your child is beginning to demonstrate a sense of awe and wonder — the experience of "joy" we spoke of earlier. A Catholic parent can capitalize on the experience of these qualities by actively exposing his or her child to the mystery and joy to be found in the Faith of the Church, especially the Eucharist. There is no better time in your child's life to begin teaching him or her about the Precious Body and Blood of Jesus. While they will not be able to grasp the full weight of what you are telling them for several years (Frankly, we are still trying to grasp it ourselves. What Catholic isn't?), there is no better time in a person's life to be able to fully enjoy the powerful, joyful, mystery of it than early childhood.

At the consecration, we make a point of quietly and reverently saying to our children from infancy on, "Look! Look at the miracle! The bread is becoming the Body and Blood of Jesus. Say, 'I love you, Jesus.' " This practice has led to some very interesting discussions with our children about the Eucharist, and has enabled us to expose them to a number of perfectly delightful resources for children. Perhaps the one that touched our children the most is the story called *The Caterpillar That Came to Church: A Story of the Eucharist* from Our Sunday Visitor Publishing. It tells the tale of a caterpillar who is accidentally carried into church in a mother's purse and is miraculously given the gift of seeing Jesus in the Eucharist. Our kids love it.

Likewise, at Mass, after receiving the Precious Body, we return to our pews and lead our children through the following prayer before we begin our own prayer time: "Dear Jesus, I love You very much. Thank You for loving us and giving us Your Body and Blood. Send Your Holy Spirit into my heart, so that I can love You more than anything, and help make me ready to receive You in the Eucharist one day. Amen." Then we parents say our own prayers.

We really didn't realize what the fruit of this could be until our son went to Easter Mass at age six and started crying afterward. We asked what was wrong and he said that he wanted to receive Jesus so much, when he saw "all those people getting Communion for the first time" (the catechumens) he wanted to be with them. He said through his tears, "I don't want to have to wait another whole year!"

This is not to say our children always love sitting through Mass, but they do love Jesus and they are developing a greater appreciation of the Eucharist every day. In our opinion, parents who do not teach their children about the Real Presence, or teach them that "It's just bread that reminds us of something special Jesus did," rob their children of the sense of joy they can experience in the presence of the Eucharist even before they can receive. It is a mistake to wait until second-grade religion class to introduce the cornerstone of our Faith to your child.

Beyond this, children can begin to lead family prayer at this age, they enjoy heroic stories of saints, and are able to fall completely in love with Jesus — so long as encouraged to do so through prayer and parental example. We will discuss more ways to foster your child's spirituality in our chapter devoted exclusively to this.

Getting Ready for First School Experience

While many children may have had some day care or other pre-school experience before this time, this age group is getting ready to begin more formal schooling. This is a good time to examine three basic questions about schooling. As far as the Church is concerned, what is the parent's role in a child's education? What can parents do to foster a love of learning in their children? And finally, how can you determine which of the formal schooling options (parochial school, public school, homeschooling) are best for you and your children? Let's take a brief look at each of these questions.

1.What does the Church have to say about the parents' role in their children's education?

John Paul II's *Letter to Families* (no. 16) tells us that parents are the "first and most important educators" of their children. This not only means that parents are responsible for teaching their children the first lessons in life, but it also means that all through the school years, parents are obliged to play an active and primary role in their children's education.

Too often, parents send their children to school with the attitude that as long as they pay the tuition bill (or their school taxes) their responsibility is complete. Clearly, this is not the case as far as the Church is concerned. Parents are responsible for overseeing their children's education, regardless of who else they may decide to involve. Practically speaking, this translates into the parent's responsibility to actively seek out educational opportunities for their children outside of school, to foster a love of learning, and at the very least, to make available to their children the resources needed to master the skills practiced through homework assignments. (We'll talk more about good homework habits in the next chapter.)

The *Catechism* tells parents that they have the right "to choose a school ... which corresponds to their own convictions" (2229). In an official document of his See, Bishop Donald Wuerl of the Diocese of Pittsburgh asserts that this right to choose a school extends to homeschooling as well. But whether parents choose to homeschool or send their children to parochial or public school, the one thing that cannot change is that the parent — not a teacher, principal, tutor, or counselor — is ultimately responsible for the child's education, both in knowledge and in virtue.

We will deal with homeschooling in a moment, but if you choose to send your children to parochial or public school, we believe that you must make an effort to be intimately familiar with your children's course of study. You cannot wait for your child to tell you what he or she learned in school today. You need to take the initiative to find out what your child is learning for yourself, not because you don't trust the teacher, but because it is the Catholic parent's responsibility to supervise their children's education. Simply put, you can't supervise what you don't know about. As your child's primary teacher — the teacher to whom your child's classroom teacher is responsible — you must know what your children are supposed to be studying in order to facilitate discussions about it, plan family field trips to support it, and offer additional activities to encourage mastery of the material. Any good teacher will tell your that school — for the most part — is not where things are learned. School is where things are taught. The learning takes place at home and in the world-at-large when the child practices what was taught.

Parents must also be active in the school community. This models to children that school is important and that the parents are interested in what is going on. Parents must be willing to give generously of their time to school functions and activities, including fundraising activities. We realize this takes a great deal of time and effort, but education in both virtue and knowledge is the primary role of parents, and if you are not going to do it entirely by yourself (through homeschooling) you must be committed to passionately supporting the people you hire to assist you in your mission (professional teachers). Just as you should never allow any activity to compete with your child's attention for school, you must never allow any activity to compete with your own ability to be an active and interested member of the school community.

2. What can you do to foster a love of learning in your child?

Early childhood is a time of wonder and awe. Everything is filled with meaning. The child of this age has a natural drive for discovery and experimentation. Parents can either encourage this and reap the benefits, or ignore/discourage it and have to spend the rest of their lives fighting with their children to get their homework done. Your call.

The first thing you can do to foster a lifelong love of learning is to not make a distinction between "school" and "play." For the child of this age, play is learning. The attentive parent can capitalize on this.

After returning home from a walk with your child, have him or her draw pictures of different things he or she sees (plants, animals, machines, buildings). Look those things up together in a good encyclopedia or nature guide. Be interested yourself in what you are reading. Model a fascination with discovery. Say, "Isn't that wonderful!" "Look at the colors." "What do you think that does?" "Let's see what it says here … I didn't know that! Wow!" Glen Doman of *Teach Your Baby to Read* fame says that the most successful babies in his program have mothers whom he affectionately refers to as "dumb blondes." That is, they get excited about everything; when they present something to their children, they act as if it is the most interesting thing in the world. In short, they model a sense of joy in the presence of learning and discovery and their children catch that joy.

When your child expresses an interest in a topic, be it history, or dinosaurs, or pirates, or cowboys, or art, or dolls, or anything, find ways to "play" that interest with him or her. Take family field-trips, draw pictures of interesting things you see in the neighborhood or on trips, read stories relevant to your child's interests, enroll in a class together, take things apart with your child (putting them back together comes later), visit educational-toy stores, play games that build skills and concentration. All of these are ways to properly blur the line between learning and play.

Perhaps the most important way to foster a love of learning is to read, read, and read some more. Hopefully, you have been reading to your child since day one. Some parents don't read to their children because "they won't sit still long enough." We say, "If Mohammed won't go to the library, bring the library to Mohammed." If he or she won't sit still, read while he or she plays around you. (And for the first three to five years of life, practice the habit of reading when you nurse. The child who associates books with the sound of his parents' animated voices and the comfort of his mother's breast is a child that will love reading all the days of his or her life.)

When you read, try to stick to books that will cause your child to think and ask questions. For example, Laura Ingles Wilder's "Little House" series, children's historical fiction, the "Great Illustrated Classics" series (at six and three, our son and daughter both loved the "Illustrated Classics" versions of *Ivanhoe* and *Captains Courageous* — though they got different things from the reading), a well-written and visually appealing children's Bible, and the children's lives of the saints we spoke of in an earlier chapter, are all examples of books that both fascinate young children and make them think. Children of this age are capable of understanding books that are years beyond their own reading level when you read those books to them. Family reading-time draws families closer together and gives family members many interesting topics to discuss.

3. What schooling option (homeschooling, parochial, or public school) will be best for us and our child?

When choosing what school setting is best for you and your child(ren), there are two basic categories to choose from: homeschooling and institutional schooling. Let's take a brief look at each.

Homeschooling

It's actually much easier than you'd think. It's legal in all fifty states, supported by Church teaching, and by nature it is flexible enough to fit almost any parent's schedule (even working parents). If you haven't thought of homeschooling before, we'd invite you to consider it now as the most intimate way you can fulfill your call to be your child's primary teacher.

First of all, homeschooling doesn't have to take much time. At this age (early childhood), the average homeschooler probably does no more than two cumulative hours (i.e., not necessarily all at one sitting) or so of sit-down class-work a day (in higher grades it usually doesn't exceed three hours a day, and much of this can be done by the child on his or her own). When you think that the average parent already spends at least an hour or two per night supervising their children's homework, you realize, again, that even the parent who sends their child to "away school" ends up facilitating most of the actual learning at home.

Some parents don't feel "qualified" to teach their children. Well, the Church begs to differ. In his *Letter to Families*, John Paul II writes that parents "possess a fundamental competence in this area: *they are educators because they are parents* [italics original]." One way to read this (though certainly not the only way) is to say that because you are responsible for your children's education either way they go, and because you have already taught your children the really hard stuff anyway (walking, using the potty, talking, love, responsibility, etc.), why not continue to do what you've already been doing all along?

There are several reasons we practice homeschooling in our own home and encourage others to at least consider it, even if they ultimately decide it isn't for them. First, it enables you to maintain that continuity between learning and play. When a child is homeschooled, everything is an opportunity for learning; every new adventure or interest can be cultivated and investigated until the next thing comes along. One benefit many homeschooling parents report is that they enjoy learning new things right along with their children. Parents don't have to know everything about a subject to teach it. After all, the best teachers model the learning process, not omniscience. If you know how to look things up somewhere, then you basically know what you need to know to teach your kids. Of course, if you would rather work with a net, you can purchase one of many pre-packaged homeschooling curricula at a very reasonable price. A pleasant range of products exists so that your homeschool program can be as structured or unstructured as you like. (To learn more about homeschooling and homeschooling curricula, we recommend *Mary Pride's The Big Book of Home Schooling* and *Catholic Homeschooling* by Kimberly Hahn and Maryann Hasson.)

Homeschooling, for us, is simply the logical continuation of our desire to foster closeness in our family. We recently attended a parenting conference in which a group of non-homeschooling mothers were complaining that since their children began kindergarten, they no longer wanted to kiss or cuddle with their parents because it "wasn't cool." Homeschoolers do not have this problem. As a family, we discover things together, we celebrate the joy of learning together, we struggle together, and we enjoy the relationship that this fosters. Do homeschooled kids ever see anyone other than their parents? Of course. (Those parents who worry about the "socialization" of homeschooled children often forget that, most of the time, "socializing" in school is strongly discouraged. Truth be told, I once got detention for it.) Children who are homeschooled have as many opportunities (if not more, due to a shorter school day) to socialize with peers after school as any other child. In fact, homeschooled children are often better socialized than their "away-school" counterparts because they are surrounded by the example of (presumably) mature, loving adults. The real benefit to this arrangement is that in spite of the many and varied friendships, activities, and interests available to the homeschooled child, the child always understands that family is the primary relationship. This is a very Catholic concept indeed, and one that seems to require special reinforcement in the post-modern world that seeks to crowd out family in favor of other, "more fulfilling," pursuits.

An additional benefit is that homeschooling makes use of focused attention to get the most out of schooling in the least amount of time. Simply put, it is efficient. One prominent homeschooling mother of ten saw to it that each of her children received a master's degree by age sixteen. Though bright, this woman's children aren't geniuses; neither is the mother an uncharacteristically inspiring teacher — her children did much of the work themselves while she supervised and directed. She simply followed a purchased homeschool curriculum five days a week, three hours a day, and worked the entire year (instead of the standard nine-month school year). Schooling this way, her kids simply finished early. Their efforts were more focused, more continuous, and more productive than their friends in "regular school."

By contrast, institutional school tends to involve a lot of down time. We recently saw one kindergarten teacher's class schedule that allowed fifteen minutes for attendance — and she only had six kids in class! Even without such (*ahem*) luxurious attendance periods, in a typical forty-five-minute class, there tends to be only twenty-five to thirty minutes of actual teaching time. This is especially true in the early grades, where much of the period involves keeping the children in their seats and getting them — literally — all on the same page.

Finally, homeschooling can optimize the parents' ability to supervise the values education of their children. While one cannot raise children in a bubble — and homeschoolers as a rule are not trying to do so — it can be a very positive thing to be able to exercise some additional influence over one's child's playmates and environment, especially at such a vulnerable age as early childhood, when the conscience is in a critical phase of development. While certainly schools teach values, they are not necessarily the values you would like your child to emulate. And even if they are, it is one thing to teach values, it is another thing to exemplify those values. We have been on enough playgrounds and in enough teacher's lounges in both professional and personal capacities to know the kind of values that are too often exemplified. It's not that schools necessarily do a bad job; many are quite adequate — even good. It's just that we believe most parents could do a better job, first because they know their own children better than anyone else and second because they are prepared than anyone else on the world to meet the unique educational needs of their children.

All this being said, there are some parents who, for very sound and admirable reasons, decide that homeschooling is not for them. What do you need to know about choosing a school if you, like most parents, are in this second category.

Choosing an "Away School"

There was a time when this section would have been easy. We simply would have said, "Find the nearest Catholic school and send your child to it." Unfortunately, it is no longer possible to make such blanket statements in an age where teachers and staff are often either openly hostile or passively dismissive toward their own mission to be a Catholic school. It is our opinion that these schools do so at their own peril, because once you take the "Catholic" out of a Catholic school you end up with a hobbled institution. Fortunately, these inferior institutions remain in the minority of Catholic schools. In fact, we are still very heavily biased in favor of Catholic schools, and we strongly recommend that you consider any and all available Catholic schools before considering other conventional schooling options (e.g., public, or non-sectarian private schools). Generally speaking, they have been shown to be more effective than their public counterparts, they typically have smaller, more orderly classes, they support the values and prayers you are trying to teach at home, and they help your child appreciate the importance of the Eucharist by attending Mass during the school week. Taking these plusses into account, however, we still recommend that you to look at all the schools in your area and determine which is best for your child (but if you choose a public school, make sure you make arrangements for your child to attend your parish's religious-education program — and that you are an active supporter of that program).

What do we mean by "best"? We believe that the best school is the school that exemplifies the values you wish your child to exhibit. When you check out a school, don't just ask the principal, "What are this school's values?" You'll just get a quote from the school's administrative handbook. Instead, visit the school. Attend a class. Watch the children and how they conduct themselves on the playground and in the hall. In all of the above, do you see the qualities you want your child to exhibit? Do you see the creativity, order, generosity, solidarity, Christian charity, discipline, and friendship that you want to see in your child? As far as academics go, most schools are about equal. Certainly class size makes a difference, as do the academic expectations of individual teachers, but since most learning occurs at home anyway, these factors often come out in the wash. Rather than looking for a school that is going to make your son or daughter the next Einstein, look for a school that is going to make your child a *mensch* — a real person. As studies have shown, and as we reported in the first chapter, emotional intelligence is a much better predictor of future success than almost any other factor. As long as you can be assured that "the basics" are being covered well, concentrate on the values displayed in the school environment.

Choose a school as if you were choosing a family member. Ask yourself, "How would I feel having any one of these students (teachers, staff) sitting at my dinner table?" You should ask yourself this question because, inevitably, your child, who does sit across from you at the dinner table, will come to think and act like the other people in the school he or she attends. You should, as much as possible, make certain this would be a good thing before you enroll your child.

Once you have found a good fit, treat your child's teacher(s) as an extended-family member. Give him or her your support, attention, and help. Develop a relationship with your child's teachers and school staff as best you can. Dr. Ratner used to encourage parents to invite their children's teachers home to dinner. This may no longer be practical in an age where families barely find the time to eat together, but regardless, it will be your job as a parent to foster as much of that sense of community between home and school as possible.

Teaching Love and Responsibility

We have already touched on the importance of giving your child small jobs to do as a training ground for responsibility, we would like to now take a moment to examine your child's continuing education in love.

Up to now, through infancy and toddlerhood, you have been modeling love by your self-donative example, sharing even your body (through extended nursing, child-wearing, and frequent cuddling) and your bed (through co-sleeping) for the good of your child. This has been a powerful example that has laid a strong foundation for attachment, rapport, and love. Now it is time to make your efforts to educate your child on the nature of love more explicit, giving words and a definition to the example you have been setting.

People often have a limited understanding of what love is. They believe it to be warm feelings, or fun, or even a sense of closeness you share with someone. And while love involves all of these things, it is much more than all of them combined.

The classic, Christian definition of love is "willing and working for the good of another." Now is the time to begin teaching your child to appreciate this definition of love. There will be many times when he or she may accuse you of not loving him or her after you have been forced to use some form of correction. The child of this age does not understand that love is something that transcends feeling. He or she believes that correction and love are two unrelated things because they feel like two separate things. While it will be years before your child will truly grasp this truth about love, that sometimes working for the good of another involves doing hard things, it is important that you begin to offer this definition of love now, so that your child may eventually grow into it.

So how, exactly, do you teach a five- or six-year-old that love is more than a feeling; that correction — especially the gentle correction you are using — is really a form of love? When your child accuses you of not loving him because you have corrected him, wait a little while for him to calm down and then approach your child with a discussion similar to the following.

You: "You know, I was thinking about something you said the other day...."

Child: "What?"

You: "Remember when you said you thought I didn't love you because I told you to stop climbing that tree in your church clothes?"

Child: "Uh, huh. I was really angry."

You: "Yes, I know. But it got me thinking. Do you know what love means?"

Child: (shrugs)

You: "Well, you love mom and dad, right?"

Child: "Yeah."

You: "How do you know you love us?"

Child: "I don't know. I guess 'cause I feel happy with you?"

You: "I'm glad to hear it. I feel happy around you, too. But do you know that I love you even when you do things I don't feel happy about?"

Child: "I guess so."

You: "See, love really means helping someone you care about become the kind of person God wants them to be. Do you understand?

Child: "Nuh, uh."

You: "Well, God wants us all to be loving, and generous, and respectful, and honest, and lots of other things just like that. And everybody who loves God is supposed to help other people be more of those things."

Child: "I love God!"

You: "Yes, you do. And so do I. And so, to help each other become the people God wants us to be, sometimes we cuddle together, and sometimes we play and have fun together, and sometimes we tell each other not to do things that are bad for us."

You can then go on to discuss with your child some specific examples of times that you were loving to each other both through fun and enjoyable ways — and through correction. Chances are, you might recall a few times that your child has appropriately corrected you (for example: for saying a "bad word" or some other such thing). Remind your child of those times and help him or her understand that he or she was showing you love by reminding you of how God wants you to act. And promise that you will always tell your child whatever he or she needs to know to be able to be happy with God in heaven — even when that means telling them not to do certain things.

Finally, tell your child to ask you, "Do you love me?" or "Could you hold me?" if he or she ever is unsure of your love in the face of correction. This will prevent your child from accusing you unjustly of not loving him or her and will continue to help your child understand what love really is — a willingness to work for his or her good, even when that means doing the hard thing. As Scripture says, "For the moment all discipline seems painful rather than pleasant" (Heb 12:11). This applies to loving correction as well. Asking your child to tell you when he or she needs that extra bit of reassurance will help you always know where you stand with your child; making you more sensitive to the times when the emotional bank-account is running low.

Fostering Your Child's Sexuality

An important part of teaching love and responsibility is continuing to foster your child's sexuality. There are some things you may wish to do to continue to encourage to the development of healthy sexuality in your child.

You'll want to continue making the fuss over babies the way you did in toddlerhood, reminding your child that "babies are a wonderful gift from God." Likewise, if you become pregnant at this time in your child's life, it can be a good idea to let your young child do things like listen to the baby's heartbeat, see the baby's sonogram picture, and participate in other activities associated with pregnancy and even delivery. While you may not wish to have your young child present at the actual delivery (although some young children we know have relished the experience of cutting the cord for their baby brother or sister), we have found that it is helpful to have the child stay close by —

rather than sending him or her away to a grandparent's home, for example. In our experience, and the experience of many parents we know, having the young child close at hand decreases the likelihood that your child will feel like he or she is being sent away to make room for the "new baby." Also, we have observed that children who either assist in the delivery or who get to hold the baby shortly thereafter have a more sympathetic relationship with the child. We cannot explain why this is; we have simply observed it many times. Young children who are kept nearby during their younger brother or sister's birth seem less likely to want to "send the baby back."

One other exercise that we might suggest is taking your children to a farm in the springtime, when lots of baby animals are being born. This is a good way to reinforce the fact that God loves to create, and that we are called to marvel and respect all that God creates.

Between ages three and six, if your child asks, "How does the baby get in the mommy's tummy?" (whether your child is referring to his mommy or the mommy horse) it is enough to say, "God puts the baby in there." This is an honest answer that both asserts the truth of creation and avoids presenting your child with information that won't make a bit of sense to him or her anyway at this point.

Finally, children around the age of six sometimes engage in innocent sex-play, like playing "doctor." These will be good opportunities to give some guidance on basic modesty. Explaining that the parts of our bodies covered by our swimsuits should be kept private will usually do the trick. Also, around this age children will sometimes play with their genitals as a kind of mindless method of self-comforting. While this can be upsetting for the parent and must be addressed, the more sensitively you handle this, the better. At this stage, it is enough to continue gently redirecting the child, the same way you would redirect other bad childhood habits that feel good but are inappropriate, like thumb-sucking, ear-cleaning, and nose-picking.

The ages between three and six are a wonderful time for parents and their children. It is the first time parents begin to realize how quickly children grow up, which can be quite a shock. But, at the same time, it is a pleasure to watch children grow in competence, self-mastery, and spiritual awareness as the years go by, a trend that will continue for the next several years. In the next chapter, we're going to take a look at the school-age years. How do you foster good study habits, healthy socialization, a stronger spirituality, and domestic responsibility?

Chapter Eight

Parenting Your School-Age Child with Grace

School Daze

Middle childhood is a time primarily characterized by the increasing role the outside world plays in your child's life. The major challenge of this stage is learning to balance and prioritize school, friends, activities, and interests with one's primary responsibilities to family.

Of course, as you've realized by now, each of these stages experiences some overlap, and this continues to be true of the transition from early to middle childhood. The middle child continues to develop his or her capacity for emotional control and purposeful action even while taking on new challenges that are unique to his or her age and stage.

At seven, the child reaches the "age of reason" with all that means, both cognitively and conscience-wise. Cognitively, the child is beginning to think in more complex, though still concrete, ways. For

School-Age

Timeframe: Approximately ages seven to eleven

Major goals of this stage:
- Continuing to develop emotional control and personal competence.
- Developing "industry" (i.e., "follow-through").
- Learning to juggle various responsibilities and peer relationships with family life.
- Learning good study habits.
- Personalizing, educating, and deepening the spiritual life and conscience.

example, where your child used to think that cutting up his or her food caused there to be more food to eat (instead of just more pieces of the same amount of food) now your child begins to understand that quantities remain the same, no matter how you slice them. Also, he or she is becoming more able to understand and accept parental direction. For example, if you notice your child of five tapping on the table, and you say, "Please don't tap on the table," your child may respond in all wide-eyed innocence, "I'm not!" Some parents respond by accusing the child of committing a bald-face lie. Really, he is not, because, in the younger child's mind, he is not "tapping on the table." He is really "playing the drums," or "having a finger fight," or some such thing — and the child believes that it should be obvious to everyone what he or she is doing. Now, at seven and up, you see a marked decrease in these sorts of exchanges as the child can understand that "tapping on the table" includes other behaviors and games that involve some sort of tapping.

The downside to all this is that some children, in reaction to their developing consciences, can become a bit sensitive to criticism, or even scrupulous. This can be frustrating for a parent, but the best thing to do is to respond lovingly with physical affection and verbal validation, taking special care to remind your child of his or her goodness.

By contrast, the child of eight tends to exhibit an increased outgoing nature, combined with a surprisingly more intense relationship with mom. In a sense, this is the child's way to check if "all systems are go" as he prepares to mentally launch out into the world, giving a more important role to peers. Some developmental psychologists suggest that this "check in with mom" before the child's first mental launching into the world plays an important role in the child's sense of security in future relationships. If the relationship with mom is fostered, future relationships will flourish, if it is discouraged, the child will lack the sense of security he needs to have successful relationships. A bit like a mountain climber who, unsure of how well he is "tied off," might be reluctant to climb even higher.

At ages nine through twelve, more and more, the child is coming out into the world and is becoming more self-motivating and goal-oriented. This is the stage where you can begin expecting a child to follow-through on tasks without your having to regularly redirect them (although some supervision will still be advisable).

Between ages nine and twelve one of the major challenges is helping the child develop a sense of priorities so that she will be able to enter adolescence knowing how to integrate a family obligations and an active social life.

Let's take a brief look at each of these goals of middle childhood.

Continuing to Develop Emotional Control and Personal Competence

Early childhood was marked by your efforts to encourage your child to try new tasks and take the first steps toward emotional control. Middle childhood, by comparison, is the age where your child begins to be more capable of completing jobs and self-monitoring. At this age, the chores you assign can become slightly more involved. Help your child take the next step toward understanding the importance of contributing as much as he or she is able in order to make daily family life run smoothly by assigning household tasks that reflect the child's increasing competence.

Though getting a middle-years child to do their jobs is still sometimes a challenge, most children of this age like feeling responsible and effective. Plus, the emerging sense of stick-to-it-tiveness allows this child to not simply enjoy trying new things, but also desire the sense of accomplishment that comes from mastering new skills. Of course, the parent should still expect himself to stay on top of things, practicing the "coaching attitude" we spoke of in the last chapter. The only difference is that now you are coaching the varsity team.

Middle childhood is an ideal time to develop or even expand the family identity-statement we spoke of earlier in the book. Through this exercise, children can be helped to see that positive personal characteristics and spiritual values are not abstract things, but tangible factors in the everyday life of the family.

With regard to emotional control, if a parent has consistently used the methods we have described in the previous chapters — especially the last chapter — the middle child should be well on the way to expressing his feelings in a respectful and articulate manner. Sometimes, however, children between seven and nine still struggle with tantrums. In contrast to the tantrums of earlier years, which were due to your child's communicative/emotional resources being exceeded by his or her environment, tantrums at this age tend to be manipulative in nature. If your middle-years child is having tantrums, you will be able to tell if they are the result of delayed emotional control or of manipulativeness by performing this simple experiment. Ask yourself whether the child's mood improves immediately if you grant the request that inspired the tantrum. If it does, chances are your child is playing you. In this case, the best response you can give is to shorten up on the amount of time you spend trying to compassionately listen to your child's feelings and move more quickly to the stage where you say, "I understand what you are trying to tell me and I have given you my answer. You may either calm down by the time I count to five, or you may go to your room (or lose whatever privilege they are having a tantrum about, etc.). One...." As far as dealing with tantrums, compassion is one thing, being played for a sucker is quite another. It's important to know the motivation behind your child's outburst so that you can give the appropriate response.

To return to the test we suggested above, if your child continues to fuss and cry even if you do give into the request, then your child probably lacks a certain degree of emotional maturity and is being overwhelmed by the strength of his emotions. You would most likely be safe to assume that the resulting tantrum is a genuine display of immaturity rather than an attempt at manipulation. In this case, your best bet is to review the tantrum and emotional-control sections of this book and shore up your child's emotional-management skills. In either case, if tantrums persist to the point where you are doubting your ability to help your child, professional help may be indicated.

Developing "Industry" (i.e., "Follow-Through")

One of the most important goals of middle childhood is developing a sense of industry, or follow-through. Being able to set goals and meet them are key ingredients of good self-esteem. While the opportunity to set and meet goals at this stage are limitless, the two chief arenas for this work are school and home life. In both cases, children, though eager at first, may exhibit reluctance or frustration when taking on a new responsibility or learning a new lesson, especially if they are not certain they are up to the task. Your response to this reluctance and frustration will determine your child's ability to follow-through on tasks throughout his life. If you become angry and frustrated with your child, eventually he or she will lose heart and feel incompetent. If, on the other hand, you don't push your child enough, he or she will never learn to push themselves to complete tasks. In either case, you run an increased risk of ending up with a child who, in adolescence, is totally lacking in the skills needed to figure out what kind of person he wants to be —

much less what he wants to do — when he grows up. So, how much do you push your child? And how much is too much?

In order to answer these questions we need to remind you of the emotional-temperature scale we spoke of in an earlier chapter. You may recall that on a scale of one to ten, with "one" representing a person on heavy tranquilizers, a "four" representing a person who is going through an average day, and a "ten" representing a person who is climbing a clock tower with an AK-47 strapped to his or her back, problem-solving ability begins breaking down around 6.5.

Keeping this in mind, you can push your child to do as much as he or she is capable of without sending your child — or yourself — over a 6.5. Past this point, you end up screaming at your child, and your child disappears to a happier place in his or her head — a place where you don't exist.

If your son or daughter is struggling to complete a task (say, a homework assignment, or cleaning her room, for example) and you want to encourage him or her without pushing to hard, try the following. First, make it clear that there is no question that you expect him or her to complete the task. It may take longer than originally planned, he or she may have to take some breaks and come back to it, but he or she will finish the work. Why? Because you believe in your child's ability to do it, and you are not about to let him or her sell themselves short. In the process, be willing to give whatever you have to give of yourself, your time, and your own effort to see to it that your child succeeds. Just be careful not to do it for him and avoid lecturing.

Second, pay close attention to both your and your child's emotional temperature. If your child is beginning to go over a 6.5 (for example, he or she can no longer think straight, is making genuinely stupid mistakes, or is becoming irritated at every little aspect of the job), or if you are getting to the point where you are starting to look for a whip and a chair, suggest a break. By a break we mean, preferably, a short recess of fifteen minutes or so during which the child can blow off some steam and the two of you can clear your heads. Though we recommend teaching your child to take appropriate breaks, we do not recommend letting your child run off to play for twelve hours in the middle of a task or lesson. Once a job is started, you should teach your child to stick with it until it is finished, but you must also teach your child how to relate to work in a healthy way. Being a good worker is like being a good fisherman in that you need to know when to work at reeling in and when to relax the line; but you don't stop until the fish is in the bucket. In the same way, we need to teach our children to approach a task with sane tenacity, integrating hard work with mentally restorative breaks until the job is completed. By following these steps consistently and faithfully, you increase the chances of your child learning the dogged persistence both the world and the Christian walk require for success.

Balancing Responsibilities, Peer Relationships, and Family Life

Socialization with peers is important, but socialization should not come at the expense of family solidarity and intimacy. In fact, children who are the best socialized often spend a significant amount of time with adults — like parents — from whom they learn manners, emotional control, and other skills that contribute to the development of emotional intelligence, of which we spoke of in the introduction.

The rule we follow in our own family, and I recommend to my clients, is that family relationships must come first, and any other activities that can be fit into the schedule without stretching or jeopardizing those relationships are welcome (this rule applies to adults as well as kids). Contrary to popular wisdom, too many activities are not good for children. Involving your children in so many activities that you don't know whether you are coming or going as a family sends the message that family is where you stop off on your way to some more important thing. Clearly, this is not the message you want to send if your goal as a parent is to teach your children to have healthy, Catholic, adult relationships.

James was a ten-year-old client who was exhibiting problems completing homework and showing a generally disrespectful attitude toward his parents. The child was involved in several after-school activities, and these often took precedence over his school work and family obligations. After a careful review of the situation and several other less-severe interventions had been tried and failed, I suggested to the parents that James needed to be grounded in the family's love before he would be capable of handling these other activities responsibly. That week the parents announced that due to James's behavior, they were pulling him out of all his activities for a time to allow him to concentrate on his behavior at home and school. However, each week that he behaved well and kept his grades up, they would allow him to rejoin another activity, so long as he continued to maintain his priorities. Within a month, James was able to work back into his other activities while keeping up his grades and being more respectful at home. Likewise, the parents were able to join in his scouting activities and so, by doing this together, the family was able to simplify their schedule while giving them an opportunity to build rapport.

On the other hand, there are some children who are not involved in nearly enough. One child, Mark, was an eleven-year-old who was all-but-addicted to video games. He was overweight, socially awkward, and lacked any clear sense of motivation. His therapy consisted of getting his parents to enroll him in the church youth-group, establish an exercise schedule, and assign chores.

The fact is, it is very important for children to spend middle childhood finding some activities or interests with which they can really identify. Doing so will serve them well in adolescence. Teens who are passionate about activities and interests like sports, music, scouts, drama, clubs, etc., tend to engage in fewer high-risk behaviors like drugs, drinking, or even premarital sex, because they have a solid sense of self-esteem, and believe they have a future that could be destroyed by engaging in such behaviors. The problem is that some parents don't start suggesting that their children get involved in such things until their children are already identifying with the "slacker crowd" at school and engaging in higher-risk behaviors. This is one case of ex-post-facto parenting you will want to avoid. Encourage your child's spontaneously occurring interests (kids in middle childhood are often big on collecting things, for example). Help your child find something to be passionate about, and help them learn to balance this with a joyful home-life. Your efforts will be rewarded when your child grows up and is able to balance his or her own family life with other personally important work or roles.

Learning Good Study Habits

As we suggested in the last chapter, while teaching occurs at school, most learning occurs at home. As far as the Church is concerned, parents must take primary responsibility for their children's education, whether they homeschool or send their children to "away school."

There are several things parents can do to encourage good study habits in their children. First, parents must take an active interest in both the work their children are doing and in the daily life of the school. This includes developing as close a relationship with your children's teacher as reasonably possible, and being a ready volunteer for various school projects, trips, and activities.

Second, parents must not passively accept their children's statements saying that they know certain subjects or "don't have any homework." You, the parent, are the head teacher, and anyone and everyone else you "hire" to assist you is merely a sub-contractor. Make it clear to your child from the earliest grades that he or she must not merely work to meet his or her teacher's standards, but must work primarily to meet *your* standards. Be familiar with your children's textbooks and feel free to test your child on his or her subjects. If you are concerned with the lack of homework your child has, assign some of your own. It doesn't matter if "the teacher said that stuff isn't going to be on the test." Education is not about passing tests. It is about learning things.

Almost universally, parents of away-schooled children complain that their students are not bringing home homework, or at least books to study. There is an easy way to solve this problem. From the earliest grades, make it known to your children that you expect at least a half-hour to an hour of homework/study per night. The earlier you do this, the less fighting you'll have to do to get it started. Then give your children a choice. They can either bring home work the teacher assigns, or they will spend that time doing work that you assign. The work you give should be relevant in some way to what your child is studying, but it should take between a half-hour and an hour to complete. It is surprising how quickly children begin bringing home books to study once parents utilize this approach. It seems that children would rather do the work they were assigned, and get credit for it, than do the work their parents assign and get no classroom credit. Using this approach, you will teach a child to be a good student without even having to nag about it. Go figure.

One thing that often makes homework difficult for young learners is that they are afraid to miss out on more fun activities while they are doing their work. One child is stuck in his room, slaving under hot sweatshop lights, while, off in the distance, he can hear the voices of his parents and siblings, dancing and singing songs of freedom, experiencing the kind of joy usually reserved for deodorant commercials. Nine times out of ten, this environment produces a kid who either intentionally doesn't bring home work, or rushes through the work he brings home so that he can get to join in the fun. To counteract this problem, we recommend having a "family homework time." During this time, parents can do their own take-home work, or other domestic paper-work like paying bills, alongside their children while they do their homework. In this way, the parents can supervise their children's studies as well as model their own work ethic. As an example, much of this book was written at the kitchenette table as our children practiced their homeschool lessons.

Even more important than supervising homework, however, is planning family activities to support what your children are learning in school. Home should be the more creative learning place, where the paperwork is de-emphasized and hands-on experience is pursued with gusto. This might sound like a contradiction, considering what we wrote above about requiring homework and home study-time, but forty-five minutes a day of formal study is hardly taxing a child to his or her limits, and if used as part of a more comprehensive home-learning program that includes trips to museums, fairs, working farms, libraries, concerts, plays, science centers, state parks, conservatories, historical sites, and other educational-yet-fun settings, in addition to craft projects, science experiments, and other home-learning experiences, paperwork fades into the background as a necessary evil.

In this same vein, we cannot overemphasize the importance of reading as a family. Modeling good reading habits in your own life, reading aloud to your children, taking turns reading to each other in the car or reserving one or two evenings a week to read as a family instead of watching television at home are all important ways to foster a love of learning. Lay the foundation for a love of learning by reading to your infant and toddler while he or she is nursing, then continue to foster your child's interest in literature by making books an integral part of your everyday life. There is a saying that the best teacher is a good book. Teach your children to have a love of good books, and they will be assured of a solid education regardless of the circumstances of their schooling.

Finally, parents should be liberal with praise for any job well done. When a child has mastered the work he has been given to do or the lesson she has set out to learn, the child should be praised, not necessarily for his or her genius, but certainly for his or her hard work and stick-to-it-tiveness. Any truly successful person will tell you that most people succeed in life not because they are brilliant, but because they are too stupid to know when to quit. Middle childhood is the prime time in life to learn that slow and steady wins the race.

Following these suggestions will not only help your children develop good study habits but also a love for learning, because they will experience learning as a way to bond with you. The greatest motivator for your child is a relationship with you. He or she will do anything to get it. Children are capable of going to great heights of heroism or great depths of pathology in their longing to connect with mom and dad. Use your child's God-given desire for an intimate connection with you to lead your child into good conduct and habits that will serve him or her well for the rest of his or her life.

Personalizing, Educating, and Deepening the Spiritual Life of Your Child

Dr. James Fowler's research on faith development discovered that the faith of middle childhood is expressed in two ways: a concern for separating truth from fiction, and the tendency to understand everything in terms of relationship.

Regarding the first point — your child's desire to separate truth from fiction — there are two basic things you can do to help your child begin to look rationally at the Faith. The first is to teach the Faith of the Church as the Truth that it is. When your child asks you if the bread and wine really becomes the Body and Blood of Christ, if Jesus really rose from the dead, if Jesus really gave Father Joe the power to forgive sins in His name, or any other such thing, you must be willing to give the unqualified "yes" answer these questions deserve. When your child asks, "How do you know it's true?" you can be confident answering, "Because Jesus, the Son of God, told us that it was true. And the Bible and the Catholic Church have proclaimed this truth for two thousand years." While you will need to prepare more complete answers to such questions as your child matures, it is enough at this stage to rely on "arguments from authority" (i.e., "You can believe it because I — a person you respect — tell you it is so") to defend the Faith because the school-age child's thinking has not yet evolved to the place where he or she can critically examine things on his or her own terms.

Now, it is perfectly acceptable to admit that you don't understand how these things happen (although you should always try to learn the arguments for why). But that is a different thing from saying that something isn't true just because it strains credulity. The fact that this table upon which our computer is sitting is not actually solid, that it is — in reality — a loose association of atoms and molecules revolving around each other with a comparatively large amount of space in between them, strains credulity as well. But it is fact nevertheless, just as the Real Presence is fact. As the Lord says in Isaiah 55:9, "so high are my ways above your ways."

For those of you who feel that this is a somewhat fundamental approach to the Faith, let us reassure you. There will be a time when your child will be able to appreciate the subtle shadings of theology, to hold two opposing opinions on a Scripture passage and work to find the most reasonable explanations of the two, and other such exercises. But that time is not now. The middle child's brain cannot handle "gray." For this child, there is only "true" and "not true." Any attempt at subtlety in this stage will most likely cause the thing you are explaining to end up in the "not true" basket of your child's mind, causing the Eucharist to have to fight the Easter Bunny and Santa Claus for elbow room. When your child asks questions about the Faith, the simple yet profound answers given in simple catechisms like Mike Aquilina's *What Catholics Believe: A Pocket Catechism* (as well as the *Catechism* itself) are really the best way to go.

Which leads us to the second thing you can do to help your child approach faith rationally. Make sure to give simple answers to your child's questions, but not simplistic ones. It is better to give your child an answer that he or she has to grow into than give your child an answer that is too easily grown out of. Likewise, don't guess at answers to your child's questions of the Faith. If you don't know how to answer your child's question, look it up. Guessing only leads to the idea that theology is not fact, but opinion. This may or may not be true of other ideological systems, but believe it or not, Catholic theology is based solidly on the same processes that guide other kinds of scientific inquiry in that each claim it advances is built upon a framework that starts with what is known and says "if this is true and that is true then thus and such must follow." In this way, Catholic theology has more in common with quantum physics (in that it is capable of making absurd but true statements by taking what is known to be true to the next step, and the next, and the next...) than mere ideology. (For a good example of this stepwise progression of theology, see Peter Kreeft's *Handbook of Christian Apologetics* and other good apologetics resources by people like Mark Shea, Scott Hahn, Stephen Ray, and Patrick Madrid).

As we said above, when looking to explain the Faith to your children, the *Catechism* and Scripture are the best places to start, but there is also a wealth of popular apologetics books and magazines that can help explain the Faith in an intelligent way to you so that you can explain the Faith intelligently to your children. *Envoy Magazine* is perhaps the best example of a popular apologetics magazine we can think of. It's eye-catching in design, hysterically funny, thorough in content, and completely unapologetic (if you'll excuse the pun) about its Catholicism. Likewise, the editor of *Envoy*, Matt Pinto, is the author of a book that explains Christian truths to kids called *Did Adam and Eve Have Belly Buttons?* It's worth a look.

Of course, even more important that teaching your child the facts of the Faith is teaching your child to have a relationship with Jesus Christ and His Church. Middle children can parrot back facts, but this does not mean they love what they are learning, and religion is the one subject that requires the student's love. Marcia, a nine-year-old girl attending Catholic school, told me that religion class was her favorite. When I asked why, she said, "It's easy." When I asked, "Do you like learning about Jesus and the Church?" she answered, "Not really. It's just easy. That's all."

Without a personal relationship with Jesus Christ and a healthy, intimate love for the Church, the facts of the Faith become empty stories to the child; catechism is like math or spelling words, all memorization and no meaning. The study of religion involves more than the formation of the mind, it requires the formation of the heart, something that simply must be done at home if it is to have any hope of succeeding. This formation of the heart is critical for the middle-childhood years because, for this child, nothing is real or relevant unless it involves relationship. Even with math and spelling, if the student likes the teacher, he will learn her subjects; if he dislikes the teacher, she could offer him one-thousand dollars to learn — and he would still refuse.

If parents want their children to grow up to be faithful, vital Catholics with a real love for Jesus, parents must first model this love and faithfulness. We must lead our children into a strong, passionate, spirit-filled relationship with our Lord so that they can understand what all the fuss is about.

Are we suggesting that every child needs to have the charismatic experience? No, of course not. But every child needs to have some experience that makes God personally real to him or her. You can facilitate this experience by vocalizing your own love for the Lord and His Church, by explaining from an early age the true power of the Eucharist and emphasizing what a privilege it is to receive Jesus at

Mass, and by inviting your child to regularly pray, "Lord, Jesus. Please come into my heart and make me Your little child. Teach me to love You more than anything, and help me always live my life for You."

We will discuss other ways to foster your child's spirituality later, in a chapter devoted specifically to it.

Teaching Love and Responsibility

Middle childhood continues to present opportunities to build on the definition of love you began teaching in early childhood — that love is the willingness to work for the good of another.

The best way to do this is by working together in your family to develop and live out a family identity-statement. This way, you can present specific examples of what it means to live out love in your everyday life as a family.

Another way to foster a greater understanding of love in your family is to ask your children to explain what the most loving choice would be in any given situation. This is especially useful in handling fights with siblings. When your children ask you to arbitrate yet another squabble, ask each one of them, "What do you think would be the most loving choice you could make in this situation?" This line of questioning has several benefits. First, it prevents you from having to sit in judgement of a situation you couldn't possibly begin to sort out even if you were Solomon's more-intelligent twin. Second, it forces your children to each take responsibility for their own part in creating and solving problems (there's that internal control we keep talking about). Finally, it helps you continually facilitate each child's understanding of what it means to exhibit true, Christian love, which is really the balance between personal strength and sensitivity (for a more thorough explanation of how these two qualities work together, see *For Better ... FOREVER!*).

Responsibility, as you have seen throughout this chapter, is best taught in middle childhood by helping a child balance all his responsibilities and interests with family life. Also, it is important to continue to encourage your children to do all they can to work for the good of the family. In middle childhood, this will not only involve doing chores, but also helping model the family rules and conduct to younger siblings.

As is true with all attempts to nurture positive character traits, praise and "catching your child being good" are absolutely essential. Be on the look-out for times when your children exhibit love and responsibility and comment on those occasions. Your child will be glad you noticed and work harder to please you because he knows he can.

Fostering Your Child's Sexuality

Catholic sexual education of the school-age child means continuing to practice all the activities we have suggested so far (in the toddler and early childhood sections) and adding three things besides.

First, this is the time when your child will be identifying with the same-sex parent in order to learn what it means to be male or female. The Church gives some guidelines for doing this in *The Truth and Meaning of Human Sexuality*:

> A growing boy or girl is learning from adult example and family experience what it means to be a woman or man. Certainly, expressions of natural tenderness should not be discouraged among boys, nor should girls be excluded from vigorous physical activity [italics original]. [no italics indicated]

Traditionally, the temptation for parents was to explain masculinity and femininity in terms of jobs, saying that men are men because they do and act A, B, C, and women are women because they do and act X, Y, Z. While this is common, it represents an improper understanding of male and female roles as the Church teaches them.

The Church teaches that male and female roles are complementary and that, to use moral theologian William May's terminology, differences in gender are best understood as differences in emphasis more than anything else. In other words, men and women are not defined so much by the jobs they do so much as they are defined by the unique ways their bodies allow them to approach certain jobs and roles. For example, both men and women are encouraged to be nurturing and loving to their children, just as God loves and nurtures us. But God gave women the ability to lactate, and so the woman will approach this job of nurturing her baby differently than the man, who will approach it by engaging in light "roughhousing," or rubbing the baby's tummy with his beard, or a million other things only a man can do through his body for his son or daughter. As you can see by this example, both men and women are doing similar work (the work of nurturing), but they are emphasizing different aspects of that particular work, this emphasis being based on the unique ways God made their bodies. (For more information on understanding the concept of complementarity and John Paul II's theology of the body, we recommend *For Better ... FOREVER! A Catholic Guide to Lifelong Marriage*, as well as William May's *Marriage: The Rock on Which the Family is Built*, and John Paul II's *Original Unity of Man and Woman: A Catechesis on the Book of Genesis*. We list our recommendations in order of difficulty, with the easiest first.)

It is almost impossible to articulate the ways these emphases play themselves out without lapsing into unhelpful over-generalizations. The fact is, stereotypes such as "women don't do yard work," or "men don't clean the house or cook," or "women should leave the finances to the men," or "men should leave the child-rearing to women" are simply un Catholic, because they fly in the face of the Church's constant admonition that husbands and wives should daily seek out more and more ways to be generous, loving servants to one another. Perhaps the best way for parents to teach their children to be men or women is to teach them how to be good, human persons first, by modeling love, responsibility, generous service, and general competence in all the tasks of daily living. Then, by allowing our daughters to work alongside their mothers and our sons to work alongside their fathers as all strive to more fully manifest Christian virtue in their daily lives, the masculine and feminine differences in approaching these things will be communicated over time. Again, whether we are male or female, God expects us to exhibit all the qualities He, Himself, exhibits, including loving attention, generous service, healthy emotionality, rationality, communicative-ness, and so on. It's just that the bodies God gave us will compel us to live out these qualities with a different emphasis.

Second, the best way to teach your children how to have loving, responsible, adult relationships is to work on having one yourself. Your marriage is the best teacher your child will ever have. Frequently, I get calls from women who have practiced extended nursing with their babies, engaged in co-sleeping, were good disciplinarians, and the whole nine yards, but their children are still serious trouble. What's wrong? Very often, what's wrong is their marriages. You can do everything right as a parent, but if you are not working to maintain a loving responsible marriage on an everyday basis, then you are shooting yourself in the foot. Remember, the whole point of discipline is to teach your children how to have healthy, adult relationships with others and the God who made them. But you can't give what you don't have. See the chapter on marriage in this book, or read *For Better ... FOREVER!* for additional information on how to make your marriage the best example it can be for your children.

Third, while John Paul II has referred to the ages between five and eleven as the "years of innocence," children are learning about and engaging in sexual behavior earlier than ever. It is not uncommon for me to hear about children having their first serious sexual experiences in fifth grade. Even if your child — God willing — is not engaging in such practices, it is inevitable that he or she will have direct questions about sex which you must be prepared to answer honestly, casually, and respectfully.

When your child asks you about sex, your attitude will convey more than your words. If you are fearful and uptight, that is what your child will remember more than anything you say. If, on the other hand, you are inappropriately jokey and disrespectful about it, they will remember that as well. As Fr. Trese suggests, and *The Truth and Meaning of Human Sexuality* teaches, it is best to approach such questions respectfully, but with real humanity and affection.

Let your child lead the discussions about sex. Don't launch into big explanations of the mechanics or even the possible sinful manifestations of sex. Keep your answers simple and to the point: "Sex is a special kind of hug that God lets moms and dads give to each other where all their parts fit together and God can make a baby. You can't make a baby with any other, regular hug. But when young men and women are ready to have children, they get married and are allowed to share that very special hug with each other. And that hug makes God very happy."

You can develop this line of thinking as the years go by, but presented early enough that your child doesn't hear things from peers first. (A specific age is difficult to say. As always, it's best to let your child tell you when he or she is ready.) This explanation covers all the bases. Sex is a divinely given good, sex is intimately linked to children, sex is the exclusive right of men and women who are married, sex and marriage are for people who are grown-up enough to want to have children of their own.

One final word on sexuality in this stage, because menses is occurring earlier and earlier for young girls. It might be necessary to cover more complex sexual issues at this age for both girls and boys. However, space prevents us from dealing with these issues here. We will discuss teaching your child a more developed approach to the Catholic vision of love and sex in the next chapter.

Having traveled though the elementary-school years, we're going to move on to what amounts to the "final exam" for parents — pre-adolescence and adolescence. What can you do to help your child exhibit love and responsibility throughout his or her teen years? How can you respectfully handle questions that arise around dating, sexuality, and the search for identity — all the while keeping your wits about you?

Chapter Nine

Parenting Your Teen with Grace

… But I Still Haven't Found What I'm Looking For

Besides toddlerhood, pre-adolescence and adolescence are the times most feared by parents. While there is no way to get through the teen years entirely unscathed, the good news is that you and your teen don't have to spend the next few years hating each other. In fact, adolescence is an important time in the relationship between a parent and child. One of the reasons the relationship between parents and same-sex teens becomes so intense is that as part of the adolescent's search for identity, he or she is going over his same-sex parent's personality with a fine-toothed comb, trying to decide what to keep and what to throw away. Assuming you have maintained good rapport with your child throughout the years, the opportunities for bonding with your teen are myriad. In fact, Martha Sears, the wife of Dr. Bill Sears (to whom we referred extensively in the infancy section) and mother of eight, once suggested in an interview that adolescence is one of the times she enjoys most in her children's lives. This is a sentiment shared by motivational speaker Stephen Covey

The Teen Years

Timeframe: Approximately ages twelve to seventeen

Major goals of this stage:
- The search for identity.
- Developing a respectful separation from mom and dad.
- Fostering the teen's own spirituality.
- Dealing with sexual issues.

and his wife, Sandra, the parents of nine children, who are on record as saying that their children's adolescence was, for the most part, a positive experience. In fact, one of their sons who is currently a teenager is following in his father's footsteps, having published *The Seven Habits of Highly Effective Teens*.

In this chapter, we'll take a look at the major issues facing this stage, with an eye toward helping everyone come out the other end alive.

The Search for Identity

The key issue for adolescents is searching for an identity to call their own. Most children at this stage have a hard time sorting out what having an identity really means. They go through phases where "being me" means wearing certain clothes or looking a certain way. This is perfectly natural and the best parental response to all but the most offensive, immodest, or vulgar of these expressions is to bite your tongue, saving your energy and emotional dollars for the battles that really matter.

Considering the confusion this search for identity can present to both parents and their children, it can be helpful for you to know what having an identity really means, so you can teach your child. In a nutshell, having a solid identity implies two things. First, that you have a clear vision of the values, virtues, ideals, and goals you want to pursue between now and the day you die, and second, seeing that your daily choices reflects the pursuit of those values, virtues, ideals, and goals. For the adolescent, the search for these values, virtues, ideals, and goals will play itself out in three ways, finding something to live for, finding activities to be passionate about, and finding a community to support them. The degree to which an adolescent can discover these things for him or herself will be the degree to which he or she will feel the all-important sense of belonging that is the basis for adolescent self-esteem. The following pages will offer some insights for parents to help their children achieve a solid, Catholic identity.

Finding Something to Live For

The biggest problem reported by adolescents in my practice is a sense of meaninglessness. As fifteen-year-old Charles once told me, "People are such hypocrites. Everybody is out for themselves. I don't know if there's anything worth believing in."

It is worth noting that Charles did faithfully attend Church with his family, but his parents, though basically good people, had a fairly casual attitude toward religion. As far as I could tell, they attended Church because it was something "respectable" people do, and they seemed to draw some comfort from going. There was no more or less to it than that.

As the world becomes more a-religious, or casually religious, a greater number of adolescents are feeling as if they have nowhere to turn for meaning. They come to view their own Faith traditions as "hypocritical" and quite rightly, because in many cases, these traditions have not been lived in a compelling way in their own homes. To be perfectly blunt, God gives adolescents an extremely low tolerance for bull. And the casual spirituality exhibited by many Catholic parents ends up looking like so much B. S. to the adolescent, who is desperately seeking some set of beliefs which is compelling enough to give his life for and to.

By contrast, the child who has been raised in a home where a personal relationship with Jesus Christ has been encouraged, a love for the Church has been modeled, and the values that comprise a family identity-statement have been both overtly defined and consistently lived out on a daily basis, tends to struggle significantly less with this sense of meaninglessness. And the earlier all this begins, the better.

Because of this, it is imperative to spend the years leading up to adolescence not merely in catechesis, but also in fostering a real spirituality in your children. This gives the child an all-important sense of participating in something bigger than himself or herself. When you deprive your children of a real and meaningful faith-relationship, you exponentially increase the chances that they will pursue dangerous and artificial means to make themselves feel bigger than life, for example: alcohol, drugs, sex, and a host of other high-risk behaviors. But, as St. Augustine wrote, "Restless is the heart until it finds its rest in thee, O Lord."

We will offer some general tips for encouraging your child's spirituality in a future chapter. Additionally, Maryann Kuharski's *Raising Catholic Children*, and OSV's anthology *Talking to Your Kids about Being Catholic*, and Bert Ghezzi's *Keeping Your Kids Catholic* and *Fifty Ways to Tap the Power of The Sacraments* are all excellent resources for learning how to nurture a meaningful, Catholic spirituality in your child.

But assuming you have given your child a solid education in spirituality and values, adolescence is a good time to help your son or daughter develop his or her own identity statement. The process for this is very similar to the process you used earlier for developing your family identity-statement. Start by leading your teen (or better still, preteen) in a discussion of "What kind of person do you want to be when you grow up?" Give your teen a list of Christian virtues (see the family identity-statement exercise, for examples) and ask him which of these are most important. Then ask your teen what it might mean to live out those values out on a daily basis. For example, what activities (schoolwork, church, youth group, personal prayer, etc.) might these virtues compel him or her to take advantage of? What circumstances (certain parties, fashions, dating activities) might these virtues compel him or her to avoid?

For parents, the real benefit to helping your adolescent develop his or her own identity statement is that it makes discipline so much easier — not magically simple, mind you — but significantly easier. How? Well, once your teen has identified the virtues, values, and spiritual ideals she wishes to pursue in her own life, you can simply refer to her identity statement when she asks for your permission to engage in questionable activities: "Will doing this make you more of a (fill-in-the-virtue) person, or less?"

Those readers who think this is wishful thinking on our part should be encouraged. I use this very intervention in my own practice for redirecting both teens and adults who are making less-than-admirable choices. In fact, using this exercise allows me to be much more direct and even in-your-face as a counselor than I could ever be otherwise, because "I am only pointing this out because you said that you wanted to be a [fill-in-the-virtue] person, and clearly, this choice would not make you that kind of person. It looks like you have a choice to make." I can be downright preachy if need be, but the amazing thing is that no young person ever resents me for it, because they know I am merely preaching their own words back to them. They can't resent me without resenting themselves. And so, sometimes reluctantly, they begin to see the wisdom and benefit of making the healthier, more-loving choice.

Chris was a sixteen-year-old client of mine who was brilliant, but hopelessly lazy. His parents brought him to counseling because he had been depressed (much more than the typical adolescent funk) for about six months, was socially withdrawn, and had recently begun smoking marijuana. Over several weeks, and after we had dealt with the drug use, I helped him develop a personal identity-statement. He seemed to enjoy the experience, even to the point of drawing his own coat of arms with the words "honor, courage, and joy" printed on his shield.

Even though his mood was improving over the course of treatment, he was still extremely isolated, saying, "School sucks. There's no one there I can relate to." I began challenging him on this. I suggested that such phrases did not seem remarkably honorable, courageous, or joyful for that matter, and that if he was really serious about living out those virtues — instead of just using them as a reason to do an attractive art project — he might have to do something about it. Though initially resistant, I kept bringing him back to his identity statement, and making use of an adolescent's inherent hatred of hypocrisy. I alternately goaded, supported, and encouraged him to become more active in his school and community. After several weeks of this, Chris was writing for the school newspaper (as well as his own short-lived "underground" school paper), building sets for the school play, playing in a band, and participating in the school's academic-games program. His mother couldn't believe the change, and shortly thereafter, he and his parents decided to discontinue therapy because his schedule was so full we couldn't find a good time to meet.

An adolescent is, for the most part, too old to be told what to do, but too young to be left alone. While there will still be times you will have to parent by "executive decision," helping your teen stay faithful to his or her own identity statement is, generally speaking, a more respectful way to motivate your adolescent to make healthy and respectful choices. Plus, it facilitates the development of healthy identity strength and of the virtue fidelity (being faithful to a particular value system), which Erik Erikson noted is the most important virtue that results from a successful transition through adolescence.

Finding Activities to Be Passionate About
In addition to finding something to believe in, adolescents thrive when they have activities they excel at (or at least intimately connect with) and causes they can make their own. Teens who are seriously committed to social hobbies like sports, music, drama, and social activism tend to do better than young people who either have no passionate interests, or whose interests are of a more solitary nature. This is not to say that all quiet teens are maladjusted — far from it — but because adolescence is such a social time, teens who are solely interested in solitary activities tend to be somewhat more given to social awkwardness and depression.

Considering how important it is to have a passionate commitment to a particular social activity by adolescence, it is a good idea to encourage your child's involvement in such activities in middle and late-middle childhood (say, at least by fifth grade or so). It has been my experience that too many parents wait until their teens are engaging in semi-delinquent behaviors before they say, "Why don't you go out for basketball or something?" The problem is, if a child isn't on his way to finding his place in his immediate world by pre-adolescence, he often feels like too much of an outsider to motivate himself to try new things. It is, at the very least, an uphill battle which may require the assistance of a professional counselor.

Regarding having a cause to call their own, this is the time when a Catholic teen should be encouraged to put his or her faith in action. If your teen is itching to "rage against the machine" (i.e., "fight the establishment"), let them rage against the culture of death by encouraging them (or even joining them — if they will have you) in the more obvious Catholic causes. Pro-life projects, social-justice activities (like volunteering at a soup kitchen or building homes for the disadvantaged), environmental-issues education, peace activism, protesting capital punishment, objecting to anti-Catholic bigotry, even Catholic apologetics (especially Catholic apologetics) are all ways that the rebellious, angry spirit of youth can be channeled into good and useful causes. Your adolescent doesn't have to do anything to get arrested, but he or she can be encouraged to find even more valuable ways to "get involved." Likewise, if you can get involved with your youth, this can be one more way to bond with a son or daughter who is becoming more and more difficult to bond with. In short, teens love a good fight. Give them something to fight for, or else they'll keep themselves busy by fighting you.

Finding a Community to Support Them

Adolescents are beginning to launch out of the nest — for good this time. It is your job to make sure they have some soft places to land. This needs to start several years before adolescence. Once your child is a teenager, you won't be able to pick their friends, but if, in middle and late-middle childhood, you put your child in activities and situations where they have a greater likelihood of associating with peers who are upstanding people and spiritually minded, you will be better off than if you didn't. Again, if you wait until adolescence to try to get your son or daughter to associate with upstanding peers who are spiritually minded, the most charitable response you are going to get from your teen will be, "What! You want me to hang out with those religious freaks!? I don't think so." If you bribe your child with unlimited use of the car for a week, you might get one or two Life Teen meetings out of them, but that'll probably be it.

Your adolescent will find a group in which he or she feels comfortable — with or without your help. As a general rule, though, teens tend not to feel comfortable in religious or spiritual groups unless they have been associating willingly in or around such groups before adolescence (or unless their best friend suddenly "gets religion"). By making spirituality a part of your everyday life as a family, encouraging your child from an early age to develop his own relationship with the Lord and His Church, and arranging to have your child associate with other children who also take their faith seriously, there is a good chance your child's faith will actually grow through adolescence instead of being tossed out with the bath-water.

Developing a Respectful Separation from Mom and Dad

Your teen will be chomping at the bit to get out into the world and test him- or herself. In general, this should be encouraged and actively supported, insofar as your son or daughter will make use of these experiences as building blocks for his or her own identity. But in spite of the adolescent's push for independence, it would be a mistake to think that teens don't need mom and dad anymore. In fact, they need you just as much as ever. Differently, perhaps, but just as much.

It is our opinion that there are three activities which should be sacrosanct in every Catholic home, especially a home with a teen or pre-teen in it. (By sacrosanct, we mean that no family member should have the option of cutting out on these activities, though guests may occasionally be welcome to join in.) The first is a family meal-time. Every day, you need to have at least one meal together — preferably dinner — where you can connect. We realize this getting more and more difficult in this busy world, but if you can't even get together as a family for forty-five minutes for dinner, then your family is probably too busy. Activities like work, sports, and clubs are meant to add to the life of the family, not compete with it. If you allow outside activities to squeeze out family time, you are sending your children the message that family life should be placed on the bottom of the totem pole. This is a lesson your child will definitely carry into his or her own marriage. Remember, for the Catholic, there is no activity more important than learning how to love, and this is done best in the family, which the Church calls the "school of love."

The second thing we recommend is having one day a week that is specifically reserved for family activities. Sunday afternoon often works best, although another day will do so long as it is consistent. As John Paul II observed in his document on the Christian Sabbath, such days are important because they give the family time to play together and reconnect before returning to weekday life. Occasionally, parents may give special permission to have their children's friends come along for their family outings or activities, but it should be clearly understood by all that the friend is joining a family activity. In other words, your child should not expect to spend the day shutting his or her family members out so that time can be spent exclusively with their friend. If your child complains, remind him that there are six other days during which he can be with others. Your son or daughter doesn't have to always love these family days, but they should be held up — at least — as an important obligation and an opportunity for the adolescent to challenge his or her own selfishness and remember where he or she comes from.

The final, but most important, recommendation is that families should attend Sunday Mass together. If outside activities cut into a family's ability to attend Mass together, those outside activities should either be worked around so everyone can attend together, or the activities should be cut. There are some readers who may balk at this. These individuals would do well to remember that the Eucharist is not fast food you grab when you can on your way to something else. It is a family meal — to be shared with your flesh and blood as well as with your spiritual brothers and sisters. If the Real Presence is not asserted as the center of your family's spiritual life, then your family is simply playing at being Catholic. Of course, friends should always be welcome to accompany your family to Church, but friends and other activities must not tear you away from attending Mass together.

By asserting these three as the essential three activities your adolescent must participate in (sometimes whether they like it or not — but often once they get there, they like it), you will help keep your teen be grounded in the love of the family. This will also decrease the chances that they will engage in behaviors that elicit more punitive grounding from you. As you may remember, grounding is often used as a strategy by adolescents to get more time with a family they perceive is threatened by outside forces, or to opt out of activities they are not certain they can handle. Asserting the importance of family life offers a more direct and respectful way to meet their needs. Plus, it gives you the benefit of staying in touch with your teen's life, something that can be hard enough to do in a good week, much less in a week where you haven't had the time to say "boo" to each other.

As with all the recommendations in this chapter, the sooner you introduce these rituals into the fabric of your family life, the less likely your teen will resist them. But if you are getting a late start, you should still enact these interventions. You'll just need more courage to see them become a reality. Don't give up. Know that our prayers are with you.

Fostering the Teen's Own Spirituality

Up until now, your child believed in the Faith because you told him or her it was true. Now, as the pre-teen and younger adolescent begins exhibiting what is known as "formal operational thought" (that is, the ability to critically analyze, think theoretically, and think about thinking itself), your child is going to be testing the Faith for him- or herself.

Considering Dr. James Fowler's work on faith development, it would be appropriate to say that there are three components which must be in place so that a teen can go from believing the Faith because you believe it, to believing the Faith for him or herself. In this order, the teen must be able to:

1. Feel the Faith.
2. Defend the Faith.
3. Apply the Faith.

Feeling the Faith

Adolescents, as a rule, rely very heavily on their "sense" of things. Though they have achieved "formal operational thought" (the ability to address complex problems and think philosophically) they have not yet mastered it, and so they rely more on their gut instincts and passions to tell them what is "true." While this is far from ideal, it is what God is giving us to work with at this stage of our children's lives, and so we might as well get about working with it.

Considering these facts, it is absolutely critical that your pre-adolescent or adolescent be given every possible opportunity to be knocked off his horse by a personal encounter with Jesus Christ and the power of the Holy Spirit — if this has not happened already. While there are perhaps many ways to foster this intense personal experience of Jesus Christ and his Holy Spirit, the way we are most familiar with — and the way that has been most effective as far as we can tell — is by finding some way to introduce your child to at least some elements of a more "charismatic" spirituality.

While we understand that "all the whooping and hollering" isn't for everyone, we cannot help but wonder, "Why not?" We freely admit that charismatic worship lacks a certain decorum, but think about it, after the Apostles received the Sacrament of Confirmation at Pentecost, they didn't exactly sit down to a lovely continental breakfast in the church basement. They went screaming into the streets, dancing and shouting and proclaiming the Gospel so vociferously that they were accused of being drunk!

Historically, strong family influence and a secular world that supported Church attendance kept teens in line until they could properly train their minds and take on the Faith as their own, but with the demise or devaluation of such structures, it becomes more necessary to give adolescents an internal, personal reason to keep them glued to the Faith. In adolescence, this internal motivation often takes the form of a fairly emotional faith; a faith that "feels personally meaningful to me." Without this more emotional expression of spirituality to latch on to, our observation is that many Catholic adolescents are either drawn into more evangelical Protestant churches, who are often more enthusiastic in their style of worship than the average Catholic parish, or alternatively, they tend to lose touch with the relevance of Church involvement until many years later, when their thinking has evolved to the point where they can prove to themselves, through greater independent study, that the Church really does have something to say. To our way of thinking, it is a shame to lose any time in the arms of the Church, and it is sadder still when young adults, disillusioned by not finding a faith to "touch their hearts" in adolescence, never return to the fold, adopting instead a "been there, done that" attitude toward Catholicism.

It would seem that even Pope John Paul II's example teaches us that we must do what we can to foster the younger Christian's emotional experience of the Faith. After all, what else is the purpose of those World Youth Day events — which have more in common with a Beatles' concert than your typical Sunday liturgy — if not to foster the notion that God and the Church do not only want to minister to people's minds, bodies, and communities, but also to their hearts and emotions?

Of course, it will be important to tie this emotionality back to the sacramental life of the Church. Good spiritual feelings are meaningless unless they are working to give your son or daughter a deeper understanding and appreciation of Christ's work through the sacraments. In this way, I was perhaps more fortunate than most. Having gone through the charismatic Life in the Spirit seminar when I was eight — even before my first confession — I came to view every sacrament I experienced as a personal encounter with Jesus Christ. And while I will not say I was never rebellious as a teenager, I never suffered the same lapses in my faith that so many of my friends did because from my earliest youth, I owned my faith on a highly personal, highly emotional level. I remember many times as a teenager when I became frustrated with this priest or that parish and desperately wanted to go to some other "more lively" church, but I could never leave the Catholic Faith because it would be like leaving my very self. I often found myself in the position where I felt tired, frustrated, struggling to understand why the Church taught that, or the people in my parish treated me like this (I have been a parish musician from my early adolescence, so I have had a lot of opportunity to be criticized in many ways and in many parishes). I would want to run away from it all, only to hear the words of the Apostles running through my head, "Lord, to whom shall we go?" In other words, I could pursue a more enthusiastic form of worship offered by a different denomination, but it would be at the expense of all the sacraments where I got to actually experience Jesus up close and personal. It was my personal and emotional commitment to the Church which allowed me to hold on until years later as a young adult, I could grasp the more intellectual and sophisticated aspects of the Church.

By developing your own capacity for an emotional faith, supporting your children in the pursuit of such a faith (for example, encouraging their involvement in things like the Franciscan University's High School Youth Conferences, Life Teen, Catholic youth rallies, and other such activities) and letting that emotionality enliven the experience of the sacraments, you are giving your children a reason to stick with the Faith until they are developmentally capable of wrapping their minds around the grandeur of the Church's more traditional theology and spirituality.

Defending the Faith

Working hand-in-hand with the development of an emotional faith is ongoing training in your teen's ability to understand and defend the Faith. Formal operational thought brings with it the teen's ability to critically examine issues and concepts. You are going to have to prepare yourself to answer — or at least know where to find the answers to — questions like: "How do you know Jesus was the Son of God and not just a good man?" "Did Jesus really rise from the dead?" "There are so many churches and each one thinks it has 'the Truth' — how do you know whom to believe?" And frankly, these are some of the easier questions they're going to ask.

If you as a parent give some sincere but hopelessly incomplete answer like, "That's just what I've always been told," or "Well, that's just how we believe, but other people believe differently and that's okay, too." Then your child's "B. S. meter" is going to read off the scale.

Case in point. When Pope John Paul II came to St. Louis in 1998, *Time* magazine ran an article about one particular "average Catholic family" who was going to see the pope. The parents were obviously poorly catechized, and made no bones about openly disagreeing with the Church on things like sexuality and other hot-button topics, but they still reported feeling excited about the pope's visit and rhapsodized eloquently about how they admired the man even though they disagreed with so much he had to say. On the other hand, their children, both teens, thought their parents were the biggest hypocrites in the world. These two young people had no sense of the importance of the pope's visit, and they had even less use for a Church they had always been taught by their parents to see as old-fashioned and out of touch with reality. The biggest surprise of the article was that the parents seemed to be totally confused as to why their children would reject their brand of Catholicism-lite; a sentimental Catholicism with no real intellectual rigor or relevance to back it up. My thought while reading the article was, "Well, who in their right mind wouldn't reject such a pathetic imitation of the real Church?" I was just saddened to think that these children might never get a chance to see the real thing.

In today's world of conflicting ideologies, it is no longer enough for a parent to offer his or her opinions about Church teaching, supportive or otherwise. We need to be able to explain why the Church believes as she does and how the Church came to hold those positions.

Unfortunately, many people who went through religious education in the post-Vatican II era don't know that there are very good reasons the Church teaches what it teaches; reasons that extend back to the earliest days of Christianity. Parents who are interested in learning more about these things should take a look at books like Stephen Ray's *Crossing the Tiber*, which demonstrates the consistency on the doctrines of the Real Presence and the necessity of baptism (and appropriateness of infant baptism) from the earliest days of the Church, and Peter Kreeft's *Handbook of Christian Apologetics*, which takes you step-by-step through questions about the divinity of Jesus, and the veracity of the Resurrection, to name but a few; subscribe to *Envoy* magazine; and of course, check out whatever *uber*-apologist Dr. Scott Hahn happens to be recording this week.

Catholic theology was once called the queen of the sciences, not because of the poor state of science "back then," but because Catholic theology is more like quantum physics than like other, less rigorous disciplines. Quantum physics makes absolutely bizarre statements about the way the universe is constructed, and few if any of these statements can be proven by direct observation. Instead, scientists build from what they know to be true and let the known truths lead them to the next truth: "If this is true and that is true, then such and such must follow." In the same way, Catholic theology starts with what is known about the created world, adds the truth of the Scriptures, examines the historical record, and builds from there step-by-step to support the precepts she teaches. It is important to understand this, otherwise you will not be able to communicate it to your children. And if you cannot communicate this to your children, you will not be able to give them what they need to make the transition from the more emotionally based faith to the more critically and rationally based faith that will sustain them in the "dry times" which every spiritual seeker encounters on their spiritual journey.

Applying the Faith

As Dr. Fowler notes, adolescence is a time when young people become sensitive to ideals; that is, the way things ought to be. They are constantly comparing how the world is with their vision of how the world should work. This is a perfect time to educate your child on the social teachings of the Church.

Challenge your teen with questions like: What would the world be like if people approached work and careers the way the Church says they ought to approach them? What would the world be like if families functioned the way the Church said they should function? What would people and relationships be like if they followed the Church's teaching on sexual ethics? How would it benefit the world to follow the Church's teaching on the ways money should be spent and distributed? How would the world be a better place if it respected life at all stages and under all conditions, instead of merely deciding that this fetus or that criminal had no right to life?

If you don't know what the Church's teaching is, or for that matter if you only think you know but aren't really sure, look it up. Start with the *Catechism*, and move onto the relevant Scriptures and documents (incidentally, the Church documents — especially the ones to come out of John Paul II's papacy — are not difficult reading, though they are wonderfully profound). You can even make a project of looking these things up with your teen so that you can learn together. After all, you don't have to know everything to be your child's teacher, you just have to have some ideas about where to look for answers. And of course, it can be helpful to seek out opportunities for you and your son or daughter to "get involved" in organizations that promote the Church's social teachings.

By showing your teen that Church teaching is not merely concerned with spiritual matters but also has social relevance, you are helping your child experience the practical wisdom of the Church. You are demonstrating that the Church is very much "in touch" with the world around it.

While being able to feel the Faith, defend the Faith, and apply the Faith is essential to any serious Catholic at any stage of life, it is critical to adolescence, where so much is uncertain and so much remains to be tested. Teens will only stick with a Church they experience as personally meaningful, solidly based on objective truth, and socially relevant. While the suggestions we offered above are merely the tip of the iceberg, we hope you will find them helpful.

Dealing With Sexual Issues

And now, the moment you've all been waiting for....

Helping your teen deal with sexual issues does not have to be that difficult, assuming you have been keeping up with the job all along. Let's review.

In infancy and toddlerhood, by practicing extended breast-feeding and other attachment-parenting practices, you have modeled the self-donative meaning of the body (a key concept for understanding the Catholic vision of human sexuality). By engaging in these practices, you have also demystified the female breast (an especially important thing for boys), demonstrating that God did not create them to be sexual objects so much as He created them to be a way to feed babies. Likewise, through extended nursing, co-sleeping, and "wearing" your young child in a sling, you helped your child get his or her "touch needs" met at the appropriate time. As a result, strong anecdotal evidence suggests that your now-teen is not experiencing quite the same degree of desperation as his or her friends are to "find someone to hold me."

In early childhood, you introduced your child to God's creation and the mysteries of birth and life by taking them to a farm or zoo in springtime (or if this is not practical, watching a video of animals being born — preferably one that has been previewed by you), and in general, talking about how wonderful God is for creating life every time your child points out a "little baby." Similarly, you have begun teaching your child emotional control, that while the emotions are good, one cannot do everything one feels like doing. You are also beginning to teach your child that love is not a feeling, but a willingness to work for the good of another, and to this end, you are encouraging your child to do as much as he or she can to work for the good of the family, finding simple ways to help around the house.

In middle childhood, you continued these lessons of love and responsibility, encouraging your child to balance family and school responsibilities with family life, teaching your child the true meanings of masculinity and femininity, and working to increase the intimacy in your own marriage so that you and your mate would be good models for marriage when your child grows up. Also, by remaining open to life, God has probably blessed you with other children, giving your older children the opportunity to play a role in the delivery and/or care of the infant(s), learning firsthand what a gift life is.

In addition to all these things you have done on your own, perhaps you have elicited help from your pastor, the Catholic school your child attends, or better still, you have made use of resources like the Couple to Couple League's New Corinthian chastity-education program for children in grades kindergarten though eight, or Our Sunday Visitor's *The Catholic Vision of Love*. In sum, you have built an exceptionally good foundation for dealing with the issues of modesty, chastity, relationships, and sexuality.

Now we arrive at adolescence and your job is three-fold. First, you need to help your child understand the importance of self-control as it relates to thought and action. Second, you need to give your child the information he or she needs on sexuality from a Catholic perspective. Third, you need to teach your child the true purpose of Christian marriage and relationships. Let's take a look at each of these.

The Importance of Self-Control

Before dating becomes a concern, your child is already beginning to experience intense sexual feelings that he or she may not know what to do with. Often, especially with boys but not exclusively, an adolescent responds to these feelings by masturbating.

Even in the absence of such folkloric "side effects" of masturbation such as poor eyesight and embarrassing palm-hair, the Church tells us that masturbation is a serious problem (see *CCC* 2352). But let's face it: Saying that masturbation is a "serious problem" raises hoots of indignation, irritation, and worse from a world that celebrates books like *Sex for One* — a popular text on the "joys" of masturbation. How could something done for one's own pleasure in the privacy of one's own room be problematic — much less, seriously so? Is it simply that the Church is a big killjoy with nothing better to do than to assail the privacy of innocent people? Of course not. So, what's the problem?

Basically, it can establish destructive sexual precedents. Granted, at first occurrence, masturbation is often the result of a basically healthy curiosity about one's changing body and the new sensations one is experiencing. In this form, masturbation, while certainly a distortion of what God created our sexuality to be, is questionably sinful (it lacks the requirement of full knowledge) and most definitely not something to send yourself — or your child — to the psychiatric hospital for (see *CCC* 2352 and *The Encyclopedia of Catholic Doctrine*, p. 432). Even so, it is not completely without danger. Since masturbation is often the first sexual experience a person has, it can establish some very negative sexual precedents that become stronger as the frequency of masturbation increases: among them that sex has no purpose beyond pleasuring oneself, that — since one often masturbates to pictures or images — people are basically things to be used to pleasure oneself, that sex is a powerful drug that can be used for venting a variety of negative emotions, and that masturbating is easier than pursuing real intimacy. Any one of these lessons can set the stage for compulsive masturbation, which is a serious problem, and, quite possibly, serious sin (*CCC* 2352).

The following tips will help you assist your children as they struggle to understand their sexuality:

1. Take a deep breath.

The first thing you need to do is remain calm. As I already pointed out, the earliest episodes of masturbation usually occur as a result of ignorance and curiosity. Shrieking about "perversion" will not make the problem go away, in fact, it will probably make it worse. The only difference will be that you won't know about it. Approach your child with the warmth and affection of a teacher whose student just added "2+2" and — try as he might — got "3.14159."

2. Teach your child the spiritual context of his feelings.

After you have asked God's help to be a compassionate teacher to His child, remember that the Holy Father tells us that God reveals Himself to us through our bodies (John Paul's *Theology of the Body*). Teach your children the true meaning of the sensations they are experiencing. Let them know that at this stage of their lives, sexual feelings are God's way of saying, "Start getting ready. I have someone in mind for you to love and be loved by. I want you to spend the next few years learning how to be a good help-mate to the one I have chosen for you."

Explain to your teen that they can waste the time God has given them to prepare for marriage by pursuing their own selfish "pleasures," or they can respond to God's call by learning more about healthy relationships, reading age-appropriate literature on Christian marriage and sexuality, and learning to be a better friend to the young men and women God places in their path.

Help your teens understand that when they experience arousal, they are feeling the voice of God speaking through their bodies. He is asking them to pray, both for their soul-mates and for themselves, that one day they may find true happiness with each other and God.

Acknowledge that the struggle to overcome selfish desires is a difficult one, but that if God is giving them these feelings, He is confident that they are capable of learning to use them responsibly. And of course, before, during and after this discussion, keep praying that your teens will grow in age, wisdom, and grace.

3. Encourage the three strengths.

Children who develop problems with compulsive/habitual masturbation tend to exhibit weaknesses in three areas: they lack mature, effective ways to express emotion; they tend to be socially inept; and they tend to be sheltered even from positive, Christian sexual education. You can't keep constant tabs on your child's genitals — God forbid — but you can encourage their healthy sexual education, socialization, and emotional facility. In fact, the Church obligates you to do this (see *Truth and Meaning of Human Sexuality*, and *Familiaris Consortio*). Sign your kids (girls and boys) up for an NFP class, buy them books on Christian relationships, encourage their memberships in clubs, teams, and other outlets where they can learn more about friendship and responsibility. Teach them how to express their emotions freely and respectfully. If you, yourself, have difficulty modeling these strengths, do some reading, some praying, or maybe even get some counseling. Teachers need to stay at least one chapter ahead of their students, or they will be dismissed as irrelevant. In fact, the wise parent will be working to develop these strengths in their child years before they see little Johnny wander into the bathroom with a copy of *Cosmo*. An ounce of prevention is worth a pound of cure.

Chastity is a skill to be taught, just like reading and math. While teaching your child this skill, keep your wits about you, your sense of humor handy, and God at your side. With the Lord's help, we can all be the skilled, compassionate teachers we need to be to help our children become the "masters of their domains."

Besides teaching self-control as it relates to sexual urges, it is going to be important to reinforce your adolescent's sense of modesty. While modesty is in part about hemlines and other fashion issues, modesty is really an interior virtue that "protects the intimate center of the person" (*CCC* 2521). By way of a humorous example, the Catholic physician/philosopher Dr. Herbert Rather once jokingly suggested that a nun could walk down the street naked and still find a way to be modest, but Marilyn Monroe could dress in a nun's full habit and still find a way to be immodest. In other words, modesty is really about how one carries oneself in relationships, and avoidance of blatant displays of raw sexuality, haughty refinement, or even pharisaical piety, all of which can lead to serious sins such as lust, pride, and self-righteousness.

The *Catholic Encyclopedia* defines modesty:

The virtue by which the individual exerts restraint over external actions, dress, and conversation. The vices that are contrary to modesty are lewdness, coarseness, and boorishness on the one hand, and excessive refinement and delicacy on the other. Modesty fosters social relations and charity, in that it ... promotes agreeable manners and harmonious relationships.

It is worth noting that while, traditionally, the Church has taught that women are primarily responsible for guarding chastity and modesty, *The Truth and Meaning of Human Sexuality* strongly warns against teaching any possible "double standard" that leaves men off the hook for exhibiting their own God-given responsibility to practice self-control. This is a welcome change, considering two factors. First, the older, less-nuanced teaching — that men couldn't control themselves, so women had a special responsibility to not lead them into sin — seemed to fly in the face of the idea that men are supposed to be pastors in the domestic church of the family. After all, one cannot reasonably assert that men are to be the spiritual leaders in Christian relationships on the one hand, and then say that men have a diminished capacity for sexual self-control on the other. Second, the older, less-nuanced teaching flies in the face of current psychological research, which is asserting that women are much more easily sexually aroused than it was previously thought. (Of course, this would also seem to be common sense. After all, those randy men throughout history had to be "doing it" with someone.)

Considering both current theological inquiry and psychological research, it is our opinion that it is entirely possible and natural to train boys to take the lead in exhibiting sexual responsibility. It is good training for the servant-leader role they are called to for the rest of their lives, it is good training for becoming faithful husbands (or faithful priests), and it is good training for the Christian walk. Of course, we are not suggesting that girls should be let off the hook, either — just that there is more than enough responsibility to go around.

The fact is, sexual modesty and chastity are attainable objectives for both men and women. Both women and men must be prepared to control themselves regardless of the stimuli around them. To suggest less is a cop-out unworthy of our Christian dignity. It also suggests a certain ignorance about the way the human mind works.

Cognitive psychology (a model of therapy that has been validated time and again by serious scientific studies) teaches that the key to mastering emotional states (like depression, anxiety, or even inappropriate arousal) is guarding one's thoughts and "self-talk" (that is, the things we say to ourselves). In essence, what arouses a person — male or female — is not the presence of external stimuli (such as a short skirt or sweet talk) so much as it is the harboring and entertaining of impure thoughts. Considering the assertions of cognitive psychology, it is easy to understand why current research is finding women to be more easily aroused than previously thought. Simply put, in a misdirected attempt to overcome the unfortunate sexual double standard that used to exist, popular culture is now encouraging girls to entertain thoughts about sex that were only culturally acceptable to boys a generation or two ago. Impure thoughts lead to impure actions, regardless of gender. Similarly, chaste, modest thinking leads to chaste and modest action. As Dominican Fr. Giles Dimock, a professor of theology at both the Franciscan University of Steubenville and the Angelicum in Rome, is fond of saying, "To the pure, all things are pure."

The Importance of Giving Catholic Information on Sexuality

When it comes to teaching your children to have healthy Catholic sexual attitudes, we cannot stress the importance of giving them the truth of the Church as early as you believe is appropriate to do so. There are some parents who would rather not tell their children anything about sex with the intention of protecting their innocence. This is a mistake. Allow us to illustrate why with the following example:

Imagine being at a party and walking around with an empty drinking glass. You want to make sure that no one fills your glass with something you find distasteful. How do you make this happen?

There are two options. The first is to walk around holding your empty glass out to the gathered assembly and saying over and over again, "Oh, no, thank you anyway," until finally someone insists hard enough and you let them "freshen your drink" with whatever vile concoction they care to pour into your glass. Or, you could simply fill your glass yourself with something you like to drink so no one bugs you in the first place. ("What's that? Freshen my drink? I've already got one. Thanks anyway.")

The same process works with sexual education. There are certain well-meaning Christian parents who think that the best thing that they can do for their children is to keep their glasses empty with regard to sexual knowledge. But nature abhors a vacuum, and inevitably, these "empty glasses" will be filled with something — probably not something that is remarkably desirable.

The only truly effective way to insulate your children against a distorted sexual education is to teach them what the Church teaches about sexuality and chastity first, so they can avoid being bothered by the things they will inevitably hear from others later. To this end, we can think of nothing better than instructing your child in the practice and attitudes behind Natural Family Planning as soon as you believe is appropriate, but at least by early puberty. Likewise, as *The Truth and Meaning of Human Sexuality* teaches, parents must lay the foundation for their children's sexual responsibility by practicing the same responsibility in their own marriages. Parents can best do this by also using Natural Family Planning in their own marriage, which allows parents to foster healthy expectations for their children's behavior, and model responsible love.

Also, it will be important to give your teen some guidance about setting appropriate boundaries when it comes to physical affection. Your adolescent needs to know how to draw the line way before the issue of sex is even a possibility in a dating relationship. In other words, help your son or daughter decide what kinds of affection are acceptable at various stages of a relationship, and help them decide what is "the point of no return" — that is, that point where the temptation to move into sex might be too difficult to resist. Some teens believe they can swim right up to the edge of the waterfall and not be pulled over in the current. ("It just happened! I didn't mean to do it!") Teach your teen that being true to the values he or she stands for as a Catholic means being able to say "no" a few miles upstream, by knowing his limits and being careful to think of his girlfriend as someone who first and foremost belongs to God, to whom he will have to account for his treatment of her — good or bad. And the same applies to young women.

But more than saying "no" to "near occasions of sin" (i.e., swimming too close to the waterfall), exhibiting a healthy sexuality means knowing what living out chastity is saying "yes" to. For example, by saying "yes" to a chaste mind and a chaste relationship, the young person is saying "yes" to:

— A life without sexually transmitted disease.
— Never having to feel as if he or she was used merely as a toy to satisfy the urges of another.

— A special sense of discovery and joy that comes from saving all the wonderful gifts of sexuality for marriage. Knowing that those gifts are being unpacked with that "one special person" who has never known another, nor will ever know another as you know each other.
— Never being haunted by the ghosts of past lovers.
— Never being tempted to use sex as a tool of revenge, a way to hurt someone the way someone else hurt you.
— A marriage where they will be able to enjoy their sexuality without guilt, because sex will not remind them of things they have done in the past about which they now feel guilty.
— Always knowing what a gift life is, because they will not have spent their formative years fearing, "What will happen to me if I (or someone I'm having sex with) gets pregnant?"

This list is just the tip of the iceberg. The benefits of practicing chastity, both of mind and action, outweigh any perceived short-term gains.

It is beyond the scope of this book to provide tips on designing a comprehensive sexual- and chastity-education curriculum to meet the unique needs of your child, but we gladly refer you to the following resources for further information and guidance:

Real Love, by Mary Beth Bonacci. A simple, practical book written in a style that will appeal to your teen. Written by a woman who has found a way to talk to teens of all denominations and backgrounds about chastity without having them laugh her off the stage. If you have an adolescent, you've really got to get this one.
The Catholic Vision of Love: A Guide for Parents, by Michael Aquilina. An excellent resource written in a simple, practical manner by a true, Catholic gentleman, husband, and father.
The New Corinthian Chastity Education Curriculum, available through the Couple to Couple League. A solid resource on chastity education from grades kindergarten through eight.
The Truth and Meaning of Human Sexuality, Pope John Paul II. A comparatively easy read. An excellent summary of the Church's thoughts on sexual education.
Catholic Sexual Ethics: A Summary, Explanation, and Defense, by Fr. Ronald Lawler, O.F.M. Cap., Joseph Boyle, Jr., William E. May. An excellent resource. A must for anyone who is serious about developing a deeper understanding of the wisdom behind the Church's teaching on sexual matters.

Besides these resources, as a way of shoring up your own understanding of how Catholic sexuality can at once be a toe-curling, mind-blowing, eye-popping, and yet profoundly respectful and deeply spiritual experience, check out the chapter in *For Better ... FOREVER!* entitled "Holy Sex, Batman! Or ... Why Catholics Do It Infallibly."

The True Purpose of Christian Relationships

The final point we want to cover in this section is how to formally teach your sons and daughters what it takes to have a real Christian relationship with a member of the opposite sex. Up until now, all the work you have been doing is foundational. Now, in pre-adolescence and early adolescence (that is, before the age where your child is intent on dating), you are going to put it all together. There are five steps to teaching your child how to think of Christian relationships:

1. Help your child develop an identity statement around which to build his or her relationships.
2. Help your child identify the specific qualities or virtues he or she desires in a future mate.
3. Seek out opportunities for your child to learn how to be friends with members of the opposite sex before you give permission to date.
4. Interview your child's romantic interests.
5. Help your child learn to check the effect of his/her dating relationships on his/her identity (i.e., "Is this person helping you become more — or less — of the loving/self-confident/honest/cheerful/godly/creative/chaste/etc. person you said you want to be when you grow up?").

Let's take a look at each:

1. Help your child develop an identity statement around which to build his or her relationships.

Earlier, we talked about the importance of helping your adolescent develop his or her own identity statement. That is, the specific set of virtues, values, spiritual ideals, and personal goals your teen would like to stand for and strive toward throughout the course of his/her life. In a sense, this is their "mission from God."

Having had your child do this exercise and identify the qualities

God wants him/her to emphasize over the course of his/her life, you need to explain what all this has to do with relationships. Basically, a Christian marriage is supposed to be about finding someone who you believe is going to help you actualize (fulfill) all those virtues that are near and dear to your heart. Teach your teens that they can know whether a person they are dating is "good for them" not just by how that person makes them feel, but by the qualities that person brings out in them. In other words, is the relationship helping your child become the more loving, self-confident, creative, joyful person she says she wants to be? Or is this relationship causing her (or him) to be jealous, to stuff her feelings and ideals into a box because her so-called boyfriend thinks they are stupid, to doubt herself, to be deceitful, and a host of other things. Teach your children that both in regular friendships and in the more intimate friendships that romantic relationships are supposed to be, the best people to associate with are the ones who help you feel you are more like yourself when you are with them. Teach your young teens to ask themselves, "Does this person I'm hanging around with (or dating) make me want to hide those values, ideals, and goals that make up my identity statement, or do they make me want to take those values ideals out, polish them up, and show them off even more?" Teach your teen that the only good friends are the ones who fall into the second category.

2. Help your child identify the specific qualities or virtues he or she desires in a future mate.

"She's awesome," gushes your son about the latest girl of his dreams.

"He's really cute!" beams your daughter about her latest crush.

Once you regain your balance, the best thing to do is congratulate your child on finding someone to feel so happy about, and then ask this gentle question:

"I'm really excited for you. Tell me, what kind of person is (s)he?"

Chances are, your child will be confused at first. Gently, ask again, "Well, you know. Is (s)he an honest person? Does (s)he love Jesus? When (s)he's around friends, is (s)he proud of you/does (s)he treat you with respect? That kind of stuff. I know you must be really attracted to him/her, and I think that's great, but what kind of person is (s)he?"

Of course, it's ideal to have this discussion before your son or daughter starts getting those crushes, but sometimes this happens sooner than we think it will. And anyway, better late than never.

Besides helping your son or daughter develop his or her own identity statement, it is essential that you spend some time helping your teen figure out what qualities to look for in someone else. This underscores the notion that friendship, especially romantic friendship, is about each partner helping the other become the person God wants him or her to be when he or she grows up. When you help your teen develop a list of virtues to look for in possible dating partners, you give your teen the tools he or she needs to decide whether or not a particular friendship (romantic or otherwise) is healthy or not. Within the first few dates, your adolescent will be able to have a pretty good idea of how respectful, honest, trustworthy, godly, supportive, etc., his or her girlfriend/boyfriend is, and make decisions accordingly. Likewise, this teaches your child to look before he or she leaps. Your child will learn to say, "I am attracted to so and so, but it takes a couple of dates — at least — before I know what kind of person my boyfriend/girlfriend is, so I better keep my eyes open and not go too fast." The fact is, children want to live up to your expectations, if you expect them to be godly and responsible, most often, they will do that.

Of course, that doesn't mean that your child won't ever blunder or occasionally bring home dates that make your flesh crawl. ("Mom? Dad? This is my boyfriend, Mad Dog. He spent last year in a Turkish prison, but now he's turned his life around and wants to give something back to the community by opening up a body-piercing salon right next to the junior high! Isn't that so cool?") But it does increase the chances that after your child sees that you won't be shocked that easily, she will begin to realize all on her own that her date isn't all he's cracked up to be. ("Mad Dog was such a fake. All that stuff he said about how Sesame Street was really a Marxist metaphor for the collective state was such garbage. Turns out he never even watched Sesame Street!")

3. Seek out opportunities for your child to learn how to be friends with members of the opposite sex before you give permission to date.

Too often, kids run right into dating relationships without ever having had the opportunity to learn what it takes to be a friend to a member of the opposite sex. This leads to teens and young adults who have a wide romantic repertoire, but have no clue of how to really relate to each other. As I show in my book *The Exceptional Seven Percent: Nine Secrets of the World's Happiest Couples*, the whole "men from Mars, women from Venus" phenomenon has its roots in adolescence, and is most profoundly felt by those men and women who, as teens, never took the time to learn how to befriend a member of the opposite sex — concentrating instead on strategies for impressing or seducing the opposite sex. As I wrote in *For Better ... FOREVER!* many men know how to sweep a woman off her feet, but they have no clue what to do with her when she's up in the air — except drop her on her rear.

To teach your child how to have the skills he or she needs to be a good friend before becoming someone's love interest, it is a good idea to encourage your teens and pre-teens to participate in activities where both genders mix freely. The best of these activities will require young men and women to work together to solve problems or complete an end goal. For example, community-service projects like Habitat for Humanity, working in a soup kitchen, volunteering at a hospital, etc., or Outward Bound-type programs (programs that use wilderness activities and rope courses to build teamwork and self-esteem), plays, school newspaper/yearbook committee, marching band, and other clubs and service groups that require members to function as a team, to learn each other's languages — as it were — and reach a goal together. Obviously, these are all important skills that translate well into long-term relationships.

Regardless, we strongly encourage you to require your son or daughter to show you that he or she has what it takes to make good friends with members of the opposite sex before giving your blessing to any one-on-one dating activities. This will serve you well, because young men and women who regard each other as friends first will be less likely to engage in any activities that would be harmful or disrespectful to the other. Likewise, it will serve your teen well, because such friendships help "Martians and Venusians" learn each other's unique languages and ways of looking at the world, so that eventually, when they are ready to marry, they will have the skills and experience they need to truly understand each other and work together as friends and helpmates — the way God intended it to be.

4. Interview your child's romantic interests.

John Ream, a Catholic father and grandfather who conducts "Effective Fatherhood Seminars," recommends interviewing the people your son or daughter is dating. While it sounds ominous (As John, himself, jokes, "The interview begins with 'Up against the wall!' "), the interview is actually a beautiful thing that his own children, and even his nieces and the children of friends, have asked him to do for them when they reached dating age.

While Mr. Ream has the most experience using the interview with the boyfriends of his daughters or other female family-members, we see no reason why a husband and wife could not sit down with their son and his beloved and conduct a similar interview. We have taken the liberty of combining Mr. Ream's interview with our own reliance on an identity statement. The result looks something like this:

The mother and father make a point of meeting the young person dating their teen (for the sake of clarity, we will use this example with a daughter, but a similar format could be used with a son). This meeting should take place early in the relationship, so that you can demonstrate that you and your daughter are holding the boy up to a higher standard of behavior right from the beginning. In preparing for this encounter, the mother and father might make dinner for the younger couple, or plan some other activity that would accommodate the casual-yet-serious nature of the meeting.

Over the course of the evening, the father should lovingly, gently, but firmly take the lead in saying to the young man dating his daughter (or the young woman dating his son), "I want you to know how happy I am that my daughter has found someone who helps her feel as happy as she does when she is with you. I've heard good things about you from my daughter, and I can tell that she really respects you. I wanted to meet you because I needed to tell you something. I love this young woman (he indicates the daughter). I would willingly give my life for her, as she is more special to me than anything I have. My wife and I have worked hard to instill values in her that will assure her of a happy and blessed life, and she, herself, says that everyday she wants to work toward being (insert the qualities of her identity statement here). I really respect her for that.

"I need you to understand that when you are out with her, I am trusting you with my special treasure. Man to man, I want you to promise me that you will never take her anywhere she could be harmed, do anything intentional to harm her yourself, or be disrespectful to the values and virtues that are important to her. Will you make that promise to me?"

This is an intense and loving action that is best handled by the father. It does two things. First, it is a public proclamation of your love for your son or daughter. You are showing the suitor the exact value of the treasure he has found. This is an overwhelmingly beautiful experience for your son or daughter, who truly feels esteemed by being spoken of this way.

Second, it sends a clear message that you are not playing around. Relationships are serious business. Self-esteem, future goals, even lives can be changed forever — for better or worse — by the shortest encounter between a man and a woman. This lets the young couple know that there is more to a serious relationship than having a guaranteed date for bowling night, that a Christian relationship is ultimately about believing that you have a better chance, with your partner than without him, of becoming the person God wants you to be by the end of your life, and vice versa.

5. Help your child learn to check the effect of his/her dating relationships on his/her identity (i.e., "Is this person helping you become more — or less — of the loving/self-confident/honest/cheerful/godly/creative/chaste/etc. person you said you want to be when you grow up?").

It is a regular occurrence in my practice for parents to bring in an adolescent son or daughter and desperately ask me what they can do to separate their teen from a boyfriend or girlfriend they believe to be a bad influence.

Unfortunately, there is little that they, the parents, can do directly. But by taking the time to help your teen develop an identity statement and a list of the qualities he or she would want in a partner, you can give your young person the tools he or she needs to make educated decisions for him- or herself.

One man we know had not developed an identity statement with his daughter yet. But he was in the habit of taking her to breakfast once or twice a month. During one of these breakfasts, the daughter began talking about how she was crazy about a new young man. After politely listening for a while, the father took the opportunity to ask her to come up with a list of qualities that she would want in a husband. She ticked off about four or five things, and then she started to cry.

"What's wrong?" asked the father.

Tearfully, she said, "I just realized that Mark [her boyfriend] doesn't have anything I really want in a relationship. Do you think he's bad for me?"

"Well, honey. I don't know. It's *your* list. I'm afraid this is going to have to be your decision. But I want you to know how proud I am of you for thinking this hard about what you want, and taking relationships so seriously. That is very mature of you."

Within the week, the man's daughter broke up with her boyfriend.

As touching as this story is, you can avoid such a close call by helping your young person come up with a wish list of the characteristics he or she would want in a mate some day. The youth can then use the first date or two to ask simple questions in the course of conversation that will help him or her decide whether or not this person meets their criteria.

Interestingly, Lisa used this exact method when she began dating me. Tired of taking a hit-or-miss approach to dating, she had made a list of the qualities she wanted in a husband and a father for her future children. In our first dates, she was able to discover a lot about me because she knew what she wanted to ask. These questions helped us found our relationship around the intention of helping each other become the people we believed God wanted us to be when we grew up. This intention — developed early on in our dating relationship — became the basis for the exceptional marriage we enjoy today.

When you have taken the time to help your young person develop an identity statement, you give him a way to check his own relationships, and you give yourself a legitimate way to inquire about the health of a relationship without seeming like a buttinsky. All you have to do is ask, "When you are with (insert name here), do you feel like he/she is helping your become more of yourself, or less?" Your young person will not resent the intrusion, because, done in the right spirit, he or she will know that you are only helping them stay true to the values they themselves have said are important.

Grounded in Love

The teen years are a challenging time for parents and teens both. Parents will do well to make sure that they are taking advantage of every opportunity to ground their teenaged children in love. Adolescents might be loathe to admit it, but they need parental affection and attention just as much as they did when they were younger. The best thing you can do to get yourself and your teen through adolescence in one piece is to give them as much affection and attention as they will allow (plus just a wee bit extra). The trick here is to let them know you aren't going anywhere, while still respecting their God-given needs for privacy and increased responsibility for their own lives.

By being generous with your affection throughout their lives, you decrease the chances that adolescence will become a terrifying time in which your teen runs around pell-mell, desperately trying to find someone to love them better than you did — and getting into all sorts of trouble in the process. When you ground your adolescent children in the love of the family and help them develop their own identity statements, you give them the security and freedom they need to make healthy choices on their own. You give them the security and freedom they need to become the young Catholic Christian men and women you always wanted them to be.

Closing Comments on Developmental Discipline — And the Five Fabulous Phases of Childhood

Well, there you have it, the five fabulous phases of childhood. As we said when we began this journey, the map we give is far from complete, but it is not meant to be a step-by-step guide for you to follow religiously throughout the various stages of your parenting career. Rather, it is meant to be a series of helpful hints and questions for thought that will help you decide for yourself the best ways to respond to your child's unique needs throughout the years of his or her life.

As your child's primary teacher, you are free to choose whatever method of parenting you see fit, and in doing so — as long as you are a basically loving, attentive parent — you would probably raise a basically good kid. But we would invite you to consider using the methods we have described throughout the first two parts of this book, because we believe that these methods represent the fullness of parenting. Keeping with Church teaching, the methods and attitudes we have described are consistent with the self-donative meaning of the body, and have been shown by research and the example of men and women who are parents many times over to help families live life as a gift in a way that other parenting models simply can't replicate. You may disagree in your gut about something you have read along the way, but the one thing that you cannot deny is that the methods we describe represent self-donative love, compassion, and high expectations of behavior, joined with the gentle discipline the Church herself uses in the Sacrament of Reconciliation. In that sense, the methods we have outlined are decidedly Catholic.

While we cannot and do not claim to have discovered the "one right way" to be a Catholic parent, we are confident that we have at least outlined "one very good way" you could manifest the mission that is Catholic parenting. As we have stated time and again throughout this book, the tips we offer are not commands you must follow if you wish to be a good parent; rather, they are an invitation to help you learn to get the most out of every stage of your child's life and your parenting career. By following them, you increase the likelihood that you and your child will enjoy a strong rapport even into adulthood, and that you will find yourself sitting next to Lisa and me on a park bench one day many years from now, saying to the young couple passing by with a babe-in-arms, "What a beautiful baby! Make sure to be present for every step of your child's journey through life. We were, and what a blessing our children turned out to be — even now!"

Part Three

A Parenting Potpourri

Chapter Ten

Soul Food: Twelve Ways to Foster Your Child's Faith Life

"As for Me and My House, We Will Serve the Lord."

For the Catholic parent, everything begins and ends with nurturing a healthy relationship with God. From the earliest days of your child's life, your first concern must be, "How can I teach this child to give and receive love, so that one day he may stand confidently under the fearsome gaze of Love Himself?"

We cannot underscore the need to help your child develop his own unique and personal relationship with Jesus Christ and His Church. We have seen many, many children who ride on the coat-tails of their parent's faith throughout childhood, only to reject the Faith in middle adolescence or early adulthood because it was simply never made personally relevant to them. These young people fall away, often never to return, because well-meaning parents made the mistake of thinking "Well, he went to Catholic school. We went to Church every Sunday. The Faith was always important to me. Isn't that enough?"

No. Absolutely not. Your faith is your faith. Your child's faith is another matter. There

In this Section ...

We'll examine some areas of special concern for Catholic parents including twelve ways to foster your child's faith life, how you can encourage vocations, handling TV and the Internet, Catholic fathering and mothering, the steps to nurturing your marriage, and tips for keeping your marriage and family life solid.

will come a time when your child no longer believes because you do, but is not intellectually strong enough to believe in the Faith because it is true. During this period, especially, your child will need to rely on an intense, personal relationship with Christ and His Church to carry him to the next stage of his faith development and sustain him through every stage thereafter. Don't wait until it's too late. Foster your own child's faith by helping him own THE FAITH today.

Throughout this book, we have attempted to give some suggestions on how to nurture your child's spirituality as he or she grows in age, wisdom, and grace. To summarize some of those suggestions and help you generate your own ideas for developing your child's spirituality, we offer the following twelve ways you and your house can serve the Lord:

1. Hold family prayer-time.

At least once a day besides meal-times, your family should take time to pray together. Use the following or a similar format: **P. R. A. I. S. E.**

PRAISE and thank God for His faithfulness and glory.
REPENT of the times each of you failed to love God or each other.
ASK the Lord to supply your needs.
INTERCEDE for those who need your prayers. Ask for the intercession of your brothers and sisters who have gone before you (i.e., the saints and the holy souls).
SEEK God's will for your lives.
EXPRESS your desire to love more and be more open to love (both God's and your family's).

This prayer time could be as short as five minutes or as long as you like, but by following this or a similar format, you are making sure all the bases are covered. Even more importantly, you are teaching your children the importance of constantly seeking God's will for your lives.

Of course, it is also important to remember that family life is itself a prayer. Everything you do for your family throughout the course of your day, when done with the intention of mirroring Christ's love to those around you, becomes a powerful prayer that not only molds you more closely to the image and likeness of Christ, but transforms your family members by Christ's love shining through you. You don't have to be a saint to do this, you just have to try to do remember to everything as Christ would do it. Begin each day as a family, praying some form of the Morning Offering. ("O my God, I offer You every thought and word and act of today. Please bless me, my God, and help me do Your will today.") Then take advantage of the grace of marriage, on which the family is founded, to help you perform the tasks of daily living — everything from taking out the trash to correcting your kids, to being attentive to your mate — as Christ Himself would do them.

2. Attend Mass together.

The Eucharist must be given pride-of-place in your family's spiritual life. Nowhere else do your children have a better chance to meet Christ "up close and personal" than in the Blessed Sacrament, and as Scripture tells us, no one who ever actively sought out a such a relationship with Christ left the encounter unchanged. Like our separated Protestant brothers and sisters, Catholics have an "altar call," too, in which we receive Christ as our "personal Lord and Savior." Our altar call is the Eucharistic meal, in which we acknowledge Christ as Savior not only of our spirits, but of our flesh and blood as well.

By teaching your child the true significance of the Real Presence, you allow your child to understand that he or she truly is a son or daughter of God, not only spiritually but literally, because like your children are your "flesh and blood," when your child receives Christ in the Eucharist, he becomes part of God's "flesh and blood." To be this kind of special member of God's family is a powerful and transformative thing — when understood properly. Though all are invited, not everyone can come to this meal. Only those who can humble themselves enough to admit that they need and desire this flesh-and-blood kinship with the Lord are welcome. Anyone who comes to the table to partake in God's family meal becomes truly (in flesh as well as in spirit) a son or daughter of God, and each person who comes to the table is given the grace needed to treat each other with the respect, dignity, awe, and love that is properly due a son or daughter of God. Protestants may well be devoted and honored friends of the King. But Catholics are among the few Christians who can legitimately claim to be the King's flesh and blood. It is time to stop taking our privileged position for granted, for as Christ told the Pharisees, "God can raise up children to Abraham from these stones" (Mt 3:9 NAB). If we will not make proper use of our inheritance, God will give it to those who will. In fact, He already does.

If you want to fully celebrate your status as a true son or daughter of the Most High God, along with all the spiritual, behavioral, and relational fruit this station bears, attend Mass as frequently as you can, every day if possible, but at least on your days off with your family (for example, Saturday mornings, vacation days). The more you go, the more you will be blessed by God's grace, and the less likely your child will neglect Mass as he or she gets older, because you have made it a central part of your life as a family.

As we consider the importance of Mass for your family, we would like to address two questions. First, what is the proper place of children at Mass? And second, how can you keep your kids well-behaved and interested once you bring them?

To answer the first question, we turn to Fr. Mark Gruber, O.S.B., a professor of anthropology at St. Vincent College. Fr. Gruber did his doctoral research living among the so-called "desert fathers," Catholic monks who live under austere conditions in the midst of the Sahara Desert and practice a very solemn, deeply reverent form of spirituality and liturgy. There, among these very no-nonsense holy men, Fr. Gruber discovered a surprising thing — that these monks loved having little children at Mass. As he wrote in an article for New Covenant:

> I cannot tell you, then, how astonished I was to see worshippers come to the monasteries with armloads of children. Their toddlers were permitted free reign in and out of the icon screen, around the altar, and even under the priest's robes!

Fr. Gruber then goes on to legitimately bemoan the less-than-welcoming attitude American priests and parishioners have toward children at Mass:

> For years, the better part of our liturgical planning has been about how to excise the little urchins from our assemblies. Regularly, I hear complaints about their racket, their crumbs, their distracting faces and sounds. Frequently, I read articles about their assault on worship and the inconsiderateness of the parents who bring them. And we are all aware that special Masses are provided to quadrant them out of the adult assembly; and the special soundproof cry-rooms are outfitted to delimit their noise.

It would seem that in many parishes across this country, no sooner does the congregation finish singing "Gather Us In" than we start herding the children so we can "Usher Them Out," all so the adults will not be distracted by their goings-on. To counter this trend, Fr. Gruber goes on to point out that according to the theology and longstanding tradition of the universal Catholic Church, children of all ages, once baptized, belong in the assembly:

> This understanding holds true of the rite of baptism and de facto holds true of the rite of Communion. If it [having small children in the assembly during Mass] makes us nervous, we may remember the classic translation of Christ's well known invitation. "Suffer [meaning, "Hey, you Apostles, get over your bad selves and let..."] ... the little children to come unto me" (brackets ours).

It would seem that the answer to the question, "What is the place of children at Mass?" is, "In the assembly with the rest of God's children participating as much as they are able." Furthermore, Fr. Gruber's experiences among the desert fathers proves that a Mass that welcomes children need not be "lowbrow liturgy." But frankly, regardless of the form it takes, almost any Mass that welcomes children is better than the antiseptic, contraceptive, roped-off, plastic-covered living-room Masses that are the norm in many American parishes.

This being said, it is important to talk about how to maintain the child's interest and behavior once you get to that "Kids 'R Welcome" church. Consider the following do's and don'ts as a good starting point.

Taking Your Kids to Mass: Do's

- Do sit up front. Children pay better attention when they can see and be seen.
- Do encourage prayer and participation from your children. Teach them the prayers and the most common songs sung at your parish, and expect them to participate as well as they can. Quietly cue your child when to sit, stand, and kneel. At the consecration, quietly and reverently say, "Look at Jesus! The bread and wine are really Jesus now" in your child's ear. Teach them beforehand to whisper, "I love you, Jesus" when the priest elevates the Body and Blood.

- Do bring quiet (and when possible, religiously oriented) toys for your youngest children. While children older than three generally do not need toys to help them get through Mass, younger children do. There are wonderful Catholic coloring books, fabric activity-Bibles, and other soft, quiet toys of a religious nature that are appropriate and educational. For some additional product ideas, call the Catholic Child Catalog at 1-800-363-2233.
- Do model prayer for your children. Model reverence for the holy place you are occupying and the miracle you are witnessing. Be attentive. Be respectful. Expect your children to follow your lead.
- Do take your children out of the assembly if they are making a disturbing level of noise for more than a minute or so. Do bring them back as quickly as possible, lest they get the impression that a tantrum will excuse them from the family meal at the Lord's Table.
- Do use the bathroom before Mass. Sick children and kids under five are exempt from this rule. Healthy children over five need to go at home or "hold it."
- Do make Sunday special. Let Mass be the first activity in a day of activities that celebrate family unity and joy.
- Do respect the decorum of your parish. While there is no reason to automatically camp out in the cry room, it's really not a good idea to let your children run around pell-mell either. The Mass must be welcoming to children, but in return, children should be encouraged to practice their "company manners" at the Lord's Supper.
- Do talk about the Mass after Mass. On your way home, talk about what the readings meant to you and how the pastor's homily applies to your life. Talk about what it is like for you to receive the Eucharist and any thoughts that might have come to you during your prayer-time after you received the Precious Body and Blood.

Taking Your Kids to Mass: Don'ts
- Don't bring loud toys, hard toys, or electronic toys.
- Don't expect perfection. You can expect your children to be their best, but they will not be automatons. Praise their good behavior, patiently and firmly redirect their lapses.
- Don't trash the priest. You don't criticize your kids in public; don't bad-mouth their spiritual Father either. If you have concerns, take them directly to the Rev. Horse's mouth — as it were.
- Don't bribe your kids with promises of doughnuts, toy stores, or outings "if you behave in church." Require your children to be re-

spectful and attentive in the presence of the Lord for the Lord's Own sake.

• Don't make Mass optional. As Kimberly Hahn, wife of apologist Scott Hahn and mother of six, says, "My children can be anything they want when they grow up, but that they will love the Lord is not negotiable." Missing Mass is not a sin because "the pope says so." Missing Mass is a sin (i.e., it damages your relationship with God) because you are refusing the Lord's invitation to dine with Him. You are telling your Father, Creator, Sustainer, Savior, and Friend that He is less important than sleeping in, or hanging out with your buddies, or pursuing a hobby. If you snubbed any other friend that way, how long would you remain friends? The Lord has set a place at His table for you. Won't you come?

No doubt you can come up with a few other do's and don'ts of your own. We leave you to it. Just keep in mind that you should not be so restrictive that you choke out any potential for joy in the experience of being at church, but you should likewise not be so *laissez-faire* that your child has done everything except attend Mass.

3. Make the Sacrament of Reconciliation a regular family ritual.

Besides Mass, take your family to confession at least once a month. Regular confession provides the accountability you need to stay faithful on your Christian walk, and it gives you the grace you need to overcome those sins you can't seem to let go of. When parents model the importance of regular confession, the children are more likely to catch the spirit of it as well.

4. Read the Bible together.

Every family has stories that draw the members closer together. Remember that time Uncle Leo lost his teeth blowing out the candles on his birthday cake? Or the time your son crashed his car into the limo on the way to the prom? Or the time you sat up all night nursing your daughter through a particularly bad fever? These stories tell us who we are, where we've come from, and suggest where we are going.

The stories of the Bible are the stories of our extended Christian family. They tell us who we are (God's children), where we come from (out of darkness into His wonderful light), and where we are going (to spend eternity with Him in heaven). Take some time to read the Bible as a family every day, whether five minutes before meals or at bedtime, or for longer periods during a family Bible-study. *God's Word Today* is a popular source of daily Scripture meditations from a Catholic perspective. You can subscribe by calling (651) 962-6738. Likewise, the Missionaries of Faith Foundation has an online family Bible-study, hosted by Scott Hahn and Jeff Cavins, called @Home in the Word, at http://www.moff.org. Of course, you could also follow the daily readings published in your parish missal. Ground your family in the Word, and the Word will be made flesh in the daily life of your home.

5. Celebrate Catholic traditions and spirituality.

Make a point of attending events at your parish like First Friday celebrations, Benedictions, the Stations of the Cross, May crownings, and other important observances of our Faith. These events are important and beautiful expressions of our Catholic spirituality. Making use of them helps remind us that Jesus must come first in our lives, not just on Sunday, but every day.

6. Celebrate the saint or feast of the day.

Check that calendar you get from your parish. On a saint's day, read his or her story aloud at a family meal. A good resource for this is Our Sunday Visitor's *Encyclopedia of Saints* or the "Lives of Saints You Should Know" series, by the Bunson family. After reading the story, ask the saint for his or her special intercession.

On minor feast days, find a way to celebrate them with your family. For some great ideas on how to do this, subscribe to *Catholic Parent* magazine, or pick up Michaelann Martin, Zoë Romanowsky, and Carol Puccio's book on instilling Catholic traditions in the family, *The Catholic Parent Book of Feasts* (both available through Our Sunday Visitor).

7. Use sacramentals.

Keep holy water in the house. Use it to bless each other on those days when you need extra help from God. Keep a crucifix in your home. Kiss your hand and touch Jesus' feet when you walk by it as a sign of respect. Keep blest oil in the house. Anoint each other when you are sick (this isn't the same as the Sacrament of Anointing of the Sick, but it is a beautiful expression of your hope in the healing power of the Holy Spirit). Keep blessed palms to remind you of Holy Week. Wear a scapular to remind you of God's covering you in grace.

Catholicism is unique for its little, physical ways of reminding us that God is always hanging around waiting for us to let Him love us better. Celebrate the uniqueness of your faith and its power to remind you that He is the God of everyday things as well as the God of the mountains.

8. Don't forget about Mama!

Remember, the Blessed Mother has never left unaided anyone who fled to her protection, implored her help, or sought her intercession. Ask her to pray for your family. We would encourage parents to pray a daily rosary for the spiritual and temporal well-being of their family, but don't stop there. Look for opportunities to have your children pray with you. Younger children sometimes balk at the thought of saying "a whole rosary!" but they might willingly say a decade, and after they get going, sometimes, they just forget to stop. When you foster your children's relationship with "Mommy Mary," as our kids call her, you give them a powerful friend who will always look for opportunities to lead them to her Son — especially when you aren't around to do it.

9. Sing God's praises.

We know, Catholics don't like to sing. Well, get over it. God loves music. He inspired the Psalms, and St. Augustine tells us that a song is prayer twice. Teach your children praise songs. Sing them on car trips or during family prayer-time (it beats the heck out of "100 Bottles of Beer on the Wall"). If you don't know any praise songs, check out your local Christian bookstore for some great children's tapes. The "Wee Sing" tapes are good, as are the songs by The Donut Man. ("Life without Jesus is like a donut ... 'cause there's a hole in the middle of your heart.") As your children get older, help them find Christian pop-groups to their liking. Contemporary Christian music is extraordinarily good and very contemporary — completely unlike the sappy church music that used to be played on Christian radio not so long ago. Check it out.

10. Lay hands on each other.

Each night, we bless our children by placing our hands on their heads and saying, "Lord Jesus, please bless this child. Send Your Holy Spirit into his/her heart, and help him/her to love You more than anything. Give him/her Your grace so that he/she can grow up to be the man/woman You want him/her to be. Amen." Then we make the sign of the cross on their foreheads.

Our children love it. They feel like they are getting a special gift from us, and they are — the gift of the Holy Spirit. Sometimes they return the favor by asking to pray over us. This is one powerful way families can make practical the idea that each Christian is called to be a priest, prophet, and king.

11. Celebrate baptisms and personal feast days.

Commemorate yours' and your children's baptisms as your "birthdays in the Church." Wish each other "Happy feast day!" on your patron saint's feast. On such days, have a special meal and ask that saint for his or her special intercession.

12. Be mushy about loving Jesus.

Love Jesus with all your heart, with all your mind and with all your soul, and don't be ashamed about it. Tell the Lord that you love Him every day. Let your children hear you say it. When you hug your children, remind them that the only person who loves them more than you is God — and give them another big hug from Him. When your children tell you that Mass is boring, don't criticize them, witness to them. Tell them how much it means to you to spend that special time with Jesus. Then pray with them — out loud — that they would learn to appreciate Jesus in the Eucharist more deeply, that they would learn to love the Lord as much as you, and that you would learn to love the Lord even more.

The other day, we were in a Christian bookstore, and a young man was strumming his guitar singing songs about the Lord. He was not remarkably talented, but what he lacked in talent, he made up for in heart, and eventually, he had the whole bookstore singing God's praises along with him. We Catholics have no excuse for not being this way. We have the Real Presence. If Protestants, who restrict themselves to a mere "spiritual communion" with the Lord, can find so much to be happy about, how much more do we Catholics — who are one with His Flesh and have the Precious Blood coursing through our veins — have to be happy about? C'mon, all you drowsy Catholic people, let's love Jesus as passionately as He loves us.

These are just a few ways that you can nurture a healthy love of Jesus and the Church. Complete the following exercise to see if you can come up with more ways you can make Christ the center of your family life.

Exercise: Is Jesus the Center of Your Family Life?

Take the following quiz:

_____ Every day, I try to view even the mundane tasks of family life as a kind of "living prayer."

_____ My family prays together every day (besides at meal time).

_____ My family attends Mass together, at least on Sunday.

_____ Our family discusses God's involvement in our daily lives.

_____ We parents share how important Jesus and the sacraments are to us.

_____ My family is conscientious about attending Mass on Holy Days.

_____ We read the Bible as a family (at least one or two times a week).

_____ We model personal prayer to our children.

_____ We teach our children the formal prayers (Our Father, Hail Mary).

_____ We teach our children how to pray in less formal ways.

_____ We encourage our children to have their own prayer lives.

_____ We teach our children the truth of the Faith.

_____ We (parents) model a deep, personal love of Jesus and His Church.

_____ We make use of sacramentals (holy oil, holy water, the crucifix, blessed items, etc.) in our home.

_____ We make an effort to attend liturgical events at our church besides Mass (e.g., Stations of the Cross, Benediction, "First Fridays," Bible studies, etc.).

_____ We go to confession at least once a month.

Scoring

No scoring. You know how well you did. Regardless of your score, make an effort to make Christ an ever more present part of your daily lives.

Exercise

1. Make a gratitude journal in which your family can list all the ways God has been faithful to your family every day. Have the kids decorate the cover, and write your entries in each day during family prayer time.
2. Write the story of your lifelong relationship with Jesus and the Church; include the most important struggles and joys you experienced along the way. Share your story with your children. Encourage them to share theirs.

Questions

1. How could you get to Mass more often? What do your think you would gain by attending more often (e.g., more grace to overcome sin or personal struggles, a greater appreciation of the Eucharist, etc.)? Make a commitment to go as a family at least one day during the week besides Sunday.
2. What role does confession play in helping you become a better Christian? How do you feel after you have been absolved? Why? How could you and your family get there more often?
3. If you were going to live your faith out more fully in your family, how would this require you to treat each other differently than you do currently?

Chapter Eleven

Sibling Revelry: Six Hints for Helping Your Children Love One Another

Charles has three brothers and a sister. "We used to fight like cats and dogs as kids," says Charles, "Once, I got so sick of Jennifer [Charles' older sister] calling me 'the infant,' I stole her bra out of her drawer. I pinned a big sign with her name on it to the cup and hung it in a tree right outside her school. She was completely humiliated. Of course she beat me to a bloody pulp. I hurt for a week after she got done with me," he says with a chuckle. "But now that we are grown-ups, all I have to do is pick up the phone and any one of them would be here in a heartbeat."

The greatest inheritance parents can give to a child is brothers and sisters. But sometimes the earlier years can be rough, as siblings try to stake out their own territories and identities while struggling to find the best ways to relate to each other. How can you take sibling rivalry and turn it into sibling revelry — a feeling from the earliest years that one's brothers and sisters are a real blessing?

Them's Fightin' Words ...

While brothers and sisters fight as a matter of course, typical bother/sister arguing is different from sibling rivalry. Sibling rivalry is a much more serious estrangement between siblings that occurs when there isn't enough parental time, attention, or love to go around. In such cases, parents might have favorites, or be very demanding, or disapproving. When this happens, the children's fights are so vicious because the stakes (parental attention) are so low.

But even simple arguing between brothers and sisters can degenerate into sibling rivalry if the parents don't have the proper tools to address this behavior. Jerry, a thirty-five-year-old phone client from New York, was talking to me about growing up with his older brother Andy. "Andy was always bigger than me. He used to call me horrible names and thump me every chance he got. Most of my childhood memories involve some aspect of being tortured by that jerk. I know my parents knew because he did it right in front of them. When I would ask for their help, they would just say that it was between Andy and me to work out. They thought it would build character, I guess. To this day I don't have anything to do with him."

And Paulette shared this story: "My parents used to leave my older sister in charge of me. Jane [Paulette's sister] hated me for it. One time when I was five, she told me there was a burglar in the house, gave me a kitchen knife, and told me to hide under the bed and not come out no matter what, or 'he' would kill me. Then she disappeared downstairs. I stayed huddled under the bed crying for several hours until I heard a car pull into the driveway. I was terrified. All of a sudden, my sister came upstairs with my parents. She told them we were playing hide and seek and that I wouldn't come out. When they saw the knife, they spanked me and sent me to bed because, 'You know you shouldn't be in the knife drawer! Next time, you listen to your sister.' I tried to tell them what really happened, but they just said I was making things up. There were about a thousand other ways my sister took her anger out on me while we were growing up. I don't know who I'm angrier at, my sister for doing those things to me, or my parents for letting it go on."

The fact is, left to their own devices, children can be capable of remarkable cruelty toward one another. They simply don't have the self-control needed to handle strong emotions or temptations deftly. It is up to the compassionate, attentive parent to facilitate a healthy relationship between siblings and not just assume that it will magically happen. The following tips will help you avoid sibling rivalry in your home and instead promote what we call sibling revelry, a genuine love and solidarity between the young members of your family.

1. Special delivery!
We have observed that healthy sibling relationships begin from day one. Too many parents pack their older children off to grandma's or some other place when their baby brother or sister is going to be born.

We have found that this simply exacerbates the older child's fear of being replaced by the younger sibling.

By contrast, when older children are given some role to play in the actual delivery of their sibling (for example, helping to cut the cord, helping to give the baby her first bath, cuddling the baby with the parents, etc.) the children begin bonding from day one. To be honest, we would not believe the powerful effect this has if we had not seen it ourselves so often. We cannot explain why this happens, but the following example might help increase your understanding of the phenomenon.

Billy, age four, was a remarkably gentle playmate and caregiver for his baby sister. He loved to sing her lullabies, help his mother dress her, and cuddle her with his mother while she nursed the baby. We asked him once, "How come you're so good with Maria?" Billy, who had attended the very end of the delivery and helped his father cut the cord, said proudly, "I helped her be born!"

While this event is not the be-all and end-all of good sibling relationships, it seems that playing some small part in the delivery gives older sibs a sense of ownership — if you will — in the sense that, "I helped make this, so I'm going to take good care of it."

2. Use the family identity-statement.

A family identity-statement is extremely helpful for negotiating good relationships between siblings. In the first place, because the entire family is committed to growing in love, service, generosity, solidarity, or any of the other qualities that make up the core of your family identity, it stops any one child as being labeled "the generous one" or "the creative one." When a family identity-statement is in place, each child, along with the parents, is expected to be as (insert qualities here) as their age and stage allows.

Secondly, it helps you arbitrate those impossible fights between siblings that are designed to be a test to see which one you love best. When your children are fighting, and can't seem to solve it themselves even after trying for a while, avoid the temptation to solve the problem directly. Instead, say to both of them, "It looks like you both need to show more (generosity, love, kindness, responsibility, etc.), because neither of you is acting in a way that works to solve this problem. What could each of you do differently?"

Once you have solicited more responsible options from each child, stay there and help them to arrive at their own solution. Then, ask them to apologize to each other for their part of the misunderstanding, and give each of them a sign of your affection for sticking with the process even though it was hard.

The beauty of this is that not only are you building solid sibling relationships, but you are also teaching your children from the earliest years the same healthy arguing strategies I work to teach couples in marriage counseling: problem-solving on a foundation of love and responsibility.

3. Watch comparisons between children.

One obvious suggestion for building good sibling relationships is to be careful of comparisons. This applies to both negative comparisons ("Why can't you be more like little Brunhilda?") and positive ones ("Edwinna is the pretty one.").

When praising your children, praise them for specific accomplishments and efforts ("I love your picture!" or "That was really a loving choice.") instead of mere personality traits ("You're so smart.").

When you praise a child in too broad a fashion ("You are so _____.") it can set up two problems in sibling relationships. The first is the "me too" problem. If you say to one child, "You are so loving (or smart, or creative, or clever)," inevitably another child is going to say to you, "Am I loving (smart/creative/clever), too?" Saying "Of course you are, honey" is fine in one sense, but in another, it undermines the fact that the one sibling actually did something specifically loving (smart/creative/clever) for which he was being praised, and it sends the message to the other sibling that she can consider herself loving (smart/creative/clever) without having to do anything to show it. Taken to its logical extreme, such empty compliments lead to adults who think themselves loving while completely neglecting their families, or adults who think themselves brilliant while under-whelming everyone by their performance.

Likewise, praise each child according to his or her ability. For example, if your ten-year-old and your five-year-old are both drawing at the table, the older child may say, "Isn't my picture a lot better than his?"

This is an impossible question, because comparing the work of a ten-year-old to the work of a five-year-old is like comparing apples and oranges. This is just another one of those Smothers Brothers "Mom likes me best" ploys. Respond to such situations by saying, "Ten-year-olds and five-year-olds are good at different things. I love all the pretty colors your brother is using, and I really like your perspective and composition."

"But which do you like better?" The child may persist.

At this point you may be tempted to say "I like them both equally," but this would be a mistake. Anyone — especially your children — can see that the pictures aren't equal. You are going to have to explain yourself more clearly, or else you will accidentally send the message that you are happy with a less-than-sincere effort. For example, the ten-year-old, hearing such a "I like them equally" comment, will think "I worked really hard, but she likes his equally as much. Next time I won't work so hard." Meanwhile, the five-year-old thinks "Mommy likes my picture as much as my brother's even though his really is nicer. It would be silly to try to do even better next time. It's perfect the way it is!"

The only way to avoid undermining your children's need to do their best is to respond by saying something like this: "What I like is when my children make their best effort. You are making the best effort you, as a ten-year-old, can make, and your brother is making the best effort that he, as a five-year-old, can make. And that's what makes me very happy."

When praising your children, avoid cheap and easy overgeneralizations. Praise their specific efforts, and specific aspects of what they've done. And always be sure to keep in mind the abilities of their particular ages.

4. Attend to everyone's needs (not necessarily wants).

"It's not fair! Allie got three hot dogs and I only got two!"

"It's not fair! I want another piece of paper too!"

"Why did you buy Terri a new dress but not me?"

Fairness as a virtue is highly over-rated. But children, when they express concerns over it, are voicing a legitimate need to know, "Do you love me as much as my brothers and sisters?"

Of course you do, but how do you demonstrate that love without giving into the silly practice of giving every child the "same" all of the time? The simple answer is to avoid the fairness issue altogether and instead concentrate on need. Through our actions and speech, parents must consistently communicate the message that "needs come before wants, and all needs will be met in this family."

For example, the child above who wanted a third hot dog should be asked, "Are you still hungry?" If the child says yes, then thirds should be given. But if the child is not hungry, and this is a simple matter of "me too," it is enough to say, "All needs will be met in this family first. Your brother was hungry, so I gave him another hot dog. If you are hungry you may have one, but if you are not, then taking it would just be greedy. Do you need it?"

In another situation at the beginning of this section, a young girl objected because her sister got a new dress. A similar reply works in this situation: "Terri outgrew some of her clothes and so she needed a new dress. Is there anything you've outgrown?" If the child says that there is, plans should be made immediately to replace the item, since "all needs will be met in this family." But if the child says "no," you may reassure her that the minute she needs something, it will be attended to, but that time is not necessarily now.

Of course, a child's wants should also be respected and responded to as generously as possible — as long as you are careful not to go overboard. It is no more healthy to overindulge children than it is to constantly deny them the little pleasures that you can afford to give them. But regardless of how much or how little you are able to give your children, the key to making each of them feel cared for is letting them know that their needs for material goods, attention, comfort, and love will always be taken seriously and responded to quickly, even if they have to wait for some of the less-important things.

Taking this approach to apportioning your emotional, financial, and physical resources among your children — rather than teaching them to constantly want more — will teach them the meaning of the word "enough." They will learn to be satisfied when their needs are met. In both childhood and adulthood, your children will be able to avoid the trap so many others fall into. Amassing and hoarding "stuff" and monopolizing other people's time and energy just so that they can feel "as good as" their brothers and sisters, or in adulthood, their peers and co-workers. Teach your children that needs come first and that their needs will always be attended to promptly, and they will learn to be satisfied with what they have, even while they are waiting and working toward some of their most important wants.

5. Be careful about how much child-care responsibility you assign to siblings.

Until a child is well into the teen years (and even then some caution may be indicated) he or she lacks the skills necessary to adequately and respectfully care for his younger brothers and sisters. He may have the best of intentions, but few things have as great a potential to turn an otherwise "good child" into a latter-day Mussolini than "babysitting" his brothers or sisters.

Bridget, the mother of two, brought her children to counseling. The oldest daughter, Leah (age ten), was being cruel to her seventeen-month-old sister. She was not being abusive, exactly, but she was playing cruel "jokes," like taking the toddler's toys away and hiding them behind her back, and tripping the child when she was trying to walk. It seemed that the oldest daughter took some pleasure in making the baby cry.

While there were several issues that came into play as counseling progressed. One factor was that the mother had too high expectations for her older daughter's ability to care for her sister. Bridget would frequently ask Leah to "watch the baby" while she went to another room to fold laundry or do other household chores. Most often it was at these times that the oldest girl would take advantage of her sister.

Instead, I suggested that the mother ask Leah to help her around the house, while the mother took primary responsibility for the baby. This met the mother's intention of trying to give the oldest child some responsibility, but did it in a way that the older daughter could handle.

In the following weeks, the mother reported that she would sit with her daughters and fold laundry together while she kept her eye on the toddler. Bridget made Leah chiefly responsible for doing the job while the mother supervised and played with the baby, but they were all together. Bridget reported that there was a marked improvement in the relationship between the siblings. "Leah likes feeling like 'mommy's helper,' I get time with the baby, and all of us get along better."

If you want to give your children more responsibility, give them chores to take care of. When they are much older (middle to late teens), you may consider giving them some responsibility over their siblings. But even then, be careful how much. Child care is not unskilled labor. It is serious work that is best left to the most mature members of the household.

6. Be generous with affection and one-on-one time.

As we have said throughout the book, there is nothing more important to the life of your child and the success of your parenting relationship than your ability to shower generous amounts of affection, love, and attention upon your children. When siblings are convinced

Exercise

Ask yourself the following questions:

1. What ways do I accidentally pit my kids against each other? Do I unfairly label or compare them?
2. When my children argue, do I give them parameters they can use to solve their own problems or do I ignore them/solve it for them?
3. What ways do I allow myself to be drawn into those "Whom do you love more?" fights between my children?
4. What are my expectations when it comes to my older children taking care of my younger ones? Am I giving too much child-care responsibility to my older children?

Try the following:

Think about the activities that your kids enjoy the most. Take out your calendar, sit down with your mate, and schedule a "date" with each of your kids to do some of those things this month. Make it an ongoing tradition.

For more information, see *Siblings Without Rivalry* by Adele Faber and Elaine Mazlish, Avon Books.

— not just cognitively but on the deepest, visceral level — that each one is loved as much as possible, fighting in the house tends to decrease markedly. This makes a great deal of sense when you consider that most fights between brothers and sisters are, at their core, about two questions: (1) How much do mom and dad love me? and (2) Do mom and dad love me more or less than my brothers and sisters? When love and affection are overflowing from both parents, siblings have little reason to have such "how much do you love me" fights, and peace reigns, more often than not.

One of the most important ways to show your affection to your children — especially, though not exclusively, in a larger family — is to make sure that you are getting some one-on-one time with each child every month. Children love having your focused attention, and those special parent-child nights are an important way to stay connected with what is going on in each of your children's lives.

Lynn, a woman we met at a conference, fondly recalled the one-on-one time she spent with her mother and father as a child. "I always looked forward to those two times a month when I would get my mom or my dad all to myself. They were both very busy. Dad had his own business and mom worked part-time in addition to being primarily responsible for the home and taking care of the four of us kids, but they always made sure that each one of us got some time alone with them each month. We might go out for dessert, or play putt-putt golf, or even just take a walk in the park, but we always talked. Well, mostly I talked and they listened. It meant a lot to me that they cared enough to take that time to just listen. I think that's why I, or any of my brothers or sisters for that matter, really ever rebelled. I mean we had our moments, but we never got into those 'I hate my parents, can't wait to get out of here' spells. Because even when things got tough, they were still pretty good. At least twice a month, sometimes more when we needed it, we had their ears and could hash things out. They were great."

Making a serious commitment to helping each child feel loved and special as an individual as well as being an important part of a larger community (i.e., family) pays off in the loyalty and obedience that will be returned to you, and the camaraderie that will be shared by all of your children because they don't have to compete to get your attention.

Chapter Twelve

Strengthening the
Three Pillars of Stewardship

Stewardship is perhaps best defined as using the gifts we have been given in a way that gives honor to God. On the one hand, stewardship requires us to take good care of the things we have and responsibly manage the resources God has made available to us. On the other hand, good stewardship demands that we not value those things more than the people in our lives, nor should we allow the conscientious management of those resources make us blind to the needs of others.

As a virtue, stewardship sits neatly between responsibility and generosity. Practiced properly, stewardship is a beautiful prayer of thanksgiving to God that not only celebrates the goodness the Lord has shown us, but invites us to share that goodness with others.

It should be obvious then that, as parents, we must actively seek out opportunities to teach our children stewardship from the earliest ages. If the child is old enough to grasp the concept of "mine," then the child is old enough to begin his education in the three pillars of stewardship; being grateful for what he has been given, taking care of (or at least not abusing) the things he has, sharing those things with others.

The following are some tips for fostering the three pillars of stewardship throughout the years.

Practice an Attitude of Gratitude

The more grateful a person is for the things he has, the more likely it is that he will be a good steward. Ungrateful people tend to have an overblown sense of entitlement which causes them to treat the people in their lives and the things they have with neglect. Practice an attitude of gratitude toward each other and God to remind yourselves that everything you have and every blessing you encounter is a gift that requires care and acknowledgment.

1. Praise God.

Every day, let your children see and hear you thanking God for the little things that go right in your day and for the simple gifts God has given you. After a long day out, as you pull in the driveway, let your children hear you say, "Thank you, God, for our home." After a nice evening with friends, say, "Thank you, God, for the gift of our friends, and for giving us a chance to share what we have with others." When you wake up, say, "Thank you, God, for this day; let me use it wisely." All throughout the day, when you happen to feel grateful, acknowledge it in a little comment to God that your children can hear. Encourage them to do the same.

Reserve time in family prayer for acknowledging the good things God has done or given you. For example, at dinner or bedtime prayers, each family member should take turns thanking God for some blessing they encountered that day.

2. Thank each other.

Make sure that you thank each other for various services you perform, the acts of kindness you experience, and the gifts you receive. As we said before, ingratitude breeds a sense of entitlement which, in turn, tells me that I can treat people and things any way I please. For example, if I don't have to thank you for letting me use your toy, then that implies that that toy doesn't belong to anyone. Therefore, I may treat it any way I wish. But if I have to thank you for giving me the toy, that implies that I am receiving a gift from you, and it reinforces the idea that the toy is special and should be cared for.

Practice expressing your gratitude to your family and you will always be mindful of what it takes to be a good steward of your family.

3. Keep a gratitude journal.

In a special notebook (if your children are young, have them decorate it) keep a special list of all the blessings your family receives. Work on it together during family meetings, at a regular meal time, or as part of your nighttime ritual. Writing things down helps us remember that every blessing we receive is a gift, which makes us what to care for those things even more.

Care for the Gifts That Have Been Given

As the parable of the talents teaches us, God expects us to care for what has been given to us, regardless of how much or how little we have. Taking good care of the things and resources God has given us is a physical prayer of thanksgiving that gives honor to God and grace to the supplicant.

1. Model care for your things and resources.
- Do you keep your home basically neat and orderly (not like a museum, mind you; that's not stewardship, that's the sin of pride).
- Do you maintain your car and home properly?
- Do you spend and save wisely? Are you careful to pay off credit cards as soon as possible? Do you pay your bills on time?
- Do you make sure not to take each other for granted? Do you care for your family by being generous with love and attention?
- Do you manage your time well? Are you pleased with the balance you have achieved between work and family?

These are all ways that we can model the second pillar of stewardship to our children. By keeping our own affairs in order, we teach our children to manage theirs.

2. Expect your children to treat their home with respect.
Whether your home is furnished by Chippendale or Chip's House O' Furniture is irrelevant. Everything we have is a gift from God and should be treated with respect. Now, that doesn't mean that we should rope off certain parts of our homes or encase our living-rooms in Lucite. After all, God give us things for people to use them. It just means that we must treat the things we have with some degree of care and respect. By all means, your home should be a welcome place for people of all ages to come and play and sit and enjoy. But you are well within your rights to teach your children — and expect other people's children — not to climb on tables, jump on the couch, color or eat where they shouldn't, and maintain other rules of civilized home life. Such rules are not stifling, they facilitate an attitude of grateful respect for gifts given.

3. Teach your children to care for their things.

While children must have the freedom to play and make messes, they also can be expected to play responsibly and help clean up the messes they make. Teach your children how to play appropriately with the toys they have. Ask them to put things away when they are done with them and have them clean up at the end of the day.

Likewise, it is important to require children to put their clothes away and keep their rooms as neatly as they are able. Though a child's age will dictate his level of ability, generally speaking, if a child is old enough to have things, he is old enough to begin learning to care for things.

Finally, teach your children to be good stewards of their friend's things by making sure they play gently with their friend's toys and help to clean up when it is time to go home.

4. Teach your children to manage their money.

Whether or not you give your children an allowance, at some point they are going to come into money. Teach them how to handle it. Require them to set aside a certain percentage for the Lord (the Bible asks for ten percent) and a certain percentage for savings. While they should maintain major decision making power over the remainder, you should be available for guidance and you must retain veto power. Some parents say, "I didn't want him to buy the Slaughterhouse Wombats CD but he spent his own money, so what can I do?" This is unacceptable. Of course, your children should be free to spend their money as they see fit (after they have met their saving and tithing obligations) but there are limits. Feel free to set them.

5. Teach your children to manage their time.

Make sure your child is managing his homework and housework responsibilities well before allowing him to engage in other activities. Socializing, playing sports, and attending club activities are all important, but they are less important than mastering basic life skills, self-care, and maintaining primary obligations to home and school.

Share the Gifts That Have Been Given

1. Model sharing.

Shamefully, Catholics are the least generous group of Christians there are, giving on average merely two percent of their income to charity compared to the Protestant average of seven percent. The

Bible asks for ten percent. How close to this commandment do you come? We must model generosity to our children if we expect them to manifest generosity. Giving to the Church is an important way we share our blessings with those who need them. God does not give us good things so that we can hoard them (cf. the parable of the man who stored up grain). He gives us gifts so that we can share them. Model sharing the wealth to your children so they will have an example to follow throughout their own lives.

2. Expect them to give to the Church.

To encourage a healthy sense of Christian generosity, start early by asking your children to give a percentage of what they make (either by allowances or gifts) to the Church. Read the scriptural passages on tithing (giving ten percent of your income) to God. Make a commitment as a family to offer this sacrifice which is befitting of every Christians baptismal priesthood.

3. Encourage sharing between siblings and friends.

Teach each child that even though something is "hers" this does not mean she has exclusive rights over it. Rather, it means that while she is the primary custodian of it (i.e. she gets to keep it in her room, take care of it, have first dibs on it, and others must ask her permission before using it) she still obliged to generously share what she has with her siblings and friends.

Some parents try to buy "the same" things for each child so there will not be any turf battles. In most cases, this is a cop-out that merely reinforces the selfishness which is common to childhood. It is much better to let each child be the custodian of different things but require each to share generously. "And what if they don't?" you ask. Simply take the thing away until the child has expressed a willingness to practice generosity. "I am taking this from you. You may not choose to be selfish with the things I give you. You may earn it back by showing generosity to the family for the remainder of the day. Do you understand what that means?" This reinforces an important lesson of Christian life. Specifically, that ownership has both privileges and responsibilities, not the least of which is sharing what you have with others.

4. Insist that your children generously offer their time and service.

Building a family that is a community of love requires that all members of the family generously offer themselves and their service for the common good of the family. First through modeling and then through direct instruction, teach your children that if they see a job within their capabilities they should simply do it. To this end, look for opportunities to educate your children about the steps necessary for completing the various tasks involved in running a home. Every child is capable of doing something to be helpful, and all persons in the family should do as much as they are able. Teach your children to ask if there is any way they could be of help before they ask to go out and play or are excused from the dinner table. It sounds like a big deal, but it is a simple thing to enforce. All you have to do is consistently ask "What are you supposed to ask before you go/get up from the table?"

Make sure you don't overwhelm them; they are not your slaves after all, but they are an important part of the family and they should play an important role in making sure the home runs smoothly.

A Word About Allowances

Among parents, there is some disagreement about whether or not allowances are a good idea. Whatever your position, we strongly recommend that if you grant your child an allowance, you not give it as "payment" for completing chores. This cultivates a "what's in it for me?" attitude that you will live to regret. Chores are one thing. Allowances are a completely different thing. Family chores are not special jobs which require special monetary rewards, they are simply a part of family life. If you are going to give your children an allowance, simply give it to them because it is one way you, as a parent, can model generosity. The only requirement you should tie to an allowance is that your child must exhibit similar generosity by making giving a portion of his money to the Church, saving a bit, and using some of it for the good of others (for example, buying a small birthday present for a friend, or getting a candy bar for his sister as well as one for himself).

Such an approach not only teaches responsible money management, it reinforces a host of Christian virtues.

How Much is That Doggy in the Window?

Pet Stewardship

Most every child wants a pet at one point or another, and pets can be a rewarding part of a child's life. But they can also be a parent's worst nightmare.

The fact is, many parents romanticize the "boy and his dog" experience as much as their children do. But unless you really want to assume primary responsibility for the care of a pet, don't fall for your child's doe-eyed yet untested promise of "I'll take care of it, Mom. I will! I'll walk it and feed it, and play with it, and love it, and call it George. PUHLEEESE can I have one?"

As we say, if you do not want to be the one left holding the leash, then you are going to have to work up to a dog or cat. Start with something simple, like an amoeba (or a mouse or gerbil). Let your children demonstrate responsibility for caring for a small thing before giving them primary responsibility for walking and feeding Marmaduke.

Our own children were desperate for a pet, and though they really wanted an Irish wolfhound (about seven thousand pounds of big, slobbering, lovable dogness) we were able to steer them toward an equally lovable, but considerably less slobbering, lop-eared bunny. After a week of cleaning, feeding, and watering the bunny, our children were re-thinking the whole pet thing. "Boy, his poopy really stinks! I'll betcha dog poopy stinks even more 'cause it's bigger!" "This thing really eats a lot! Does a dog eat this much?" "I have to water it again? Already?"

Even so, we made certain our children kept up their responsibilities toward their pet until it was called by God to bunny heaven after a mysterious and disturbingly sudden death some six months later. Though we were all saddened by his passing (honest) we all learned a valuable lesson. We weren't quite ready for the wolfhound experience. The children were able to make this decision for themselves based on their experiences with Cuddles the bunny.

Before you acquire a pet, clarify what you really want. If you are looking for the "boy and his dog" experience and don't mind being the one who ends up being the primary caregiver, then by all means jump right in. But if you are serious about making your children care for the animal, you are going to have to work up to the experience. Do yourself, your children, and your future pet a favor by seriously considering your ability as a family to adequately care for any four — or more — legged borders.

Stewardship in Sum

Stewardship is an important Christian virtue that affects every aspect of daily life from how much we are able to be grateful for what we have, to how willingly we share our gifts with others, to how well we preserve our gifts and resources for future enjoyment.

Tonight, take a moment with your family to consider what you have and how you are treating it. Could you be more grateful, more, generous, more responsible? What steps will you as a family take to be better stewards of the gifts God has given you?

Remember, stewardship is not just about "taking care of your stuff." Ultimately, stewardship is a physical prayer of thanksgiving for God's Providence in your life. It is one more way you can worship in the domestic church that is your family.

Chapter Thirteen

I Want My MTV?
Catholic Parents and the Media

Generally speaking, there are two camps in Catholic circles when it comes to dealing with television and the Internet. The first group believes that we would all be better off if a nuclear bomb destroyed all forms of telecommunication, *especially* TV and the Internet. The second group wishes they could have a fiber-optic cable and a microchip surgically implanted in their visual cortex so that they could watch everything — including the "Paint-drying Channel" — while surfing the 'Net in their heads, mouse-clicks replaced by eye-blinks.

And then there's us.

We believe that television and the Internet are an important part of everyday life. There are few research tools as powerful as the Internet, and there are some wonderfully educational and entertaining programs on television. Of course, they are buried amid five hundred channels of "When Jerry Springer ATTACKS!" (insert blood-curdling scream here) but they are there if you know where to look. Culturally speaking, television has replaced the ancient tribal custom of sitting around the campfire

We would like to thank Charles Beaudry, principal consultant for The Ridgefield Group, a business consulting and Internet-development firm that has several major Catholic organizations as clients, for his "responsible surfing" suggestions. Visit their Web site at:
www.RIDGEFIELDGROUP.com.

listening to the village storyteller. Now, our stories are told around the warm glow of the HDTV. Mourn the change if you will, but there is no use denying that, as far as contemporary society is concerned, being both media savvy and pop-culture fluent are important indicators of socialization and intelligence.

Even so, as parents it is necessary to model and teach healthy TV-viewing and Internet habits. The following do's and don'ts can be a good starting place for making sure that technology serves your family, instead of the other way around.

TV and Internet DO's

- Do set limits. Have clear rules about what kinds of television shows and Internet sites are and are not permitted. Post them. TV and Internet privileges should be tied to faithful compliance with these standards.
- Do monitor your children's use of the Internet. It is best if you can set-up the computer in a common room of your home (as opposed to a child's bedroom). Know where your children are, on- and off-line.
- Do model responsible viewing and surfing. The Internet sites you visit will be stored in your computer's memory and your child can
- access them. Don't think they won't try to go where you've been.
- Do discuss the programs your children watch and the sites they visit. Ask specific questions. "What do you like about that show?" "What did you learn on that site?" "What do you think about the way that TV character behaved?" Avoid the temptation to lecture. Use these discussions to lead your children to develop their own healthy viewing and surfing habits.
* Do require your children to check any questionable sites or programs with you first. View them yourself or with your child before giving permission for your child to view them alone.
- Do require your children to use nicknames instead of their real names on the Internet. Predators abound and can access your home address with as little info as your child's last name.
- Do turn the TV or computer off if it is interfering with your child's ability to listen to you, socialize, or fulfill responsibilities in a timely manner. Leave it off until your child is demonstrating more responsible self-management. Use your own discretion for the length of time television or Internet privileges should be suspended.

TV and Internet DON'TS

- Don't let your children give out any personal information of any kind on the Internet, ever (including name, age, grade, name of school, address, phone number, friends' names, etc.) — without checking with you first.
- Don't ever permit your child to set up any face-to-face meetings with Internet contacts unless (1) you are aware of the plans first and (2) you plan to chaperone the meeting.
- Don't neglect your spouse, children, or domestic responsibilities due to excessive TV or Internet use. Chat rooms can be especially addictive. Monitor your own responsible use of technology so your children have a good example to follow.
- Don't just leave the TV on for noise. Turn it on only when there are specific programs you are interested in watching. Then turn it off. Instead of always reaching for the remote, talk to each other. Play games. Do arts and crafts. Bake. Go outside. Do anything but sit there having your brains sucked out by the idiot box.
- Don't trust Internet-filtering programs to supervise your child's surfing habits. These are imperfect devices at best which can inexplicably screen out good sites and still let undesirable sites be accessed. Nothing can take the place of an attentive parent.
- Don't use the television as a babysitter. This is extremely tempting and very common, but still unadvisable. As much as possible, encourage your children to draw, use clay, play games, read, or do similar activities when you need them to be occupied and quiet. In a pinch, use familiar, quality videotapes instead of television when more creative options are not available. Familiar videos are preferable because you will not be surprised by show content or inappropriate commercials. Regardless, be careful not to overdo it.

Accidents Happen

While we strongly advocate firm limits and consistent parental supervision of television and Internet use, sometimes your child will encounter inappropriate shows and undesirable sites regardless of your best efforts. It is best to handle such circumstances calmly and rationally. When your child encounters something disturbing or undesirable on television or the web, it is best to calmly and rationally initiate a discussion with comments and questions like:

"I feel sad that you had to see that. What are you thinking about it?"

"What did you think of the choices that TV character made?"

"How does this show/site fit with our family identity-statement? ... Why do you think so?"

"Do you think that God would be pleased, or disappointed, with that show/site? Why (or why not)?"

"If a person were to watch/visit shows/sites like that all the time, how do you think it would affect them? (Or wouldn't it?)"

Of course, you can use similar questions to address concerns over any form of media (for example movies, comics, supermarket magazines, radio, tapes and CDs, and computer games). Just remember, the point of such conversations is not to lecture your children on the lurking evils of the world. Even *The Truth and Meaning of Human Sexuality* cautions parents against this approach to "protecting" their children's innocence, suggesting that it is counterproductive to developing healthy attitudes. Rather, the point of such conversations is to gently solicit your child's feelings and thoughts about the experience, and learn how your child would like to handle similar circumstances in the future. Such questions also help you learn how your child thinks and, over time, allows your child to show you what skills and information he still needs in order to develop his own internalized criteria for determining what is appropriate, what is inappropriate, and why.

Questions to Ask and Things to Do ...

1. Have your family make a list of your favorite television programs. Discuss the value (or lack of value) of these shows. If, after this discussion, your family decides to continue watching these programs, make a commitment to leaving the TV off unless these programs, or a similar show, are on.
2. How much computer time is enough? Clarify this with your children. Post the rules for good TV and Internet management right next to the TV and computer.
3. Discuss. What ways does your family let technology come between you? How could you make better use of this time to foster family relationships?

Chapter Fourteen

BOO! — Coping with Childhood Fears

Cody, age four, is afraid to go downstairs to get his teddy bear for bed: "There are monsters downstairs by the door!"

Virginia, age eight, is suddenly afraid that her parents are going to die: "Please don't go out with daddy tonight. You might have an accident."

Matt, age ten, is painfully shy. He has a hard time trying new things and almost begins visibly shaking when around people he doesn't know.

Janice, age eleven, learned about germs in health class. Now she refuses to eat anything and is constantly washing her hands.

Childhood fears are always difficult for both the parents and the child. The child feels crippled and incompetent, and the parents feel frustrated and helpless. After all, no one likes to see their child suffer. And of course, the problem is made worse if the fear is accompanied by the teasing of peers. What can a parent do to help a child overcome his or her fears without being too pushy and making things worse?

The following five tips can offer the concerned parent a place to begin in helping a child conquer his fears, using the acronym **B. R. A. V. E.:**

BE aware of the child's emotional temperature (maintain your own).
RUN to the Lord.
ASSESS what's needed to conquer the fear.
VISUALIZE a way through the fear.
EMPATHIZE.

Let's examine each of these:

Be aware of the child's emotional temperature (and maintain your own).

Childhood fears can be very frustrating, especially for parents. An odd mix of concern, love, embarrassment, and our own fears of inadequacy as parents often lie behind our attempts to "help" our children overcome their fears.

As a consequence, the most popular question I receive in my practice as asked by parents of children with fears is this one: "How hard should I push my child, and how hard is too hard?"

The best answer to this question is that it is acceptable to encourage a child to face his or her fears, but you must never push so hard that it raises your emotional temperature scale or your child's over a 6.5. You may recall that over a 6.5 you and/or your child begin losing touch with reason. You begin to feel hostile, and you are tempted to say and do things that you would not otherwise do. Past this point, you can easily become abusive to your child, if not physically, then certainly verbally. Similarly, past this point, your child's fears become more and more intractable, as they are now adding the feeling of being terrorized to the feeling of being terrified.

When your sense is that either you or your child is coming close to the 6.5 mark, stop. Take a break. Don't throw your hands up in disgust and roll your eyes at him. Rather, say, "That was a good effort. Sometimes you feel strong, sometimes you feel afraid. But I'm proud of you for trying." Then spend a minute or two helping your child calm down.

Run to the Lord.

The Book of Jonah says, "Out of my distress I called to the LORD, and he answered me" (Jon 2:3).

Teach your child to turn to the Lord when he or she is afraid. Lead him or her through a prayer for courage that, depending upon the child's age, may go something like this: "Dear Jesus, I know that You have not given me a spirit of fear, but a spirit of strength and a sound mind. Send Your Holy Spirit into my heart and give me Your courage. Keep me safe in Your arms and make me strong. Amen."

Also, teach your child to ask his older brothers and sisters in heaven (i.e., the saints) for help. Of special note is the Blessed Mother (or "Mommy Mary," as she's known around here). The Memorare teaches us that "never was it known that anyone who fled to your protection, implored your help, or sought your intercession was left unaided." Inspired by this confidence, we teach our children to "fly unto her" the "virgin of virgins, our mother." A simple prayer of "Mommy Mary, please hold me," or even a Hail Mary or the Memorare itself, are very beautiful and powerful prayers that invite the Blessed Mother to carry the child to the feet of her Son, who will shower him or her with protection and love. Or, for those times when the monsters under the bed or fears of the playground bullies call for a less nurturing, more forceful response, St. Michael the Archangel is a good friend to have: "St. Michael the Archangel, defend us in battle, be our protection...."

Teach your child to be a "prayer warrior," as it is known in certain Christian circles. Help him discover how to confront the spirit of fear with the Spirit of God, and he will learn that he can — as St. Paul teaches — "do all things in him [Christ]" who strengthens him (Phil 4:13).

Assess what is needed to overcome the fear.

In most cases, what is most needed is more maturity on your child's part, and more patience and affection on yours. Childhood fears tend to decrease on their own as time goes by, peaking between three and eight and decreasing thereafter, as long as the parents don't make it worse by labeling the child early on as "a wimp" or some other negative appellations that the child can come to identify with. Under most circumstances, even more serious presentations of normal childhood fears (like a fear of water, new experiences, new people, etc.) tend to decrease as time goes by, and the child feels more competent. In the meantime, it will be important to enhance your child's sense of competence in those areas in which he can succeed, so that he will have a foundation of strength to draw from when he is forced to confront those things he is afraid of.

If you would like to take a slightly more active approach to particular fears your child may have, you should use solution-focused questions to determine what is different when your child is less fearful of that thing he or she is usually very afraid of. For example, if your child is afraid of the dark, is he less fearful on nights that the hall light is on, or you are walking in the dark with him? If your child is afraid to go to school, is she less fearful on the days when her father gets her ready than her mother? On days where there are no quizzes? That her friends are going to be there? Likewise, on the occasions that your child is less fearful and more comfortable in a crowd, is he better rested? Talking about something he knows about? Familiar with the people? Unfamiliar with the people? You don't have to know why these particular differences create a change in your child's level of fear. It is enough to recognize that this difference is somehow significant and replicate it.

You might also ask your child what it would take to help him overcome a particular fear. Don't just assume you know the answer. Sometimes simply listening to your child explain his concerns helps take some of the bite out of the problem. At the very least, it will give you some insight into the ways your child is thinking about the situation and suggest some possible interventions. Keep in mind, though, that most childhood fears are not rational, and therefore do not respond to simple advice-giving or lecturing. Be patient. Most likely you will have to go through this with your child more than once, and even then what will make the real difference is not that your child will have "gotten it," but that he or she has outgrown the particular fear. Affectionate listening is the best intervention available to parents.

When fears persist beyond a point that you believe is developmentally appropriate, or at level that you consider is unacceptable, seek a professional opinion or contact the Pastoral Solutions Institute at (740) 266-6461 for additional information.

Visualize a way through the fear.

You might recall our discussion of relating styles in an earlier chapter. It would seem that children who are most prone to childhood fears are the ones with a primarily visual relating-style. These children tend to have very vivid imaginations, as well as the ability to "see" the possible consequences (real or imagined) before they happen. This tends to make them more cautious than other children.

By contrast, children who are less fearful tend to have a more kinesthetic relating-style. This is due to the fact that these children tend not to "see" the possible consequences of certain behaviors until they are already feeling those consequences. So, for example, the visual child might decide that he had better not climb a particular tree, because he could imagine that once he got up there, he might not be able to get back down. Alternatively, the kinesthetic child, feeling confident about his climbing ability in general, would have no problem taking on the tree in the first place. Only once he had gotten to the top and began trying — unsuccessfully — to climb down would he begin to feel incompetent and the panic would set in. In other words, the child consistently bites off more than he can chew because he has a difficult time visualizing the consequences.

All of this would seem to indicate that there is a strong visual component to childhood fears. Because of this, it is possible to fight fire with fire; that is, to use visualization to fight the visual component of the fear.

For example, some parents from our parish brought their five-year-old in to see me. The boy was terrifying himself with thoughts of monsters in the hallway. A very simple intervention cured him in one session. First, I prayed with him. Then, I asked him to imagine a "friendly monster" that would be his protector. This imaginary monster should be unquestioningly devoted to him, but also be stronger and more capable of fierceness than the worst "bad monster" he could think of. He giggled at this. I asked what he was imagining and he proceeded to describe a creature so fearsome that it even scared me to think about. But he said he was laughing because "the monster wants to be my pet and so I'm rubbing his tummy and he's purring!" Next I had him "make a movie" in his head that showed the monster (whom the boy named "Big Enemy Shredder") attacking the other monsters he was afraid of, making the hall safe for his friend. The young boy was ecstatic.

From that point on, the boy was no longer afraid of the monsters in the hall; in fact, as he went through the house, and even the basement, he would often pretend to be "Big Enemy Shredder" fighting off the monsters, and having a great time doing it. Teach your child how to use his imagination for his benefit, and you will be on the road to teaching your child how to master his own fears.

Empathize with your child.

As I suggested above, the most powerful intervention parents have at their disposal are affection and patience. When your child shows you his fears, let him know that sometimes you get afraid too. Tell him how you overcome, or fight against, those fears. You may also remind your child that even Jesus was afraid in the garden of Gethsemane.

An important lesson for all children is that being brave doesn't really mean never being afraid; it really means doing what needs to be done in spite of feeling afraid.

Perhaps the best lesson you could teach your child is that even more important than overcoming a particular fear is the willingness to keep trying. And let him know that you love him even when he is shy or afraid.

How Do I Know If I Need More Help?

Does your child exhibit a level of fear or shyness that is stopping him from enjoying life? Do your child's fears or shyness significantly inhibit his friendships, school performance, or other important activities? Is your child resistant to your best efforts to talk to him about his fears, or try any of the suggestions you make? Have the fears persisted at the same level of intensity for more than six months? If you've answered "yes" to any of these questions, it may be helpful to seek the advice of a professional. Contact the Pastoral Solutions Institute for more information at (740) 266-6461.

Fortunately, though, these kinds of fears are fairly uncommon. For the most part, a healthy dose of affection and patience, with an extra bit of prayer and a willingness to listen thrown in, is all your child will need to grow up confident of his abilities to face whatever needs to be faced.

Chapter Fifteen

We Can Work It Out: Catholic Parenting in a Two-Career Family

Married for ten years, Nick and Sara are the parents of two children. Nick is employed as a human-resource manager for a pharmaceutical company and Sara works as an oncology nurse at a community hospital. Members of a large, suburban parish, they called me at The Pastoral Solutions Institute to discuss a concern of theirs.

Sara: "We're probably like most families. We enjoy our work, but we want our kids to be healthy and secure. It's also important to us to be able to pass on our faith."

Nick: "We're both active in our parish. I serve on the council and Sara sings in the choir. We'd like our kids (ages seven and five) to see the Church as important part of their lives, too."

Sara: "The reason we decided to call was that we've read a lot of books on balancing careers and kids, but we were wondering if the Church has any insights on how to run a family where both parents work. It seems like most of the things we read from Catholic sources are more relevant to more traditional families. Can you offer any thoughts?"

Work is an important part of life. And for many couples, having one parent at home is not an option, for one reason or another. Is it possible to still do the kind of parenting we describe in this book even when both parent work?

Though it presents it own unique challenges, the answer is, "Absolutely, yes." In fact, when two parents work outside the home it is even more important to use the methods we describe to encourage the children's sense of self-worth, to maintain the priorities of the family, and to protect the family's sense of solidarity in light of the many commitments and responsibilities that are tugging at the individual members. Regardless of the structure of the family and the various roles the parents play, there is no reason at all any family should feel unable to use loving-guidance discipline or follow attachment-parenting practices.

Consider the following tips to be a launching point for your own discussions dealing with the unique challenges you face as a two-career family.

Remember Your Family Identity

Life is chaotic, even more so in families where both parents work. Sometimes it is all you can do to get through the day and get a meal on the table. Considering this, it is even more important for you to have a family identity-statement to help you remember that there is more to life than getting through the day; that family life, first and foremost, is about helping you become the people God wants each of you to be. By concentrating on your family identity in spite of multiple outside pressures, you will be able to maintain your priorities and remember that no relationship outside of family is as well-equipped to help you achieve the goal of becoming a more loving, self-donative person. You and your kids will be able to keep from getting sucked into the all-too-common belief that true fulfillment is found outside the home in the work-a-day world, where everyone is replaceable and the bottom line is all that matters. You and your children will be constantly reminded to find yourselves in the loving service your family identity calls you to offer at home on a daily basis.

Be Conscious of the Relationship Between Home and Work

Having personally meaningful work or roles is essential to good mental health, as long as you are able to set appropriate limits. In other words, of course you should love what you do, but that cannot be an excuse to build your life around work instead of around the people whose souls God has called you to nurture.

A woman we know is an extremely busy interior designer. She loves her work, and she loves her husband and children, but she has a difficult time balancing the two. She shared the following with us: "I overheard my son talking to his friend about a field trip. His friend asked if I was going to chaperone the trip, and my son said, 'Nah, mom's way too busy to go. I didn't ask her.' The worst thing about it was that he didn't even seem to be bothered by the idea. Mom was too busy, so he wouldn't even ask. Somebody else might say that he was well-adjusted, that he was respectful of my needs. And of course, he is. But I felt like I was teaching him that mom was too busy to be there — and that was okay. Well, it's not okay for me. I want to be there, and I want him to feel sad when I can't. I want him to miss me. I want him to know that I'm never too busy to meet even his smallest need. But I realized that often I am. "

Many parents find themselves in a similar bind. In such times it can help to remember that the Book of Genesis tells us that the necessity of toil was created long after the command to love was given. For the serious Catholic, the Catholic family ethic must supercede the Protestant work ethic. We must do the work we believe God is calling us to do, but do it in a way that respects our vocation, our call to be a father or mother who plays the most important role — second only to the saving work of Jesus Christ — in perfecting our mate and our children in love. Catholic fathers and mothers must develop the attitude that we are working to live, not living to work. This is not to say that we are obliged to embrace holy poverty — though some may be. Rather, this is to say that we need to know when to say "enough." And to do this, we will rely on the qualities given to us in baptism and articulated in our family identity-statements.

Practice Attachment Parenting

If you have an infant or a child under three, we cannot stress enough the importance of using as many aspects of attachment parenting as you can (e.g., nursing, co-sleeping, carrying the child as much as possible, being generous with affection, being sensitive to their cues, and practicing loving-guidance discipline).

If you are a working mother who would like to nurse her infant, contact the La Leche League for tips on how you can have a successful nursing relationship. If your child is past the nursing age, but still in early childhood, you may still wish to practice co-sleeping. Many working parents find that co-sleeping provides a great way to give their child the extra cuddle-time and security he needs, even when the parents and child are separated for longer periods throughout the day. And of course, no child ever outgrows the need for generous physical affection and loving, gentle forms of correction.

Engage in Family Hobbies

One other challenge of the two-career family is that often the children are as busy as the parents. Each child has his or her activities which he or she must be bussed to and from six or seven hundred times a day. All for the sake of the children's socialization.

I recently read a case study of a nine-year-old who was having panic attacks and bed-wetting episodes. The parents were convinced that the child would need some kind of medication to help him calm down. As therapy progressed, however, it was discovered that the child was so busy going to various lessons and activity groups that he didn't have time to ride his bike and play with his friends. He was stressed because his family never stopped rushing him from one thing to the next. Once his parents relaxed his schedule, giving him more time to be with them and to be a kid, the symptoms were resolved.

A well-socialized child is a child who is socialized to the family. Of course other friendships and activities can play an important role in your child's development, but these should play a secondary role to the lessons learned by being together as a family. Politeness, solidarity, teamwork, loyalty, responsibility, can all be taught best at home. Before you sign your child up for one more thing, ask yourself about the strength of your own family relationship, and add to or subtract from the extra-curricular activity list accordingly. If all is well on the home front, and your family can handle the commitments, by all means, sign them up. But if there is a constant struggle at home to make connections with each other, then it is time to scale back.

One way to meet the need for an extended social network while maintaining a healthy respect for the primacy of the family is by taking on hobbies that you can do as a family. Join a gym together. Be in a play together. Serve at church together. Serve the community together. You don't have to all be doing the same things when you get there (for example, some of you might act in the play while the others work on the sets), but being generally in the same place at the same time helps you build a sense of togetherness.

Hire Jobs Out and/or Do Jobs Together

A common complaint is that most of a two-career family's time is eaten up by the work they do out of the house and the work that remains to be done at the house, leaving little time to build relationship. The simple answer to this problem is to hire out as many of the jobs as you can, and those you can't, you should tackle as a family.

Regarding the first point, it is possible to hire someone to clean, cook, cut your lawn, or do just about anything that needs to be done, but you cannot hire someone to love your kids. While you could probably hire someone to play with them and to make sure they don't get killed, you cannot hire someone who will truly love them like you can. To this end, all parents, but especially two-career parents, need to give special weight to maintaining family rapport even over and above getting the chores done.

Of course, you can use the family chores to build rapport as well. Some working parents feel guilty making their children work at home because, "We get so little time together, I don't want to have to spend the time that's left doing chores." As a result, what often happens is that mom and dad (or probably just mom) do all the housework in addition to their work outside the home, and the children become spoiled because they never have to do anything.

If you cannot afford to hire out certain chores, then do them as a family. Pick a specific block of time, assign jobs, and let everyone know that once the jobs are done, you will celebrate by having some special fun family-time. Think of getting chores done as "the home team winning the game," and afterwards, celebrate accordingly.

Find Ways to Recharge Your Batteries

Every parent needs some time to his or herself once and a while. The problem is that in two-career families there is so little time to go around that parents feel guilty taking this time.

In some ways, this guilt is appropriate, as it keeps you from taking too much advantage of the temptation to just run away from home (which we've all experienced from time to time). Of course, there are days when you just need a break, and this is perfectly acceptable. Remember, Scripture tells us that even Jesus was eager to get some time away from the crowds to pray and think by himself on occasion. When you feel your batteries are running low, find simple ways to recharge them while your mate, or if necessary a sitter, takes some time with your children. Later on, return the favor for your partner.

Think About Why You Work ...

We would be remiss in this section if we didn't ask you to think about why you work, and whether your work outside the home is actually helping you meet those goals. For example, many people believe they need the second income to make ends meet, but several studies show that once expenses like child care, a work wardrobe, lunches, travel, and other miscellaneous items are deducted, a family tends to keep only ten percent of the second income. For most people, this amount simply doesn't make that much of a difference.

Others work because their self-worth depends upon it. While personally meaningful work and roles are important to healthy-identity strength, one must be careful not to get the sum of one's identity from what one does. When you are dependent upon your work to define your self worth, you leave yourself open to being taken advantage of by employers who couldn't care less about your home life, and you leave yourself open to conveying the attitude that your career is more important than your spouse and children. And of course, they're not.

The key for both men and women who work outside the home is remembering that as Christians, who we are is best represented by the values we hold and the priorities we exemplify in every day life — not the jobs we do. It takes real courage to live this out, but the effort brings its own rewards in the form of greater rapport at home, inner peace, and a deeper, spiritual view of life, instead of a merely survivalist one.

Chapter Sixteen

Is Eight Enough?
Planning the Size of Your Family

Few things are more misunderstood than the Church's teachings on sex and family planning. While it is beyond the scope of this book to go into this in great detail (for more information on this subject please see *For Better ... FOREVER!*), we would like to offer a cursory examination of some of the more basic points, especially how they relate to planning the size of your family.

Responsible Parenthood: A Balancing Act

The Church's teaching on family planning is summed up with two words: "responsible parenthood." You can find this phrase in several major documents of the Church, especially *Humanae Vitae* and *Familiaris Consortio*. Basically, responsible parenthood boils down to this.

> On the one hand, Marriage and conjugal love are by their nature ordained toward the begetting and educating of children. Children are really the supreme gift of marriage and contribute very substantially to the well-being of their parents.... Hence, while not making the other purposes of matrimony of less account,... the couple ... should regard as their proper mission the task of transmitting human life and educating those to whom it has been transmitted [that is, the children already born.]
>
> *Gaudium et Spes*, No. 50

On the other hand:

> ... While a child is a great blessing, it is sometimes very important for parents to give careful thought to the size of their families. Husband and wife "will thoroughly take into account both their own welfare and that of their children, those already born and those which may be foreseen. For this accounting they will reckon with both the material and the spiritual conditions of the times as well as their state of life. Finally, they will consult the interests of the family group, of temporal society, and of the Church herself. The married partners themselves should make this judgement, in the sight of God."
>
> *The Teaching of Christ*, quoting *Gaudium et Spes*, No. 50

Though each of these quotes from *Gaudium et Spes* has a slightly different focus, both uphold the belief that there is no greater gift that God gives to us than our children, and there is no greater inheritance that we can give to our children than siblings. As our son once told us, "Brothers and sisters are friends who never have to go home."

God, being generous and loving, invites us to share in the joy He experiences when He creates life. As the *Encyclopedia of Catholic Doctrine* says, "God is a lover." God loves loving (it's what He does best) and so He creates more things and people to love.

And yet, as the orthodox Catholic moral theologian Janet Smith writes, "Catholics are not obliged to have as many children as their bodies can bear." God, though Himself unlimited, understands that we, being creatures, have limits. Since each person's limits are different, God invites us to be open to life in two different ways. The first is through a willingness to bring children into the world, and the second is to build a life-giving love in our marriages. Balancing these two ends of marriage (unity and procreativity) is where Natural Family Planning (NFP) comes in.

NFP gives couples the opportunity to practice two sets of virtues that are equally important to the Christian walk. For example, when a couple is pursuing conception, they are expanding their generosity, their abilities to identify with the Fatherhood of God, their trust in divine providence, and their opportunities to practice sacrificial love, to name a few. Likewise, when couples practice this openness to life responsibly (by practicing NFP) they grow in self-control, temperance, prudence, chastity, and a host of other virtues.

When a couple practices NFP they discern each month which set of virtues God is calling them to exercise in their marriage. Through prayer and intimate communication, the couple ask each other if this month God is calling them to celebrate their life-giving love by conceiving, or if God is calling them to work on strengthening their marriage in other ways so that in the future — perhaps next month — the couple will be able to celebrate a love so powerful that, as Scott Hahn says, "in nine months it has to be given a name."

This way, the couple is always thinking about God's unique plan for their lives, and they work together closely to protect both the unitive and the procreative ends of their marriage. In both cases, the couple is always open to life (unlike couples using artificial birth control, who tend to assume they are not having children unless there is some dramatic change), and they practice this openness responsibly, making sure that while they don't give in to selfishness and close themselves off to children, they also give serious, prayerful thought to the state of their marriage, their health, and the continued well-being of the children they already have before they conceive. And since these factors can change dramatically from month to month, the NFP couple prayerfully re-evaluates their circumstances each month with the intention of asking, "What — if anything — can we do to be ready to accept a new life from the Lord?"

To help you decide whether you are ready for your next child we ask you to prayerfully consider the following areas of your life:

Your Own Heart

Is your heart in the right place when it comes to the blessing of children? Do you believe that children are a gift? Even if you aren't sure that you want another child right now, would you be willing to consider the possibility if you felt God leading you to have another child? If you were pregnant today, would you be welcoming to the new life God has blessed you with? Such attitudes are absolutely necessary if you want to grow in the generosity Christ requires of his followers. As Scripture says, "Whoever receives one child such as this in my name, receives me" (Mk 9:36).

The State of Your Marriage

God creates because He loves so much and so powerfully, that life spontaneously bursts forth from His being. This is the model for Christian conception. Getting pregnant is not a duty you owe the Church, and it is certainly not something you do to try to breathe life into a flagging marriage. A husband and wife should be so full of God's love and their love for each other that they joyfully celebrate a love so powerful that in nine months it has to be given its own name. Theologians tell us that it is this way that the family models the Trinity itself.

Are you and your mate secure in your marriage? Are you and your mate good witnesses of love to the children you already have? Are you and your mate in agreement about wanting to have another child? (You will both have to be enthusiastic parents, after all.) Is the love you experience in your marriage powerful and fulfilling — a mirror of the love God has for each of you? Are there any ways that God might be calling you to strengthen the unity you experience in your relationship? Are both of you prepared to be active, attentive parents, or is one of you going to be absent mentally or physically from the parenting partnership?

Is the love you and your mate share already vital and powerful, but you've been holding back on conceiving for less-than-noble reasons? How might adding another life to your family help each member of the family reach for those virtues (like trust, generosity, patience, solidarity, etc.) God wants you to pursue? How could working better together as parents help you actually increase the intimacy you share in your marriage and family life?

Such questions help you protect and celebrate both the unitive and procreative purposes of your marriage. On the one hand, asking questions such as these will help prevent you from celebrating a sick kind of romantic love that shuts out the world, including children, and on the other hand they will also help you avoid the dangers of using your parenting role as an excuse to avoid developing the kind to powerful, fulfilling, unitive love God is calling you to celebrate in the daily lives of your marriage.

Your Health

While the Church teaches that our bodies were made to practice life-giving love, the Church does not teach that we are obliged to be pregnant unless we are in a coma (and even then, a really bad coma). To this end, it is important to honestly, seriously, and prayerfully consider questions of health. Are you physically capable of meeting the needs of a new baby while attending to the needs of your other children? Do you feel that you are at the end of your tether with the children you already have? Are you experiencing a mental illness or serious stresses that would not merely "stress you out" but would actually prevent you from loving a baby the way God would have you love him or her?

Your Children

Do you feel that the children you have are securely attached? Or do they need more time in your arms or at your breast? Do you have good rapport with the children already born to you? Do you have a "problem child" whose needs you would not be able to attend to if you had to care for a baby at this time?

On the other hand, do you think that a new baby would give your children (and yourselves) an opportunity to expand your generosity and bear witness to the beauty of human life?

Your Social Supports

How much outside help and support do you need to function well as a family? Whether this is a little or a lot, are you getting these needs met?

Your Finances and Temporal Needs

For most families in the West, financial and temporal concerns are the least justifiable reasons for postponing a pregnancy. However, it is still an important question. Are your financial and other resources adequate to meet your needs? (Not your every whim, mind you. Your needs and perhaps one or two of your most important wants.) If not, what steps do you need to take to rectify this situation?

The Deciding Factor: Prayer

Answering "yes" or "no" to any of the above questions should not necessarily prevent you from trying to conceive, nor should it necessarily make the decision to conceive a *fait accompli*. The questions above are merely a starting point for discussion between you and your mate. The real deciding factor in all cases is prayer. You and your mate must continuously and prayerfully discern God's will for your life and marriage. God's ways are far above our ways. In some circumstances, through prayer, God will compel you to ignore all cautionary signs and throw yourself completely on His providence, and the baby that results will be an amazing blessing to all concerned. For others, through prayer, God will make your heart heavy, preventing you from moving ahead with your plans for another child even though all the signs seem right. At such times, it can be helpful to enlist the prayer support of other couples, an organization like the Couple to Couple League, or a supportive priest.

Most times, though, God asks us to use the intelligence he has given us to make the best decision possible. If you want more information on how to discern God's will for your life and family, we recommend the book *What Does God Want?* by Fr. Michael Scanlan, from Our Sunday Visitor Publishing. It is a simple but comprehensive look at discernment that can help you hear God's voice more clearly in your everyday life.

Holiness by the Numbers

The one thing we would encourage our readers to avoid is an attitude of judgmentalism toward others for either having "too many" or "too few" children. It is uncharitable and un-Christian to pick on couples for having children, just as it is completely unacceptable for you to look down your nose at those who have fewer children than yourself.

You simply don't know what others have gone through. That childless couple who look like the stereotypical selfish yuppies may have had five miscarriages. That couple with one or two children may be experiencing secondary infertility. Alternatively, that couple with twelve children may just be the people you want to be like when you grow up. In any case, you would do better to keep your comments to yourself. Or, if you must ask questions, be sure to phrase them charitably and with great humility. As *Gaudium et Spes* says, "The married partners themselves should make this judgment [about their family size] in the sight of God." No couple has the right to criticize or pressure another couple to have fewer or more children than God is calling them to have. It is the height of pride to ordain yourself to do what the Church, in her wisdom, prevents herself from doing.

There are, however, three things you can do to support couples regardless of what God is calling them to. The first is pray. Pray that all the families you know will be open to as many children as God wants to give them, and that they will be the kind of parents God wants them to be to the children they already have. While you are praying this, you should also assume that your prayer is being answered by God Himself, and resist any self-righteous desires to help God along through indiscriminate advice-giving, unless you know beyond a shadow of a doubt that such help would be well received.

Second, you should be willing to support the families you know through prayer and acts of service. Talk is cheap. And so is prayer without action. One client of mine is a mother of eight whose husband abandoned her. Each of her "very Catholic" nine brothers and sisters were ready with advice about what she should do (Don't you dare get a divorce!), but not a blessed one of them came through with any offer of real temporal, domestic, or financial support. In fact, they disassociated themselves from her, saying that she "was buying into the culture of divorce" and they didn't want her to negatively influence their own children. In fact, this woman didn't want to divorce her husband, but due in part to the lack of support she received from her family, she was eventually forced to seek a civil divorce, because that was the only way to compel the husband to meet his financial obligations to the family he left behind.

When dealing with the other families in your life, it would be much better to keep your mouth shut while at the same time keeping your eyes and arms open, ready to come through with hand-me-downs, meals, child care, or anything else a family might need — not only to get through a rough time, but also to help them function at their best.

Finally, we need to make a fuss over all children. We frequently read letters complaining about "those couples who have their token child and then stop." Or "those contraceptive couples who have their boy and girl and don't want to spoil their matched set." What a terrible anti-life message this sends. Does that one child somehow not count? Are those two children any less precious in the sight of God? Do any of us really know the minds of those parents, the things they may have suffered, or the plan God has for their lives? If, on the other hand, a certain openness to life is lacking in that couple, do you really think they will be converted by your judgmentalism?

We also read letters from couples who complain about others who "have too many children." "How," these people ask, "can those parents attend properly to those children's needs?" How indeed. Ask them. You just might learn something that God wants to teach you through their witness. Likewise, rather than clucking about how irresponsible you think a couple is being, better to say to that family, "You are witnessing so strongly to your respect for life and love of children. What can I do to support you?"

In any case, the correct response is to rejoice in what life is there

— just as God does — and offer what help you can give to support all families of all sizes at all times.

Questions for Discussion

1. Do you practice Natural Family Planning? If not, why not? Are you sure those reasons are based on fact rather than just opinion? Why not find out from the horse's mouth what NFP really involves? Call the Couple to Couple League today (513) 471-2000. Don't do it because "the pope says you should" or because I say you should, but because you need to experience for yourself the powerfully positive effect NFP can have on both your sex lives and your marriage as a whole. Don't rot in your own ignorance. Find out how you're missing out.

2. Are you open to life? If you were pregnant today, would you welcome the child as a gift even though you might be scared or worried?

3. Do I express judgmental attitudes toward other couples for having either "two few" or "too many" children? What can I do to overcome this prideful, sinful tendency?

Try This at Home

Think of a family you respect. What can you do to make their lives easier or more pleasant? (Not necessarily because they need the help, but because you want to generously support their witness.) Do you have any clothing or toys that your children have outgrown but theirs would appreciate? Could you make them a meal and bring it over — just because? Could you send them a letter telling them what a great witness they are to you?

Catholic families need to support each other in their mission to be "civilizations of love." What can you do to support those families who are living that mission well, or assist those families who are struggling?

Chapter Seventeen

There's No Place Like Rome: Fostering Vocations

"Why would I want my kids to be nuns and priests? I want grandkids! And talk about thankless work! No way."

These are honest reactions that many Catholic parents have about their children becoming priests or religious. But we would encourage you to re-think such notions for a minute. While only God can call a young man or woman into religious life, there is a great deal you as parent can do support, or discourage that call.

Why Would Anyone Want to Be a Priest?

So, why would anyone want to be a priest anyway? First, because a priest gets to bring the Eucharist to the Church. He is the only one who can. He is prayed over by a man, who was prayed over by a man, who was prayed over by a man who was prayed over by Jesus Christ Himself. It is this transfer of Christ's actual touch and blessing from generation to generation that enables a person to preside over the bread and wine becoming the Body and Blood of Jesus Christ. Jesus Christ told us that "unless you eat the flesh of the Son of man and drink his blood, you have no life in you" (Jn 6:53).

The Eucharist is the chief instrument of our salvation, given to us by Christ Himself: "This IS my Body. This IS my Blood" (see Lk 22:19; Mk 14:24). Only a priest has the privileged place of feeding the faithful the food without which, Jesus tells us, their souls cannot live.

If a man came up to you and said, "I want to give you the power to save lives," wouldn't you jump at the chance? How much more should we teach our children to respond positively to Christ's invitation if He says to them, "I want to give you the power to save souls." If all a priest ever did was consecrate and distribute Communion, he would be doing the most noble work of all. In our opinion, contrary to popular belief, the vocation crisis is not due to the celibacy requirement, but rather to a general devaluation by "Joe Catholic Layman" of the Eucharist and the importance of the priestly role as it relates to consecration. If the Eucharist is not the Body and Blood of Christ, then the priests become nothing more than counselors-of-the-cloth, and poorly qualified ones at that. But priests are not primarily counselors, they are primarily *consecrators* — celebrators of the Eucharist. You will note that among those Catholic groups that do give the Eucharist its proper place of honor, vocations are actually increasing. Regardless, while this line of thinking helps understand the dignity due the priestly vocation, it doesn't explain the value of religious life. Let's take a moment to examine the next point.

Okay, Fine, But Nuns and Other Religious Don't Get to Consecrate ...

Why would I want my kids going to a convent or monastery?

Good question. The other thing that priests get to do, along with all religious, is give their whole selves, all their talents and work, to the Church-at-large. Lisa and I often wonder if all those workaholic, high-powered, married professional people out there haven't missed a calling to religious life.

The world is full of people who work sixty or seventy hours a week serving the community and love it. Fields like medicine, law, social work, the arts, sales, and marketing are chock-full of deeply committed professionals whose work, ministries, and even self-esteem would flourish if they didn't have to call it a day at the end of their shift. People who would thrive if they could just work into the night saving one more life, overseeing one more act of justice, ministering to one more needy person, touching one more heart with God's beauty, or "selling" the Gospel to one more hungry soul.

The fact is that many of these same people are lousy marriage material. They are so distracted by their work or passions, that there is little passion left for a spouse or children. God doesn't stop making people like this because He needs them, but being a person who is intent on giving his or her entire life to a particular work or ministry means that he or she is a person who would probably be best served by religious life. As a religious, you are able to give the overwhelming majority of your time, talent, and energy to serving the world. You are able to take all of those gifts, talents, and passions God has given you and use them for the good of the whole world — without the "distractions" of family life (mind you, we don't think of family life as a distraction, but if many of the people we are talking about were honest with themselves, they would have to admit that they do).

Religious life makes sense for the young person who is consumed by a passion or interest to the point of distraction. Marriage is really intended to be a powerful ministry for those of us who don't have a particularly strong interest in saving the whole world ourselves. Sanctification in marriage comes from learning how to have intense, vulnerable, one-on-one relationships within the family, along with all the self-donation, self-sacrifice, and joy that this involves. But sanctification in religious life comes from donating your whole self to God for the world's benefit. Religious life allows a person to use the talents he or she has been given by God primarily for the good of all. While there is an important community aspect to religious life, as a rule, the relationships fostered by convent or monastic life are less intense than the relationships marriages are supposed to be, specifically so that they don't distract a brother or sister from doing the work he or she has been called by God to do.

In recent years, there has been an unfortunate blurring of the roles played by clergy, laity, and religious. Rather than "opening up ministry to all" as presumably was intended, these sloppy boundaries have simply confused people. They have prevented young men and women from discovering the kind of lifestyle God intended their personalities for, and have caused them to bite off more than they can chew, leaving a string of wounded husbands, wives, and children in their wake while they are out saving the world — not for the glory of God, but for the glory of capitalism.

We believe that as the Church continues to meditate on Pope John Paul II's document which defines the distinct ministries of laity and religious, there will be a surge of healthy, vital people entering seminaries, monasteries, and convents. In the meantime, teach your children to be in awe of the Eucharist, to love Jesus like crazy, and to develop their talents to the fullest. And if God touches their hearts and wants to use them as part of His plan to save the world for Himself, get down on your knees, thank God, and pray that He would give your children strong voices and powerful ministries.

Chapter Eighteen

Dad's da Man!
Five Steps to Being
a Great Catholic Father

Thomas called me at the Pastoral Solutions Institute because he wanted to be a better father to his three young children than his dad was to him. As we talked on the phone, Thomas said, "It isn't as if my dad was cruel to us. It's just that he was a shadow. He worked long hours, was active in the community — everybody thought he was a great guy — but he was never home. And now I find myself struggling to make a connection with my own kids. I want to have the kind of relationship my wife has with them, but I'm not sure how to make that happen."

The ministry of fatherhood is unique and powerful. I believe that fathers are primarily responsible to God for building the "communities of love" the Church tells us our families are supposed to be. But this can be a tall order, especially when so many of us, like Thomas, have no blueprint. I offer you the following tips as a starting point for becoming the kind of father God is to us; the kind of father God is calling us to be to the children He has entrusted to our care.

1. Be the pastor of your family parish.

Catholics consider the family to be "the domestic church." This means several things, but perhaps one of the most important ideals conveyed by this phrase is that each family must be centered around a deep love of Christ. Fathers play a central role in making this happen.

Ancient Hebrew tradition made it the father's responsibility to teach his children the Law of God, the Torah. Further, as we pointed out in the introduction, psychological research supports this tradition, having found that children who grow up to exhibit the highest levels of moral virtue as well as a healthy spirituality learned to do so at their father's knee. These same studies suggest that even when the mother is active in teaching the Faith to her children, her efforts are severely hampered — even nullified — if the father is not leading the way.

Sacred Tradition and solid research agree. Catholic fathers must be the pastors of their family parishes. This begins when we pursue a close, personal relationship with Jesus Christ both in personal prayer and in the Eucharist. And it continues when we take the lead in encouraging family prayer, and function as the primary teachers of the Faith in our homes.

2. Love your wife.

Fr. Theodore Hesburgh, past president of Notre Dame, is credited with the following famous quote: "The best thing a father can do for his children is to love their mother."

Of course love involves giving tokens like the traditional flowers, cards, and candy, but it is so much more. The Christian definition of real love is "willing and working for the good of another." Every day, we must ask ourselves, "What can I do to make my wife's life a little easier, more enjoyable, more grace-filled?" and then we must do it. Not only because she deserves it, but because our Christian dignity demands it. Doing this serves the "prime directive" of Christian discipline: teaching our children how to have healthy adult relationships with others and the God who made them.

St. John said that anyone who says he loves God but hates his neighbor is a liar (see 1 Jn 4:20-21). We cannot legitimately consider ourselves Catholic, Christian men unless we give every drop of energy we have to loving — that is, daily working for the good of — our closest neighbors, our wives and children. What can you do for yours — today?

3. Foster family identity.

Part of being the pastor of your family parish is making sure that your family has a vision, a plan for where it is going and who each of you — parents included — wants to be when you grow up.

Sit down with your wife and children today and do the family-identity exercise in chapter two. Post your family identity-statement in a prominent place in your home so that all can see what your family stands for, and take primary responsibility for helping your family, yourself included, stay on-task.

4. Love and serve your children.

We all want obedience from our children. But as you learned in the introduction, true, Christian obedience (as opposed to fear-based, blind obedience) is best understood as a loving response to having been loved first. As St. Thérèse wrote in her *Story of a Soul*, she never wanted to do anything to offend her parents because the love and service they showered upon her compelled her to offer nothing less than her best behavior.

Of course, God "commands" our obedience in the same way. He is constantly reaching out to us, showering us with love so that one day we might wake up from our sin-induced trances and say, "God really does love me. I can trust Him. I will follow Him." As the children's Bible-school song says, "O, how I love Jesus, because he first loved me."

Mirroring God our Father, we earthly fathers must work to expand our capacity for love, affection, and service for our children. We must take the time to play our children's games. We must kiss them, cuddle them, gently correct them, and say that we love them at least a thousand times a day. We must be demonstrative with the pride and joy we feel when we look at our little ones. To paraphrase the great Catholic apologist and child psychologist Fr. Leo Trese, it is not enough to have love for a child, we must show that love, or it will be as if the child was never loved at all.

Boys especially need a father's demonstrative love. Even now, there is a cultural bias against boys with regard to displays of fatherly affection, but God created every human being to need love more than anything else. Babies — including boy babies — will refuse food and drink to the point of death if they are not kissed and cuddled enough, and even older boys show the effects of a lack of affection. It is my professional opinion that the reason so many parents experience boys as more troublesome than girls is that in many homes, boys are typically shown less affection than girls, "since they need it less." I am convinced of this because I have seen boys who have grown up in homes where they, with their sisters, experienced generous physical and verbal affection from their fathers. The very well-done book *Raising Cain: Protecting the Emotional Life of Boys* by Daniel J. Kindlon et al.

(Ballantine Books, 1999), presents solid academic support for the observations I am reporting here.

The fact is, boys who are raised in affectionate homes are no more troublesome than their sisters, and they display just as much emotional and communicative ability as their sisters. At the same time, these young men are in no way effeminate. They are "all boy" with regard to their interests and games, but they are capable of more love and sensitivity than boys from less-affectionate homes, they are better with younger brothers and sisters than boys from less-affectionate homes, and they are better behaved to boot. In short, the generous affection of their mothers and fathers is helping these boys not only become men, but Christian gentlemen.

5. Heed God's call to growth.

Earlier in the book, I quoted Peter DeVries, who once said, "The value of marriage is not that adults produce children, but that children produce adults." Through the grace of marriage and family life, God calls each Christian father to grow up — to be perfected in love. But growing up can be hard work for us fathers. Sometimes, rather than facing and challenging our weaknesses, our lack of patience, our limited capacities for affection, our feelings of incompetence, our dislike of the chaos and noise of childhood, we retreat into work, friends, community involvements, or "important" ministries. ("I'm sorry, Hon. Gonna be home late again; that client/meeting/friend-in-need/committee called today. They really need me!")

Yet God continuously brings us back home at the end of the day to remind us that there is nothing more important than learning to love our closest neighbors; nothing more important than being perfected by the work of love, without which we will be poorly prepared to join in the feast of love at the Heavenly Banquet.

Embrace the weakness, incompetence, vulnerability you feel in the presence of your wife and children. Experience these feelings as the voice of God calling you to grow up — to be perfected in his love. Doing this can be a fearsome task, but it is a task worthy of a true Christian man compelled by the love of Christ to "Take up your cross and follow me."

Chapter Nineteen

A Woman for All Seasons: Being an Attached Mom

We've spent much of this book discussing how this kind of self-donative, attachment-style parenting is beneficial for your children, and your family as a whole. But I — Lisa — think I can hear some of our women readers saying, "Wait a minute. Hold the phone. This is all very well and good for the rest of the family, but it sounds like a lot of this work lands in my lap. Attachment to my baby, extended nursing, baby-wearing, open availability to my young children, maybe even homeschooling. Where do I come in? I've got an education, a career, interests of my own, and a stake in staying sane. What about me?"

Good questions! These are issues every mom who has answered the call to this kind of parenting has had to wrestle with, not just once but at each stage of your child's/children's development. As a mom who has gone through it myself, I will try to address some of those concerns in this chapter.

First off, I sympathize with any concerns you may have about your education and career "going to waste." You worked hard for it, and with the whole world screaming, "You must have it all!" it can be pretty hard to walk away from. My personal answer to the screaming masses is, "Yes, you're right. I can have it all — all in God's time." You see, Scripture tells us that there is a time and a season for every purpose under heaven (see Eccl 3:1). As women, it helps to see our own lives according seasons. Think about the seasons of any given year. Spring, summer, winter, fall, all have their own rhythms, their own joys, and present their own challenges. God gives us each one to enjoy, in its own time. The joy of making snowmen, or cuddling by a warm fire in winter, is followed by the pleasure of making sandcastles at the beach in the summer, and each activity, enjoyed in its own time, can bring a sense of well-being to our bodies and spirits.

However, imagine for a moment what it would be like to experience these activities out of their appropriate time — sitting on a beach in fifteen-degree weather, during a northern gale, trying to joyfully build a sandcastle. Or desperately trying to keep your snowman from melting on a hot August afternoon by wildly flapping paper fans and packing it with ice cubes. Obviously, most of the joy of the activities are lost. In fact, quite a lot of unnecessary stress is gained.

Do these examples seem humorous, ridiculous, or even a little crazy to you? Perhaps. But they are, in fact, illustrative of exactly what our society encourages women to do with the seasons of our lives. We each have our own seasons — a time to be a student, a time to be a new bride, a time to be a mother, a time to have a career and/or a time to share the accumulation of our life's knowledge with others. (A good scriptural illustration of this can be found in Titus 2.) With these seasons, we are also given choices to make. We can fully embrace each season for what it offers us, enjoying each moment so that when the season passes we have no regrets. Or we can try to overlap each season, trying to appreciate all these joys at once, only to find that we can't adequately keep up with any of them, and greatly increasing our stress in the process.

I don't believe that God calls us to this kind of insanity. He is, after all, a God of order. If you are in the season that calls you to motherhood, focus on that season. Embrace all your child is, and all God is calling you to be as a mother. You will experience many wonderful things, including the realization that your mind will not atrophy as a stay-at-home mom, provided you throw yourself into loving your children, nurturing your children, and teaching your children from infancy on up, instead of letting your children rot in their diapers while you watch the soaps or dust your knick-knacks one more time. In other words, the secret to feeling fulfilled as a mother is learning and doing what it takes to be a professional mom.

By surrendering to God and your motherhood, you will call into play all the gifts, intelligence, and creativity God has blessed you with. By savoring this season you will find a peace, a joy, and a level of self-discovery that simply cannot be found in the work-a-day world.

"Does that mean that I never get to work at my career?" you might ask. No. There are many options available to you. While the most preferable of these is postponing your outside career until the children are out of the nest, and then returning to the work world with the wealth of skills and knowledge you have gleaned from your years of "professional motherhood," other choices include having a home business, so that you are still present in the home and available to your children. Likewise, in the twenty-first century there is an increasing number of other options for the mother who must work, for example, telecommuting or job-sharing. (Optimally, such outside work would not begin until you have seen your child/children through the critical first three years.)

Of course, with all but the first of these choices, you are bringing in elements of other seasons into your time as a mother, and as I suggested above, there are certain personal and relational costs that accompany such a choice. I have found that rather than enriching your life, bringing these other seasons into your motherhood disrupts the Zen of mothering — if you will. Important aspects of your focus may be lost, some of the peace and renewal of the present season relinquished, as you get caught up in the world of deadlines and bottom-lines. As Sirach 51:30 says, "Work at your tasks in due season and in his own time God will give you your reward" (NAB).

As for finding time to maintain your own interests and staying sane, of course you have a right — even an obligation — to do both. Let's take a look at each of these points separately.

Pursuing Your Interests as an Attached Mom

Pursuing your own interests as an attachment mom is much easier than you may think. If you are just beginning your parenting career with a new baby you will be amazed how much freedom you can enjoy, provided you use the attachment style of parenting we have laid out in this book. Your new baby is completely portable, much more so than if you would use a more detached Western approach. Allow me to use a personal story to illustrate. Our second pregnancy, the first to result in a live birth, had been very difficult. I was, for all intents and purposes, confined to my house for the duration. When Jacob arrived in the world we were ecstatic, mostly because we had a beautiful healthy child, but also because the "confinement" was over. We had some money saved, and we knew babies traveled for free, so after my time of postpartum recovery, we began some major traveling, some for business, a little for pleasure. One such pleasure trip was a cruise when our son was only six months old. It was a breeze. We packed enough diapers for a week, popped the baby in the sling, and off we went! We had a wonderful time as a family, swimming and sightseeing. We were even able to take in a few nightclub shows, because with the baby in the sling, nobody even noticed that he was there, or that I was nursing him to keep him content and quiet.

However, upon returning home I ran into a old childhood friend, a Washington litagator, who was also a new mom. When I told her of our trip, her reaction was, "How in the world did you take a BABY on a cruise?! How did you manage to tote all those cans of formula, the port-a-crib, the baby swing?! And how did you manage to get any time alone without a nanny along?" (I'm serious. Those were her exact words.)

Similarly, a couple of months later when I asked my sister if she and her family would like to join us on a trip we were taking, her response was, "Oh no, I couldn't possibly do that. My daughter can only sleep in her own crib. Nowhere else. We have to choose between not going anywhere or leaving her behind, with her grandmother." One of the gifts that attachment parenting has given us is never having to make such choices. Wherever we might be, our children are always right at home. Their food (at least as infants and toddlers) is always in ready supply at my breast, their comfort is in our arms, and their bed is wherever we decide to sleep as a family.

You will probably find that you can pursue a great many of your own interests with your child in a sling, because unlike other "baby carriers," a sling keeps your baby close to your breast while allowing your arms and hands to remain free and your back to remain unstrained (and there are no steel bars sticking into the back of your neck like with those metal-and-canvas contraptions). Additionally, in a very short time your child will be able to make the transition between always needing mommy, to being able to feel content with daddy for longer periods of time. Especially if he is a sling-wearing, attachment dad.

Protecting Your Sanity as an Attachment Mom

As for staying sane, most of what I've written in this chapter will go a long way toward the sanity factor, but there are a few more suggestions I'd like to make:

1. Honor your husband.

Work on your marriage and letting your husband know he's still your sweetheart, no matter how busy you may seem with the children. Buy him cards, or make him one while your little ones are drawing or doing some project of their own. Even a sticky note with "I love you" written on it, placed on the bathroom mirror so it's the first thing he sees in the morning, will go a long way to letting him know he hasn't been supplanted by the children. (For more on making your marriage everything God wants it to be, read my husband's book *For Better ... FOREVER!* I promise he really does practice what he preaches.)

Honor your husband, too, with his share of the child care. As much as your children need you, they also need a deep relationship with their dad. They can only achieve that if you get out of the way and let them work it out together. Do not hover and constantly tell your husband how you would do it. He's not you and he has a right to his own style with his children. It may take an enormous amount of tongue-biting and restraint on your part at first. But the fruit it will bear in your family will be worth it.

2. Get the support you need.

Because this style of parenting is not yet the norm in the West, you may get a lot of conflicting advice. It is important to balance this with a steady influx of supportive input. Some of this input can be achieved in person by joining organizations like La Leche League. Not only will you find other women with whom to share ideas, but your little ones will meet other children who are being parented by the loving-guidance approach. (A real boon when helping your offspring gain those hard-to-learn negotiation skills.) You could also try starting your own sharing group. You will meet a lot of other nursing moms just by the interest you evoke by wearing your baby in a sling. Invite them to join you for a discussion group. For example, pick one of the many wonderful parenting books in the La Leche League catalog , and get together for a discussion group/play date in the park.

Another way to get support that does not require as large a commitment from you is through supportive reading materials. The above-mentioned books are wonderful, and there are also some wonderful magazines that support attachment parenting. Among them are *New Beginnings*, which comes to you free with your La Leche League membership; *CCL Foundations*, again free with your Couple to Couple League membership; *Mothering* magazine, an eclectic publications that will refresh your spirit (and the ads will supply you with a host of other resources). Having these periodicals magically appear in your mailbox is like having a supportive best-friend show up just when you need her most.

3. Partner with your husband to meet your needs.

Some attachment moms forget to do the basic things to take care of themselves and their home, so invested are they in the care of their child. While this investment is basically good, it is important to remember to see that your needs are being attended to so that you won't burn out. Your husband should play an integral part in this. He will have increased responsibilities for taking care of the house, or seeing that there is someone besides you to do it. He will have to take more responsibility in meal planning. He will become, at least for a time, primarily responsible for maintaining the romance and closeness in the relationship — helping you remember that you are not only a mother, but also a woman, with all that that means.

Most importantly, your husband will need to help you do what needs to be done to help you feel "put together" most days of the week. At the very least, you and he should work out a way for him to be with your baby while you get a shower and do some basic make-up. You might not look like Cindy Crawford, but, with your husband's help, you'll at least look human. And some days, that can make all the difference.

Due to the fact that attachment parenting causes wives to lean more on their husbands for domestic and emotional support, and causes husbands to expand their capacity for generosity, especially when it comes to their work around the house and picking up the slack in the romantic areas of the relationship, attachment parenting often propels couples to enjoy an uncommonly rewarding and intimate partnership. In fact, it's hard not to fall more and more in love with each other when you and your husband are taking such good care of each other and your children on a daily basis. As Mother Teresa once said, "The fruit of love is service." As we have observed in our own lives and the lives of other attachment-parenting couples, the fruit of service — is intimacy.

4. Relish your relationship with your child.

Beyond all outside helps, the greatest preserver of your sanity will be the deep and abiding relationship that is built between you and your child as the attachment process builds. Unfortunately, mothers who choose a more conventional style of parenting will not often attain the same depth of relationship and do not reap its rewards in the more challenging times of parenthood. A good illustration of this would be a woman I knew several years ago. Carol had chosen a more conventional approach to mothering, saying that, among other things, she "wanted her husband to share in the feeding of their child," that her chosen style would "afford her more freedom," and that therefore she would experience a greater "sense of sanity" in her new role. Unfortunately, her son was allergic to the formulas they fed him. Becoming more and more agitated from the physical discomfort he was feeling, he cried harder and seemed "angrier" with each passing day. Carol found this behavior extremely difficult to bear. To help her cope with the stress, she would leave her son in the care of others more and more frequently in order to "get a break." Unfortunately, this simply led her son to cry more, because as Carol told me, "He is really clingy. I guess he's just in a lot of pain, but I just can't take it anymore. I have to get out for at least a couple hours every day or I'm going to crack up." It wasn't until her son was entirely off formula, somewhere near the end of his first year of life, that the crying and screaming began to diminish. By then Carol confided to me in tears, "I can't believe I'm admitting this, but most of the time I don't even like my own son. I feel very angry about his behavior over the last year. And frankly, it's not much better now. He's not in the same kind of pain all the time, but he still whines and cries a lot. I'm not sure why. Being a mom isn't all I dreamed it would be when I was pregnant. I used to think about all the cuddling we would do during our first year together and how much we would love each other. Oh well. My husband and I have decided to enroll him in full-time day-care. We think we'd all be happier with less time together, and after all, we want to make sure he's getting the proper socialization."

Carol's story grieves me to this day. There is no reason something like this should ever occur. Don't get me wrong. I'm not saying that if you attachment parent you will automatically get the "Ivory Snow baby." What I am saying is that attachment parenting will afford you the relationship that will keep the challenges you might be presented with from escalating out of control. For example, Donna, the wonderful woman who first introduced us to attachment parenting, also had a very "high need" baby in her second son. He was, as it turned out, even more allergic than Carol's son. Although it was sometimes exhausting to cope with his reactions, Donna's relationship with her son became one of the most loving and bonded I have ever seen. Because she was attachment parenting, Donna was able to see that her son was not always angry or crying, and when he was "reacting" to an allergen, she was able to comfort him, and love him through it. Remarkably, because she was getting to know her son so intimately, she began to notice that there were even connections between his allergies and the things she ate that were apparently passing through her breast-milk. In light of the deep rapport she was establishing with her son, she did not find it at all difficult to adjust her own diet in order to eliminate the offending foods. And her sensitivity and perceptiveness — facilitated by the close bond she and her son had — paid off in the form of a baby, though who still highly allergic, was much more peaceful. By the end of their first year together, they had built up a deep sense of trust, understanding, and love that not only shone in both their eyes, but went on to serve them well in later years.

If you use the suggestions laid out in this chapter, trusting God and the instincts He has given you, it is my firm belief that you will discover more joy and fulfillment in your role as a mother than you ever dreamed possible.

The Church teaches that our fulfillment is found in love. But love can only flourish when it is given your full attention. Attend to each season of your life fully, and fulfillment will follow.

Happy mothering!

Chapter Twenty

The Most Powerful Parenting Tool ...
Your Marriage

The ultimate goal of parenting is to teach your children how to give and receive love. The best way to do this is to have a great marriage, one that is founded on self-donative love, generous affection, mutual Christian service, respectful, healthy attitudes toward sex, and the belief that because of your mate's influence in your life, you have a better chance of becoming the person God wants you to be when you "grow up" (and vice versa).

You could be the best parent in the world, but if you don't model a healthy, vital, fulfilling, Catholic marriage to them, you are undermining your best efforts. Children can grow up to be healthy, productive members of society even if they do not experience a mother and father who love each other, but they will be missing an important component of their education. Think of it this way. Imagine going to medical school. First, you will attend classes where you will learn all about the human body, and disease and its treatment. After your coursework is done, the next step in your education is the internship, during which you will go into the field, so you can watch other doctors and see how things are really done.

But what if you were denied the chance to watch other physicians do their stuff? Or what if you spent your internship observing incompetent physicians? What would that do to your ultimate ability to practice medicine well? Even if you had a great classroom education and were a brilliant student with strong convictions, you would begin your professional life with a serious handicap.

In the same way, you can teach your children all the "theory" about being a loving, Christian person by being a good parent. But the "internship experience" comes from watching you and your mate do your stuff and do it well.

It is beyond the scope of this book to go into great detail about what you need to do to have a great Catholic marriage, but we recommend *For Better ... FOREVER! A Catholic Guide to Lifelong Marriage*. In it, among many other things, you'll discover the one thing that guarantees the lifelong success of a Christian relationship, the secret to really understanding (and being understood by) your mate, the five paths to a truly fulfilling, deeply spiritual and profoundly Catholic sexuality, and a "marriage maintenance schedule" to help you with the care and feeding of your relationship.

The following five steps to building a marriage on Christian love are drawn from that book.

1. View marriage as a partnership in your Christian identity.

Christian marriage is more than a guaranteed date for bowling night. Marriage, like any sacrament, is concerned with your sanctification, specifically by helping you fulfill your spiritual identity.

Everyone searches for an identity: "Who am I? Why am I here?" Pagans have to spend a lifetime figuring out the purpose of their lives, but the answer to these questions is right under the Christian's nose. When you were baptized, you were given an identity. God took qualities such as love, generosity, wisdom, understanding, fortitude, all the gifts and fruits of the Holy Spirit, and all the theological and moral virtues, from the center of Himself and indelibly etched them into the core of your being. Sacramental marriage presents a life-changing opportunity for a husband and wife to actualize the identities they were given at baptism. What better chance does the average person have to practice being loving, generous, compassionate, etc., not to mention increase his ability to be more humble, Christ-like servants?

If you want to open yourself to all the grace God is offering you through your marriage, ask yourself the following questions:

1. If you were going to exhibit your baptismal virtues more consistently in your married life, how would you have to act toward your spouse? Your kids? Would you have to be more patient? More affectionate? Less critical? A better listener? More supportive? Less quick to anger? More understanding?

2. What ways do you consistently refuse or neglect to serve your mate? What specific steps does your Christian identity compel you to take to correct your present lack of generosity? Do you need to come home earlier? Not go out so much? Look for more ways to be helpful? Be more mentally available when you are home? Anything else? How will you achieve these goals?

Viewing your marriage as a partnership in Christian destiny means that you and your mate daily look for opportunities to exhibit your baptismal virtues, and that you encourage each other daily — by example — to be more loving, more generous, more compassionate, and better servants to one another. Why should you do this? Because it is every Christian husband's and wife's job, second only to the saving work of Jesus Christ and the free will of their mate, to see that their spouse arrives properly attired at the heavenly banquet.

2. Challenge your comfort.

Too many people view marriage as an institution of convenience. They say, "Thank God I never have to be romantic/work out of the home/wash the dishes/put gas in the car/etc., ever again. That's what my spouse is for." WRONG! Marriage is not an invitation to be taken care of; marriage is an opportunity to serve.

How good a servant are you? What jobs do you push off on your mate, not because you are physically incapable of them, but because you don't like to do them? Without having first been asked, how often do you do things you know will make your mate's life easier? What is your partner constantly after you to do or change about yourself that you don't/won't because, "Who do they think they are, anyway?"

May we remind you who they are? They are the image of Christ, and whatever you do to them, you do to Him.

3. Be more loving than good sense allows.

Christ says, "When someone slaps you on one cheek, turn and give them the other, when someone takes your coat, give them your shirt as well.... If you do good to those who do good to you, how can you claim any credit? Love your enemy and do good.... Be compassionate.... Do not judge.... Do not condemn.... For the measure you measure with will be measured back to you" (see Lk 6:27-38).

This Scripture is the essence of a great, sacramental marriage. It is far too easy to be loving to our mates only when we feel like it, or when we think they "deserve" it, or when they have done something nice for us, or when we want them to do something nice for us. But Jesus tell us that pagans do this, not Christians. As a Christian, you must become a more loving, compassionate, romantic, generous, attentive, caring person, not because your mate deserves such generosity (He or she probably doesn't. Who does?), but because that is the person you want to be when you grow up, because that is the person God is calling you to become. When you die and God asks you how well you lived out your spiritual identity in your marriage, do you really think the Almighty is going to accept, "Well, Lord, I would have worked harder if only my spouse had been more deserving of the effort," as an answer? Not bloody likely. Meditate on the parable of the unmerciful servant and you'll understand what I mean.

4. Redeem and celebrate your sexuality.

Now a bit of good news. Being Catholic does not preclude you from having an incredible sex life. Many popular books and articles assert that great sex is synonymous with spiritual sex, and the Church teaches us how lovemaking can be a powerful and important aspect of any "married saint's" prayer life.

Celebrating a truly awe-inspiring, Catholic spiritual sexuality begins by realizing that, through the Incarnation, you and your mate have been given the innate dignity of a god (see *CCC* 460). First and foremost, you must make certain you do nothing to offend your own or your mate's "god-hood." For example, you must never try to use your mate, or resent them when they refuse to be used. Likewise, you must never use your sexuality as a mere toy, or as a means of artificially inflating your own ego. Why? Because all of these things are simply beneath your dignity as a son or daughter of the Most High.

Catholic Christians who practice spiritual sexuality view their lovemaking as a soulful prayer that communicates their deepest selves, an act that physically manifests the love God has for them (see the Song of Songs), empowers their love to create life, and functions as a path to self-esteem through self-mastery. If you want to know the whole, unadulterated, mind-blowing, toe-curling, sanctifying, awe-inspiring, orgasmic truth of real Catholic sexuality, call your Diocesan Family Life office for information on a Natural Family Planning class near you. Or call the Couple to Couple League at (513) 471-2000.

5. Pray your marriage.

The popular wisdom says we can't be saints because saints spend hours praying in church, and what married person has time for that? But you live in a church (your family) and there is no end to the holiness you can achieve by worshiping God in your "domestic church." Every mundane or dramatic thing you do in your marriage has the power to transform yourself, your mate, and your children into more loving, more Christ-like, more saintly people, because every act of loving service draws you closer to actualizing your identity in Christ. Prayer isn't something a married person does; it is something a married person is. Everything a Christian spouse does in the context of his/her marriage is a prayer. Being present to your mate mirrors God's loving presence to him/her. Serving your mate in the simplest ways, especially when you don't feel like it, helps you identify with the loving service Jesus performed for you on the cross. Being a generous lover physically manifests the all-consuming passion of God's love. Supporting your mate in the pursuit of God-given dreams, goals, and values, especially when it causes you to stretch more than you wanted to, emphasizes your esteem for the God who both dwells within you both and calls your to greater fullness and holiness. Think about your own relationship. I am sure you can find a million other examples of the married person's "little ways" to becoming perfect in love.

Let It Shine

Saints are transparent. When you look at them, you see God's love shining through. As a married person, when you protect your mate's God-given dignity, encourage the dreams, goals, and values He has placed on his or her heart, and generously love your partner even when comfort or "fairness" tells you not to, God shines through you. And the more your mate can see God shining through you, the closer you are to becoming a married saint.

Striving toward such a marriage gives your children a powerful example of the kind of people they need to be when they grow up. If you're interested in learning more about having the kind of marriage that makes the angels smile and the neighbors sick with jealousy, pick up a copy of *For Better ... FOREVER!* Or if you'd like private lessons, call the Pastoral Solutions Institute (740) 266-6461.

Chapter Twenty-One

Your Family Maintenance Schedule

Cars, boats, homes, gardens, all have them. In fact, just about every valuable thing has them. Why don't families have maintenance schedules? Most people know how often they have to change their oil, till their garden, rotate their tires, replace their furnace screens, etc., but do you know how often to "oil" your marriage?

Follow the schedule below for a well-maintained relationship.

Regular Family Maintenance

Do the following as indicated:

Everyday
1. Pray. Ask God to help you become the parent He would be to your children. Pray together as a family. Bless each child by laying hands on him/her and praying over him/her.
2. Ask yourself, "What can I do to make my spouse's and children's life a little easier or more pleasant today?"
3. Find small ways to demonstrate affection. Catch your kids being good. Be generous with kisses, hugs, compliments, and calls from the office. Play with your children. Review their homework and chores. Praise them for jobs well done. Tell them you are proud of them.
4. Take some time to talk with your mate. Catch up on the news. Solve today's problems. Address issues with the children. Discuss plans for future.

Every Week
1. Attend Mass as a family at least once per week, more often when possible.
2. Set aside one day for family fun and relaxation.
3. Have a family meeting that includes prayer time and maybe a short Bible or catechism lesson. Sing praise songs and don't be ashamed to show your children that you love Jesus. Also, use this time to check in with your family identity-statement, address any general concerns, and make plans for the week.

Every Month
1. You and you mate should each get one night out alone with each of your children. Do something that they enjoy, but make sure it is an activity that allows for conversation.
2. Have a date with your mate. If your children are developmentally ready for a short separation (over three), hire a sitter and go out on a date. If your children are younger, hire a sitter to supervise your kids with a video while you and your mate enjoy some quiet time in another part of the house.

Every Three Months
1. Review the discipline chapters in this book. What techniques have you forgotten about? How might these be helpful to you at this time? What skills do you still need to develop/practice? How, specifically, will you develop those skills?

Every Six Months
1. Ask your mate how you could be an even better parent. Receive any suggestions gracefully. Talk about how you and your mate could be a better parenting team.
2. Read a book together on some aspect of marriage and/or family life.

Once a Year
1. Go on a retreat together. Or, spend a whole day in a favorite park or other place with your spouse and children playing, praying, and discerning what God has in store for your family in the coming year. Review your family identity-statement. What changes/additions so you need to make? How can you support each other in the pursuit of these goals?

Following these recommendations will help you assure the continued growth and health of your marriage. And if you ever need any help, please feel free to call on us at the Pastoral Solutions Institute (740) 266-6461.

Epilogue

Parenting is a tough job, but it is a beautiful ministry. As Christians, we are called to practice the corporal works of mercy. Every day, parents have myriad opportunities to feed the hungry, give drink to the thirsty, comfort the sick, and shelter the homeless, and we don't even have to leave our homes to do it. In this way, home life is both a prayer and an exercise that allows you to become more Christ-like if you surrender to it.

If all we have done throughout this book is give you some tips for helping your children behave, then we have failed you. Even more important than outlining a plan for raising "good kids," it has been our not-so-hidden agenda to show you how everything you do as a parent, from the way you choose to feed your baby, to the way you celebrate love and build affection in your family, to the way you work together to complete chores, to the way you discipline your children, has a spiritual significance.

Family life is itself a prayer. Founded on the graces of marriage, family life is first and foremost an exercise in opening yourselves up more fully to God and perfecting each other in his love. While things like formal prayer times, Eucharistic Adoration, retreats, other spiritual exercises, and Church activities are important, even essential, parts of the full-course meal that is the Christian life, the meat of the married Christian's meal is being an exceptional mate and parent. If Christianity is not at work in your home, it is not truly at work in your life. When you get off the couch and play with your children, serve and model affection and respect for your mate, turn off the television or computer and talk to each other, cut back on work so you can "be there" more fully, complete household chores together, celebrate family joys, correct wrongs firmly but with love and justice, build and guard each family member's character and basic dignity, and express affection generously, you are, as St. Thérèse might say, practicing the "little ways" you can become more like Christ.

Christ said, "Love your neighbor." If you are married, then there is no higher call than to spend your days and nights loving your closest neighbors: your spouse and children. There is no higher call than working together as a family to perfect each other in love. As we conclude, we offer you our sincere prayer that God in His great mercy and providence would bless you in this good work and may you and your house always live to serve the Lord.

> *May God bless you and keep you,*
> *May God make His face*
> *to shine upon you,*
> *May God grant you peace,*
> *All the days of your Life.*
> *Amen.*

Appendix One

The Natural Institution of the Family

By Herbert Ratner, M.D.

Nota Bene: This is an abridged version of the critical and influential work *The Natural Institution of the Family* by Catholic physician and philosopher, Herbert Ratner, M.D. At the time it was presented before the Tenth Convention of The Fellowship of Catholic Scholars, Dr. Ratner, a former Director of Public Health for Oak Park, Illinois, was a visiting professor of Community and Preventive Medicine, at New York Medical College, New York. It is reprinted here with the kind permission of Dr. Brian Donnelly, a pediatrician who edits *Child and Family*, the academic journal founded by Dr. Ratner. (Dr. Donnelly is also a Pastoral Solutions Institute advisory-board member).

After several sections in which Dr. Ratner defends the rightful place of science (including social science) in theological inquiry and illustrates how nature asserts the monogamous (traditional) family unit as essential to the survival of the human species, Dr. Ratner turns his attentions to what nature has to say about infant attachment and family life.

Delivered at the Tenth Convention of The Fellowship of Catholic Scholars, September 26, 1987, Los Angeles, California.

Introduction

Unity of Reason and Faith

... Truths from the natural order obtained by reason have an intrinsic harmony with the truths of the natural order obtained by faith, resulting in a unity in which each help the other to a greater understanding so that together they complete the teachings necessary to achieve the good human life, both temporal and eternal.

Jesus, for instance, tells us to love our neighbor. But Jesus does not instruct the mother how to love her closest and dearest neighbor, the newborn. Thus the mother is not told to nurse or breast-feed her baby. The Son, respectful of the Father, assumes that with eyes to see, with milk dripping from postpartum breasts, with hungry suckling lips rooting in search of the mother's teats, the woman can figure this out for herself.

In passing, it should be noted that the norm of breast-feeding is a striking example of a constant of nature not dissimilar from norms pertaining to sexual morality. The arguments that *avant garde* theologians use to justify a change in the laws of sexual morality can *a fortiori* be applied to breast-feeding. One can claim that breast-feeding is "historically conditioned," that "alternative life-styles have developed," that "cultural and social conventions have changed," that "empirical social data" negate its value, that "advances of the behavioral and social sciences provide new understanding and insight," that "the importance of natural processes do not lie in their brute facticity," and that we now have "more accurate scientific information," all of which negates the norm of breast-feeding.

The fact remains, however, that after thirty-seven years of permissive bottle feeding, the American Academy of Pediatrics along with other international pediatric associations saw fit to reaffirm the norm and superiority of breast-feeding in 1978. [Editor's note: In 1998, The American Academy of Pediatrics expanded their recommendation of breast-feeding, encouraging mothers to nurse for at least the first year.]

It should be seen from the above that we have inadequately taught that the truths of nature are one with the truths of religion and that both are intended for our happiness not only in the hereafter but on earth as well. Having forgotten that philosophy is the handmaiden of theology, we have allowed God the Father, Creator of Heaven and Earth, to become the forgotten person in the Trinity. We profess belief in a Trinitarian God, but we are ignorant of or recalcitrant to the teachings the Father has revealed to us in nature even though we know by faith that God authored both the Book of Nature and the Book of Scriptures. In a sense, we ignore nature and tend to replace it with sacraments, as if once grace is possessed, nature is irrelevant.

Survival of the Family

... Nowhere is philosophy as handmaid to theology more applicable or pertinent [than in its role of integrating science with faith to teach the skills necessary for the survival of the family]. Philosophy has a persuasive influence with believers and non-believers alike. It can convince all fellow human beings of the wholesomeness of traditional theological positions on marriage.

Every pagan, then, even though he does not identify with God in a personal way and though he may profess that the world has resulted from the blind forces of an evolutionary process, is still exposed to God the Father through the Book of Nature. That is why many pagans have a stronger and healthier family life than many Catholics, despite the absence of the sacrament and its attendant supernatural grace. Even some Communist countries have a greater dedication to the traditional family than that shown by many western democracies with a Christian heritage. It is also true of many primitive societies.

The following are some highlights, briefly sketched, of nature's teaching on the family....

The Family as the Primary Teacher

Parents are primary teachers. The profound formative influence of the first six years of life is universally recognized. During these pre-school years, the primary teaching function of the family is not the elevating of the I.Q. but the nurturing of emotional maturity. Its work is to temper emotions, to order the emotions to proper ends, and to lay the foundation for cultivating the cardinal virtues. Without emotional stability the best of human intentions are thwarted and the way is open to divorce, alcoholism, drugs, juvenile delinquency, precocious and faithless premature genital sex and other indices of a sick society.

Because love holds together the delicate membranes of human society and is the basis of our relationship with God, the chief need of the child is to experience love leading to a healthy self-love and to be able to love others as he has learned to love himself. Since love is taught essentially through a one-to-one relationship, nature sees to it that the vast majority of babies come one at a time, so that each child has his or her private tutor of love. For this task, nature has selected the mother. As a female, her capacity to care for the newborn is unique.

Although the human male and female share a common nature and its attendant equality, dignity, freedom, and personality, man and woman are not identical in soma and psyche. They differ in bodily parts and psychological dispositions, in the balance of hormones that give rise to natural inclinations, and in the interplay of the two components of the intellect: understanding and reason — the intuitive and the discursive. These differences set the female apart to be the primary caretaker of the newborn.

Since nature fashioned the mammalian female to be the prime nurturer, the key to the woman's special qualities is the infant — the *raison d'être* of nature's formation of woman as woman. T. S. Eliot, echoing Aristotle, states the principle: "The end is where we start from." A woman's task requires of her a certain congruence, complementariness and reciprocal fitness with the infant, for the natural togetherness of the nursing couplet is far more than a lactational relationship. Nature finely attunes the woman to the total physiological and psychological needs of the helpless, inarticulate, withal responsive human being — the baby. This makes possible a two-way affective connaturality which, with or without cognitive knowledge, generates an interpersonal, loving relationship.

Touch

The soft, smooth skin of the infant bespeaks the soft, smooth skin of the woman. As we, out of solicitude, envelop the baby in soft, smooth coverings, so, also, with even greater solicitude, does nature. What baby, if given a choice, would prefer to be cuddled and cherished by a rough-skinned, hairy and stubbly male? Touch, the most fundamental of the senses, and a major means of communicating love, is facilitated in man by furless skin, and is enhanced in the woman and infant by their mutual tactile softness. Both Aristotle and Aquinas point out that the correlation of soft skin and intelligence reflects the gnostic function of touch:

> ... In respect to touch we far excel all other species in exactness of discrimination, that is why man is the most intelligent of animals. The difference to touch and to nothing else accounts for the difference in natural endowments;

men whose flesh are soft are well endowed (*De Anima* Bk. II, Ch. 9, 421a 20-25).

> ... In those who have bodies of better disposition, their souls have a greater power of understanding, wherefore Aristotle says, that it is to be observed that those who have soft flesh are of apt minds (*Commentary*, ibid., lect. 19, N484).

If these philosophers are correct, and much modern thinking is supportive, the intelligence of each member of the nursing couplet is superior to that of the adult male. No one exceeds the infant's prodigious ability to learn, nor the mother's ability to understand, a function that outranks and outreaches the reasoning mind.

Hearing

The infant's ability to hear only high tones bespeaks the woman's soprano voice. This explains why adults, universally, raise their voices to get a baby's attention, and why males are conspicuously unsuccessful in lullabying babies to sleep. Furthermore, since hearing matures earlier than vision, the mother's voice is familiar to the baby. During the last trimester of its gestation, the child in the womb hears its mother's voice daily. This probably explains why the most effective and earliest stimulus to elicit a smile from the baby is not the face, but the mother's voice.

Smell

The scent of the baby bespeaks the discriminatory olfactory acuity of the mother. As the lover desires to smell good to the beloved, nature wants the baby to smell good to its mother. In the early postpartum period, some mothers' olfactory ability is so enhanced that they speak of a unique fragrance emanating from the baby. Often, they liken it to the fragrance of roses. This heightened olfactory ability enables the mother to identify her newborn by smell. With even more certainty, the newborn is capable of recognizing its mother by smell within a few days after birth.

Sight

The infant's need to have the mother's face in focus bespeaks the woman's protruding breasts, unique amongst primates. The human face is the most expressive of all mammal faces and is the major source of the infant's security during its long immobilized dependent state. Research shows that the newborn is responsive to the face from birth. The response is initially elicited by the eyes and forehead, and, subsequently, by the full face. This coincides with the focal length of the newborn's vision which is about nine inches, a measure that approximates the distance from the baby at the breast to the mother's eyes and face. In contrast to the perceptual ability of primates whose young are mobile and clinging, the eyes of the immobilized infant, during the early months of nursing, are steadily fixed on the mother's face. When the Psalmist pleads to God to turn His "shining face" upon him, he echoes the acceptance the nursling seeks from its mother, its source of security.

Cradling Arms

The infant's need to be held, carried, and comforted bespeaks the woman's cradling arms, arms that contrast significantly with the throwing arms of the male. The difference is not only evident in sports, but is even seen in the way children carry their books: boys at their sides; girls in front of them with flexed arms. The girls' inclinations to encircle and encompass foretells the future cradling of the nursling close to heart and breast in an initiation of a bosom friendship.

Intuition

The infant's inability to communicate verbally and conceptually bespeaks the woman's ability to communicate through a modality of "feeling": of knowing and loving through the intuitive, the poetic, the experiential and the affective. These non-conceptual modes of communicating result in a preternatural form of knowledge, a primary knowing common to all but most necessary in the inter-communication of the nursing couplet. In Pascal's words "... the heart has reasons of its own which reason does not know."

The natural togetherness of woman and infant constitutes a predominantly spiritual, sensorial gestalt. It is the infant's need to survive and thrive that preordains the special characteristics of the woman *qua* woman.

Unisex is a great slogan. But it goes counter to the remarkable gift nature has bestowed upon woman. She is the infant's spiritual womb, the womb with a view. If it can be said nature abhors a vacuum, it probably can equally be said that nature abhors a unisex.

Fidelity

All mammals are automatically faithful to their young by determinative instincts. Human mothers, on the other hand, have free will and can accept or reject motherhood in whole or in part. Since mammalian newborns are dependent upon mothers for nourishment and nurture, nature implants in the mammalian mother the basic motherly characteristic of fidelity. This faithfulness carries over to her spouse, to her church, to all of her activities. She is even faithful to such organizations like the March of Dimes, who exploit this trait by making her feel needed.

The most damaging consequence of the increasing trend toward working mothers who leave the home to work during the baby's formative years is the relinquishment of the child to a day care center where the child is raised as if it were part of a litter of offspring. If nature intended young children to be raised in litters, they would have come in litters. This is another example of how we must read nature for the guidelines of family life.

Major authorities now universally agree as a result of studies of the past fifteen years that, for the optimum personal maturation of the child, the child needs the fulltime attention of the mother or a fulltime mother substitute during the first three years of life. Young women must appreciate that their life span in developed countries is now over seventy-five years. Not everything in life has to be accomplished in the early years of marriage. There is enough time for career fulfillment after children are off to school. And dedication to children in their dependent years accelerates their independence and, in turn, liberates parents for additional activities.

More than that, the mother/infant relationship, which in the natural order is the child's first sustained human association, becomes the prototype of the child's future relationships with others. If the child experiences the fidelity of his prime caregiver especially when it is during the period when his needs are greatest and which when met engenders in him security, confidence and trust, that example will remain with him for life. It becomes the pattern on which all future friendships are based, a pattern which even paves the way to his relationship with God. The fidelity of the mother to her child fortifies the child's natural inclinations to the fidelity he possesses as a social animal. In its absence, insecurity and distrust abound and affect him all through life.

Maternal Attachment

It has been demonstrated that immediately following childbirth (and for some days or weeks thereafter) the mother is in a unique psycho-hormonal state which is propaedeutic to her maximal attachment to the newborn, an attachment which has lasting qualities. This attachment or bonding process is analogous to the imprinting phenomenon found in lower mammals, an imprint which lasts until the young mature and have no further need of the mother. Breast-feeding, started immediately after birth, is nature's normal and foolproof mode by which this attachment is fostered and intensified. It converts mother and infant into bosom friends.

Obstetrical technologies, imposed on normal childbirth, intercept and disrupt nature's subtle processes with loss of nature's beneficence. It is now believed that disruption of the normal attachment process has led to an increase in child abuse, premature use of the nursery school, demands for day-care centers, and, in general, to an increase of parental indifference and parental delinquency. Nature cannot forgive; it can only retaliate.

Christian maternity services, from not appreciating God the Father's script, succumb to obstetrical technologies as avidly as secular maternity services. Actually, the great medical advances rooted in the restoration of nature's norms and the recapture of nature's wisdom in developed countries have originated primarily not with Christian but with non-historians. These advances include natural delivery, the elimination of routine episiotomies (as if God was not able to make a functional perineum for man), rooming-in, birthing centers, home deliveries, breast-feeding, and maternal-infant coupling to enhance maternal attachment.

Several years ago at a medical convention a Jewish friend of mine, a professor of pediatrics at Northwestern Medical School (Chicago), knowing that I was a convert to Catholicism said to me:

> What puzzles me about my study is that the incidence of breast-feeding is no different in nuns' hospitals than in secular hospitals. I cannot understand it. I thought the nuns would have a greater feeling and respect for God's wonderful creation.

Apropos of this, we have reprinted [in an issue of *Child and Family*] a remarkable homily of Jeremy Taylor, the great seventh-century Anglican theologian on "The Duty of Nursing Your Child in Imitation of the Blessed Mother." In it, he terms the refusal to breast-feed a sin against nature. Some contraceptionists are now asking if artificial contraception is a sin, why is not the artificial feeding of newborns also a sin?

Women today who are rediscovering their womanhood and nature in the area of childbirth and child rearing are turning more and more away from technology which attempts to override nature. In the 1870s, when the baby carriage was invented, there were perceptive physicians who said: "The baby carriage is no substitute for a pair of strong, loving arms." Today, mothers carry their babies in slings of one kind or another. They prefer to keep their babies close to their bodies because therein lies the baby's security. When in touch with their mothers, babies are in touch with the world; when not in touch, they are out of touch with the world.

The Value of Children

Young couples getting married today are nowhere more ignorant than in their failure to appreciate the significance of children in marriage. Family life programs including Catholic programs stand under special indictment for neglecting to inculcate in couples the gift, the pleasures and the value of children. Kierkegaard said: "The trouble with life is that we understand it backwards but have to live it forwards." Our goal should be to educate the young so that they understand life as they live it forward and thereby help them make prudential judgements. The greatest regret of American married women toward the end of life is that they hadn't had a child or hadn't had more children. Authentic prudential judgment is based on objective reality; not an evasion of reality. It is not a circumventing of reality so as to make it conform to one's subjective desire. Secularized prudence is overly concerned with the price to be paid not the value received; it is overcautious in regard to dangers or risks. True prudence approaches judgment making with a trust in the providential order and includes hope in the final decision. The following are some reminders of the objective reality associated with marital decisions.

1. Children are a gift biologically as well as theologically. Man is a relatively sterile animal. Couples flock to birth control and family planning clinics in their twenties but switch to sterility clinics in their thirties. Babies for adoption are at a premium. Test tube babies and surrogate mothers measure their plight.

2. The time-span from age thirty-eight to age fifty-eight or from age fifty-eight to age seventy-eight is no longer and no shorter than the span from age eighteen to age thirty-eight. But that which gives pleasure in life tends to differ for the respective age groups. What seems more of a chore and intrusion in one's personal life when one is young becomes far less a chore and intrusion as one grows older. Children become more and more important to a person with advancing age. The joys of grandparent-hood are well known. Children are seen as a blessing where once they may have been viewed as a hardship. In countries with sharply reduced birth rates we are now hearing of the sufferings of a grandparentless society. Even death itself becomes more bearable when the dying are surrounded by loved ones. One does not go through life feeling always like a teenager or young adult, yet what one does in these earlier years may preclude the joys of later life.

   Certainly God does not expect the young couple to embark on marriage preoccupied with grandparenthood and death, but God does expect a couple to avoid doing what would rob them of the happiness which should come with the later stages of life. In this context, couples should be attentive to the core principle of *Humanae Vitae* of preserving the integral oneness of the unitive and procreative aspects of marriage. D. H. Lawrence makes the point poetically: "We are bleeding at the roots, because we are cut off from the earth and sun and stars, and love is a grinning mockery, because, poor blossom, we plucked it from its stem on the Tree of Life, and expected it to keep on blooming in our civilized vase on the table."

3. The choicest gift one can bequeath to a child is not material possessions but another brother or sister.

4. Parents do not live forever, and children have each other after their parents pass on. At family reunions the children, now uncles and aunts, have the opportunity to pass on family stories which give the grandchildren a sense of roots, of their unique heritage.

5. Children mature parents more than parents mature children. For most adults parenthood is the road to maturity. It is capable of converting the selfish into the unselfish.

6. The large family is the best preventive against loneliness which is so all-pervasive in modern society. One can go on. A persuasive case can be made for having children early in marriage and spaced with the interval which nature ordinarily arranges in the breast-

feeding mother, an interval of approximately two years. This affords each child a life's orbit wherein he can more readily relate to his brothers and sitters. This point has been elaborated in the following passage from "Man Against Nature: Nature's Subtleties and Nature's Prescription":

Nature's prescription not only shortens the obligations of the preschool period, (1) it brings youth to child-bearing and the arduous early child-rearing years, (2) it permits children to grow up with more intimately shared lives, (3) it closes the generation gap between parent and child, particularly valuable in the adolescent years, (4) it lengthens the joys of parenthood and grandparenthood, (5) it allows for leeway in case of obstetrical misfortunes and tragic events, (6) it gives parents the opportunity to reexamine their goals while reproductive options are still available, and (7) it rids the couple of the fear of an unplanned pregnancy with each love act, permitting them blissfully to ignore birth control for nine years or more during the period of greatest sexual activity.

If the ecologic era bears any message it is this: when nature is treated well she reciprocates. Nature is for us, not against us. All she asks is that her highest achievement, man, be tractable to her teachings — that he be responsive, not rebellious. By following nature's prescription, man not only protects himself against his worst enemy, himself, but he regains his best friend, nature, the nurturer and guide to a happy life on earth.

References
1. Pascal, Blaise. *Pensées*. In (Ed.) Trotter, *W.F. Everyman's Library*, Fr. 327.
2. A Cicero character in *De Finibus* v. 41.
3. Quoted by John Cardinal Newman, *The Idea of a University*. Longmans, Green and Company, New York, 1925 Discourse IV. p. 78.
4. Ratner, H. "Nature, Mother and Teacher: Her Norms." *Listening*, 18:197-199, Fall 1983.
5. Canadian Pediatric Society and the American Academy of Pediatrics, "A Joint Statement. Breast Feeding: A Commentary in Celebration of the International Year of the Child," 1979. *Pediatrics*,

62:591-601 (Oct.), 1978. Reprinted in *Child and Family*, 17:24462, 1978.

6. Thomas Aquinas. *Summa Theologica*. Trans. by the Fathers of the English Dominican Province. Burns, Oates & Washbourne Ltd., London, 1932, Third Part (Suppl.), Q. 49, a. 3. Reprinted in Child and Family, 16:112, 1977.

7. Ratner, H. and Deitz, H. The Youngest Member of the Human Family: A Biography. In Sneed, M. (Ed.), Human Life: Our Legacy and Our Challenge. McGraw-Hill, Inc., 1976, pp. 3-9.

8. Timasheff, N.S. "The Attempt to Abolish the Family in Russia." *Child and Family*, 16:242-252.

9. Levi-Strauss, C. "The Family." In Shapiro, H.A. (Ed.), *Man, Culture and Society*, Oxford University Press, 1971.

10. Talalay, P. (Ed.), *Drugs In Society*. John Hopkins Press, Baltimore, 1964, p.34.

11. Nagera, H. "Day-Care Centres: Red Light, Green Light or Amber Light." *Child and Family*, 14:110-136.

12. Hellbrugge, T. "Early Social Development and Proficiency in Later Life." NA. M. T.A. Quarterly, 4:6-14, (Spring) 1979. Reprinted in *Child and Family*, 18:120-130, 1979.

13. Ratner, H. "The History of the Dehumanization of American Obstetrical Practice." *21st Century Obstetrics Now!*, NAPSAC, Inc., Chapel Hill, NC, 1977, pp. 115-46. Reprinted in *Child and Family*, 16:4-31, 1977.

14. Ratner, H. "Medicine: An Interview" by Donald McDonald. One of a series of interviews in the American Characters Series by the Center for the Study of Democratic Institutions, The Fund for the Republic, Santa Barbara, CA, May 1962. Reprinted in *Child and Family*, 11:4-14, 100-10, 276-86, 363-75, 1972.

15. Taylor, J. "The Duty of Nursing Your Child in Imitation of the Blessed Mother." *The Whole Works of the Right Rev. Jeremy Taylor*, D.D. Heber-Eden Edition, London, 1865, Vol.11, pp.72-Si. Reprinted as "The Duty of Nursing Children in Child and Family" Reprint Booklet, *The Nursing Mother: Historical Insights from Art and Theology*, 1969, pp.19-29.

16. Quoted by Virginia Adams, "Erikson Sees Psychological Danger in Trend of Having Fewer Children." *The New York Times*, Aug. 4, 1979.

17. Spence, J. "The Purpose of The Family. In Purpose and Practice of Medicine," Oxford University Press, 1960. Reprinted in *Child and Family*, 8:26-35, 1969, p.26.

18. Ratner, H. "The Family: Nature's Institution." In C. Anderson and Wm. Gribbin (Eds), *The Family in the Modern World*. The American Family Institute, 1982, p.13.
19. Lawrence, D.H. "A Propos of Lady Chatterly's Lover." In Moore, H.T. (Ed.), *Sex, Literature and Censorship: Essays*. Twayne Publishers, New York, 1953, p.104.
20. Ratner, H. "Man Against Nature: Nature's Subtleties and Nature's Prescription." *International Review of Natural Family Planning*, 2:11-7, 1978. Previously published in *Child and Family*, 8:290-1, 1969; 9:2-3, 99-101, 1970, and reprinted in *Child and Family Reprint Booklet, Child Spacing*, 1982.

Appendix Two

Ten Reasons I Can't Spank: A Catholic Counselor's Critical Examination of Corporal Punishment

By Gregory K. Popcak, MSW, LCSW

(This is an edited version of an article originally published in the *Cheerful Cherub*, a magazine devoted to Catholic parenting.)

> The birch is used only out of bad temper and weakness, for the birch is a servile punishment which degrades the soul even when it corrects, if indeed it corrects, for its usual effect is to burden.
>
> — St. John Baptiste de la Salle,
> *On the Conduct of Christian Schools*, France, 1570

"How do you feel about corporal punishment?"

Few questions evoke as strong a reaction as this one. I know many good Catholics on both sides of the issue, those who feel strongly about using corporal punishment, and those who feel equally strongly about not using it. If ever there was an issue that should not be decided on the basis of feeling alone, it is this one.

The following is my journey. It reflects the research, thoughts, and prayerful consideration of a conservative Catholic, psychotherapist, father of two, and author on marriage and family issues. Ultimately, this article is the foundation upon which my wife and I build our commitment to disciplining our children without corporal punishment.

I do not presume to think that I have discovered the final answer to one of the most divisive issues in Catholic parenting, but I do think that I have uncovered some truths, or at least some nagging questions, that deserve to be reckoned with if you are a parent who has chosen to use corporal punishment in raising your children.

Whether or not you agree with my conclusions, a Christian's decisions must always be guided by a properly formed conscience. Such a conscience is developed by considering the well-informed positions of those who support and reject our own way of thinking. Whatever conclusions you ultimately draw, I ask you to consider the following ten reasons why I believe that are irreconcilable differences between Catholicism and corporal punishment.

1. Jesus' own example was discipline, NOT punishment.

There is an important distinction to be made between discipline and punishment. Jesus' own ministry favored discipline over punishment.

Punishment's main goal is to stop the present occurrence of inappropriate behavior. Anything else is gravy. It is less concerned with the future than with "Stop that right now!"

Literally, punishment means "to cause to undergo pain." At its very roots, it has nothing to do with teaching. Punishment establishes a police/suspect relationship between punisher and the punished. Punishment relies heavily upon the notion of external control. That is to say, the parent is very pessimistic regarding the child's desire, ability, or willingness to behave properly, so the parent himself becomes the child's limit and consequence. Punishment tends to assume that "they" (children) are bent toward evil (or at least no good) and are out to manipulate "us" (the police/parents). Punishment can lack in consistent application because the meting out of punishment tends to be subject to the mood of the parent. Its forms change over time — what punishments "work" at one age do not work at a later age. The philosophy that supports punishment asserts that compliance with the law for the law's own sake ("blind obedience") is a virtue. Spanking is the chief example of punishment. It is the height of external control.

Discipline assumes a teacher/student relationship, or rabbi/disciple relationship if you prefer. The Latin root of discipline, *discipuli*, means "student."

Discipline's main objective is to teach the offender what to do instead of the offense, rather than merely stopping the offense. For example, where punishment would say, "Don't speak to me like that! Go to your room!" discipline would say, "I know you are angry, but you may not speak to me that way. You may say (such and such) if you like. Now, tell me again, respectfully, please."

Discipline is less concerned with teaching compliance with the law than it is with teaching how to have deeper, more respectful, and loving relationships. Discipline recognizes that "Love does no wrong to a neighbor, therefore love is the fulfillment of the law" (Rm 13:10 NAB). The philosophy of discipline asserts that blind obedience, rather than being a virtue, is often pharisaic and hypocritical. Discipline does not assume malicious intent on the part of the offender. It assumes that the offender is ignorant of an appropriate/meaningful way to meet personal needs. Discipline has a deep regard for consistency. It assumes that the tools which helped me control my behavior when I am three should also help me control my behavior when I am thirty. As such, discipline seeks to only use those interventions that would be appropriate means by which to create change in adult relationships.

Discipline believes that good behavior is a teachable skill, not unlike math or reading. Because of this, it makes use of the tools that a good teacher would use. Tools like good relationship/rapport building, teaching stories (emotional word-pictures), following through with logical consequences, real-life examples, personal sharing (disciplining), redirecting, practice, and giving information in respectful, repeated, and varied ways. People who use discipline correctly do not necessarily differ in the number of limits they establish, so much as in the dramatically different ways by which those limits are taught and enforced.

Certainly you can see that Jesus' ministry was one which espoused discipline over punishment. Discipline recognizes that violence is not a good teaching tool. Imagine the following happening to you. Your child comes home from school and says that he was spanked because he missed a math problem. You call the teacher to say, "What were you thinking?"

The teacher responds by saying, "He did not do the problem as I taught him to."

"You should have told him again!"

"I told him plenty of times. He should have listened the first time."

You press further, "Even so, what do you think he really learned?"

"Well, you can be sure he won't make that mistake again!"

What do you think of this teacher? Was he a good teacher? I don't think so. I wonder if God thinks the same of us when we use corporal punishment to "teach a lesson" to His children, who are on loan to us? The Holy Father refers to parents' "mission as educators" ("Gospel of Life"). If we are educators, we must use the tools the best educators use. We must first use the tools the Holy Father himself enumerates, such as, "word and example ... cordial openness, dialog... " ("Gospel of Life"). These are the tools of choice. Corporal punishment is curiously absent.

Jesus himself never used violence on people. When he became angry at the money changers in the temple, he turned over their tables, and he cracked a whip at the sheep and oxen alike (see Jn 2:15). NOT THE PEOPLE. Even in this most dramatic account of Jesus' anger, he does not turn the whip on the offenders, who are fully accountable and culpable adults.

There are those parents who say, "If I don't spank, my children's salvation may be at stake. Spanking is an act of love that will bring them closer to God." Yet, on the one occasion when Peter attempted to use violence as an act of love on God's behalf (in the garden of Gethsemane) — to "save" Him — Jesus called Peter "Satan." Christ could not have given a more definitive response to violence — even when dressed up in the language of "love."

You might say that a spank on the bottom is hardly the same as a sword on the ear. In one sense, no, but in another, violence is violence, regardless of degree, just as sin, whether venial or mortal, is offensive to God. As always, Jesus said exactly what He meant. There is no occasion or excuse for Christians using violence on His behalf.

2. Scripture does not support spanking.

The Old Testament does have two references to corporal punishment, which are the mainstay of its proponents' biblical defense. These are Proverbs 23:13 and Sirach 30:1-3. (In some translations, such as the NAB, the Sirach verse refers to discipline and education.) Yet, even Proverbs, taken by itself, is questionable, particularly when viewed as the rationale for a parent's disciplinary foundation.

I say these references are questionable because contextual interpreters of the Bible (Catholic scholars — as opposed to literal interpreters) wonder if "rod" is not used metaphorically, as in a shepherd's rod. A shepherd would never beat his sheep — they are too precious and delicate. Also, could a "rod of violence" be used to bring comfort, as in "Thy rod and thy staff, they comfort me" (Ps 23:4)? God's truths do not contradict each other. A shepherd uses his rod to gently guide his flock — not to strike them. (A note on sheep husbandry: It is known that the fright of sudden noise alone can induce in sheep a shock which suppresses fertility. A sheep's guardian, whose job it is to protect the economic value of his herd, is aware of the sensitivity of his flock's constitution.)

"Rod" may also be understood as a unit of measure that figuratively refers to the Torah (like our term "scales of justice"). In other words, we can interpret the Proverb: "Spare your child the 'rod' (the Torah), and they won't 'measure up.' "

Ultimately, the Old Testament must be understood through the prism of the New Testament — the fulfillment of the law. Indeed, the Fathers of the Church, saints and prelates from St. Hilary of Poitiers, St. Cyprian, St. Ambrose, St. Martin of Tours, and St. Leo, consistently declared that the severe sanctions of the Old Testament were abrogated by the mild and gentle laws of Christ. The New Testament has a very different way of dealing with sinners than did the Old Testament. As an example, let us examine the parable of the prodigal son.

A son hurts his father deeply by abandoning righteous ways and pursuing a life of sin and folly. This the father knows. In response, does the father hunt down the child to give him a beating for the "open act of willful disobedience?" No. The father, being a wise man, allows his son to experience the logical consequences of his actions until he is so racked with sadness, estrangement, and guilt that he comes running back to his father. The father then throws a party for the prodigal son. To celebrate the son's immoral behavior? No, to celebrate the victory of love over sin.

Some punishment! Is God a pushover? No. He simply does not add any harm he could do to us to the harm we have already chosen for ourselves. The father of the prodigal concentrates on a more important motivator: building a relationship that is so strong, so undeniably loving, that the son will never want to "leave His house" again.

Through the wisdom of Christ's new mandate (see Jn 13:34), we must learn the methods that will allow us to deal with our children's transgressions the way God deals with ours. To do less is to diminish in our children's eyes the very love of God. To do less is to live out the role of the servant in the parable who, forgiven his debts by the just

King, exacts punishments upon those who owed Him (see Mt 18: 21-35).

When God reaches out to us with arms of love and forgiveness, but we treat our children to physical punishment, we are acting the part of the ungrateful servant. Will not God be faithful to His word and "forgive us our trespasses as we forgive those who trespass against us?" (see Mt 6:12).

3. The Universal Church does not model corporal punishment.

The family is the smallest unit of the Church. It is frequently referred to as the "domestic church." The domestic church must take as its model the "Church Universal." By Universal Church I do not mean one or two people, even well-known or influential people, who claim to speak for the Church. Rather, I refer to "The True Church, the Whole Church, and nothing but the Church," to coin a phrase. What does the Universal Church have to say about corporal punishment? To properly examine this question we must recall the venerable theological phrase, "*Lex orandi, lex credendi*" ("As the Church prays, the Church believes"). In other words, if you really want to know what the Church, the Mystical Body and extension into this world of Christ Himself, has to say about something, look to the way she prays, or at the nature of the sacraments.

How does the Church "pray about," or treat, sinful behavior? She employs the Sacrament of Reconciliation. When we do wrong, we go to our mother, the Church, for forgiveness. She hears us, holds us, forgives us, and, finally, as penance for our sinfulness, she sends us to spend time in prayer, learning, and discipleship at the feet of the Master.

When I was young, I used to think that praying was an awfully stupid punishment. It would be stupid punishment, but instead, is meant to be wise discipline.

By sinning, I have wounded the relationship I have with God. So now, having confessed my sinfulness and been forgiven, I spend some quiet time with my Heavenly Father who counsels me, comforts me, and holds me in His arms. Heavenly Father has dealt with me firmly. He has seen that I have been disciplined. He has done so by allowing me to experience guilt (the loving conviction of the Holy Spirit), the anger of those I have hurt, and the other natural consequences of my actions. This is what the Holy Father means when He embraces filial fear, or the "fear of all that is an offense against God," and rejects servile fear, or the fear of physical reprisal, as a means of gaining souls for God (*Crossing the Threshold of Hope*, p. 226).

It is prideful and wrong to ordain ourselves to do more than Holy Mother Church, herself, is ordained by God to do. In review, her disciplinary process is as follows:

1. An offense occurs;
2. We experience loving conviction by the Holy Spirit (guilt);
3. We may experience the logical/natural consequences of our behavior;
4. We repent and receive forgiveness through God's ordained priests;
5. We spend time rebuilding our relationship with God through prayerful penance.

If the Church does not add to our suffering by physical punishment, how can we parents, in fulfilling our sacramental mission as "priests" in the domestic church, do so to our own children? There have been periods in Church history when penance included corporal punishment of the most excruciating nature. The sad legacy of the Inquisition is testimony to this fact. Yet, as the Church grew in age, wisdom, and grace, she abandoned such practices for those which more closely modeled the ministry and commandments of Christ. Modern Catholic scholars reflect this conviction when they say that this legacy of corporal punishment "... reflect[s] neither the spirit nor the methods Christ who said: 'Learn of Me, for I am meek and humble of heart' " and that the Church should not "employ physical force to coerce the mind of man.... Our only instruments in the domain of conscience must be reason, God's grace, human kindness and love."

4. Spanking flies in the face of good science.
   The Church respects good science because it simply describes the natural order created by God. To deny the validity of scientific inquiry, and the truth and relevance of its discoveries, is to turn a blind eye to a part of God's revelation to man.

This validity of science extends fully to the study of human psychology. The *Catholic Encyclopedia* defines it as "the science of mind and behavior ... concerned with the investigation of behavior and [human] experience by means of controlled observation, experimentation and measurement." The role of Catholic psychologists is to practice their profession to the highest scientific standards and interpret their findings in a way consistent with the principles of their faith. God's supernatural and natural truths cannot conflict. It is predictable, then, that modern psychology and the tenets of the Catholic Faith are utterly harmonious on the subject of discipline.

Yet, this harmony is not spelled out in so many words. As a result, many advocates of corporal punishment dismiss out of hand even the most common-sense findings of psychology in pediatric development, marriage, and family dynamics if it does not support their position. In turn, any who recognize its wisdom are deemed to be allied with the modern forces of evil, especially secular feminism and anti-family humanism.

The Church, through the Holy Father, has this to say: "Marriage and family counseling agencies by their specific work of guidance and prevention ... offer valuable help in rediscovering the meaning of love and life, and in supporting every family in its mission as the 'sanctuary of life' " ("Gospel of Life"). In saying so, the Church is also validating the science upon which this counseling is built. Let me elucidate what this science has discovered about corporal punishment:

- Spanking has been found to increase deceitfulness, noncompliance, oppositional/defiant behaviors and violence in children.
- Research consistently demonstrates that corporal punishment creates and maintains "willful defiance" and other unmanageable behavioral problems. (Thus, the notion that "willful defiance" deserves corporal punishment is exactly counterproductive.)
- Children who are spanked have lower-average intelligence scores, and demonstrate poorer school performance. This is not necessarily because they are less intelligent, but because they are more reluctant to demonstrate their intelligence for fear of being "wrong" and, as a result, harshly judged.
- Spanked children show less creativity and are less inclined to take healthy and appropriate risks, yet are more likely to take inappropriate risks.
- Children who are spanked demonstrate a diminished ability to say "no" in personally demeaning or dangerous situations (including drug use and sexual situations) — especially when encouraged by peers.
- Spanking has been shown to increase violent/bullying behavior (especially in boys) and shyness (in girls).
- Children who are spanked have higher rates of constipation of the

bowels, depression, substance abuse, suicidality, anxiety, and irrational fears/phobias.
- Long-term studies indicate that girls who are spanked show a greater risk of ending up in abusive marriages; boys who are spanked have a higher-than-average chance of becoming abusive spouses.
- Adults who were spanked as children tend to be less happy in their marriages.
- Adults who were spanked as children tend to be more rejecting of the religion of their parents.

All of the above have been attributed to commonly accepted levels of spanking. These are the scientific findings of the profession. Ignoring or disbelieving these findings does not make them less true. The fact is, any mental-health professional who recommended spanking would be as suspect as a physician who, when asked about the dangers of cigarettes said, "Smoke 'em if you got 'em."

Granted, not every child raised in a home where corporal punishment is exercised develops the above symptoms. This fact often leads to the common objection, "I was spanked as a kid and I turned out all right." Be this as it may, there are also many children who did not develop cancer in spite of being raised in homes where both parents smoked, and many children who did not die in car accidents in spite of their parents' drinking and driving, but this does not mean that we should recommend such practices as being in the best interests of public health. In other words, just because you happened to dodge a bullet doesn't mean the bullet is good for you.

5. Spanking is violence.
Webster defines violence as "physical force used so as to injure." Having scientifically established that spanking does cause injury (although, in most instances, not immediately perceptible), it follows that spanking is a form of violence.

The Holy Father, in his recent encyclical the "Gospel of Life" condemns violence of all forms. He quotes *Gaudium et Spes*, which condemns any action which "violates the integrity of the human person, such as ... attempts to coerce the will." This pertains with specific accuracy to the objective of many Catholic parents to "break the will" of the child.

In fact, "attempts to coerce the will" are categorized among "torments of the body and mind" which involve it as a participant in the greater culture of violence which the Church rejects. Certainly, the human will must be channeled, trained, and disciplined (see "Childrearing" in the *Catechism*), but spanking does not train so much as it coerces and subverts the human will. What parents must appreciate is that the same will that motivates a "no" from a two-year-old is the same will which, if properly formed but not broken, will effectively say "no" to drugs, premarital sex, and the other temptations presented throughout life.

About the culture that must exist in the family which espouses and lives the "Gospel of Life," The Holy Father says this:

> It is above all in raising children that the family fulfills its mission to proclaim the Gospel of life. By word and example, in the daily round of relations and choices, and through concrete actions and signs, parents lead their children to authentic freedom, actualized in the sincere gift of self, and they cultivate in them a respect for others, a sense of justice, cordial openness, dialog, generous service, solidarity, and all the other values which help people live life as a gift ("Gospel of Life").

The evidence is compelling that corporal punishment does not instill in our children or lead them toward any of these qualities. In fact, it tends to cultivate deceitfulness, violence, fear, and a rejection of parents' authority and religion as arbitrary and nonsensical. Finally, the Church tells us that we must not resort to violence out of expediency. Consequences for wrongdoing must be "in conformity to the dignity of the human person" (*CCC* 2267). So strenuously does the Church maintain this that she protects even apostates and heretics against the loss of basic human liberties. "Religion, being a matter of free will, cannot be forced on anyone," wrote Lactantius. Centuries later, St. Bernard's rule, "*Fides suadenda, non imponenda*" ("faith by persuasion, not by violence") reflected this conviction. For the unrepentant, their eternal punishment would suffice. Spanking does not pass St. Bernard's test: The violence which is at the core of spanking makes it inherently offensive to the dignity of the human person.

6. Spanking as sin or occasion of sin.

Most parents who spank are unaware that spanking can cause pervasive and deep harm to its recipient. As a result, they do not manifest the willful intent required to commit a sinful act. However, as

Catholics, we are called upon to use an "informed conscience" in choosing our actions. We have available to us the doctrine, Tradition, teachings, and advice to improve upon and modify our decision-making ability in accordance with our Faith.

We must do what we can to understand what is expected of us. (This corresponds to civil authority's dictum "Ignorance of the law is no excuse.") For example, the Church's position on birth control is very clear and very easy to ascertain. While it is conceivable that Catholics of good faith are unaware of this teaching, a simple line of inquiry at their parish would enlighten them. It is incumbent upon all Catholics of good faith to try.

The Church's position on corporal punishment is not as obvious or immediate. However, this must not deter Catholic parents from evaluating their actions in the light of Catholic teaching and conforming it accordingly. In the case of corporal punishment, the comprehensive body of Scripture, Tradition, and contemporary papal teaching is compelling.

Corporal punishment, regardless of intent or application, is misguided and counterproductive. As such, the debate among proponents of corporal punishment over how and when to use it is irrelevant. (Some fervently hold that it must occur at the time when the parent is provoked by the wrongdoing; others are equally adamant that punishment must be withheld and meted out dispassionately. Both sides find the other's inappropriate.) However, a point of agreement within both camps is instructive. Most parents who use corporal punishment admit to having struck their children "unjustly" (i.e., through some fault of their own, rather than the child's). This mistake is certainly one all parents have made, regardless of admission; and one most admit is sinful. If spanking unjustly is sinful, then the risk of sinning by spanking at all is unacceptably high. As Catholics, we are obliged not only to avoid sin, but to avoid the near occasion of sin, and entreat the Lord to "lead us not into temptation." Especially, we must avoid the temptation to do harm to the least of His children.

7. God's justice is subject to His love.

Parents who use corporal punishment often defend it by saying, "God is a God of justice." Certainly, but His justice is subject to His love. If this were not so, could any of us, in light of our own sinfulness, justify our existence, much less the precious gift of Jesus' passion, death, and resurrection? How telling is Scripture: "If you mark our iniquities, then who could stand?" (see Ps 130:3) and liturgy: "*O felix culpa, quae talum ac tantum meruit habere Redemptorem"* ("O happy fault, which gained for us so great a Redeemer").

Scripture tells us that the greatest of the spiritual gifts — of which justice is one — is love. Love is defined for us:

> "Love is patient; love is kind. Love is not jealous, it does not put on airs, it is not snobbish. Love is never rude, neither does it brood over injuries. Love does not rejoice in what is wrong, but rejoices with the truth. There is no limit to Love's forbearance, to its trust, its hope, its power to endure" (1 Cor 13:4-7).

Does spanking meet this definition of love?

The Holy Father says: "Before all else, it is Love that judges. God, who is Love, judges through Love" (*Crossing the Threshold of Hope*, p. 187). We must fear, he continues, offending this pure love through sin. "The authentic and full expression of this fear is Christ Himself. Christ wants us to have fear of all that is an offense against God." Again, Christ is the model of the behavior of love which we are commanded to emulate (*mandatum*): meek, humble, ever patient, yet unwavering. The Holy Father says, "This love, according to the words of St. John, drives out all fear (see 1 Jn 4:18). Every sign of servile fear vanishes before the awesome power of the all-powerful, all-present One" (*Crossing the Threshold of Hope*, p. 226).

In administering justice in our homes, we do not have absolute dominion over our children (although it can appear temporally that we do), but, as Pope John Paul II says, "Man's lordship is not absolute ... [it is] ministerial: it is a real reflection of the unique and infinite lordship of God. Hence man must exercise it with wisdom and love, sharing in the boundless wisdom and love of God" ("Gospel of Life").

As Christians, we are not called so much to be the administrators of His justice ("Judge not, lest ye be judged" [Mt 7:1]) as we are called to be the embodiment of His Love, perfected in humanity — and for humanity — by Jesus: "Love one another as I have loved you" (Jn 15:23). St. Francis de Sales instructs us in this Christ-like love when he says, "All things need be done by love, not force."

8. Spanking does not respect the gift of will.

The Church, Scripture, and good science teach us that the will is a good and essential part of our humanity. We Catholics have what might appear to be a hopelessly optimistic and respectful attitude toward the human will. Scripture tells us that from our creation, the will is given to us as a gift from God. The Holy Father and the Church have endorsed the goodness of the human will. Science has described the will as essential to survival and continuation of our human species. As Catholics, we hold a unique place in the support and defense of the dignity of the human person, and the will is integral to the definition of our human condition. We are responsible for living and educating our children to live in a way that respects the will — and its prominent role in the process of right living. To do less, to give in to non-Catholic pressure and influences which instruct us to "parent" in a manner which is demeaning or harmful to the will, is to deny this uniquely Catholic perspective toward our humanity.

Perhaps more so than many of our separated Christian brothers and sisters, we are given the grace to respect the gift that is the will. We are required to use this grace to live this dignity out in the everyday life of the domestic church.

9. Spanking conflicts with the Church's teaching on the "age of reason."

Spanking is used most often on children who are younger than the age of seven, which is the age of reason as defined by the Church. Most supporters of corporal punishment admit that spanking tends to lose its "effectiveness" past this age.

The problem in this regard for the adherents of corporal punishment is twofold. First, the Church uses the time before receiving the Sacrament of Reconciliation as a time of education. Just as, during this period, a child gradually learns and improves his language and motor skills, so does he learn the fundamentals about right and wrong and the use of will to choose right. Second, she does not hold the child culpable of sin. This means that a child cannot sin until he can fully grasp the meaning of his actions. In the wisdom of the Church, this requires "full knowledge of and participation in a sinful act."

Any form of punishment which serves to debilitate the will, or works to subordinate it to the will of another, and which holds the child culpable before the age of reason is in conflict with the God-given nature of the child and the teaching of the Church. Spanking is both destructive of the necessary educational process and punishing of those who are innocent of it.

10. Catholic luminaries in child-rearing oppose spanking.

Catholics whose life's vocations involved the care of children, and who received graces to fulfill these vocations, categorically oppose corporal punishment. St. John Baptist de la Salle, St. Benildus, St. John Bosco, St. Elizabeth Seton, Fr. Flanagan, Dr. Herbert Ratner, and Dr. Maria Montessori are prominent examples of Catholics whose love and wisdom helped shepherd thousands of children on a path to God, and who saw corporal punishment as antithetical to this mission.

It is true that there are Catholic saints who prescribed ritual mortification for themselves and their followers. Yet, these examples are concerned with self-discipline and adult spirituality. St. Francis flung himself naked into a briar patch to "crucify his flesh" for having impure thoughts. I daresay he would condemn such treatment of an animal, much less a child.

There are others who speak in passing of the corporal punishment of children. An acquaintance once told me that his grandfather was taught by one religious sister who was being elevated to sainthood. Said the grandfather, "That woman spanked me so many times my butt could be a third-class relic!" Even so, these are generally instances which reflect the disciplinary psychology of the times, and do not, nor are they intended to demonstrate, a systematic, theological/scientific child-rearing methodology which is designed to reflect the fullest teachings, objectives, and promises of our Faith. This latter mission was the vocation of those good Catholics whom I previously mentioned.

Conclusion

Well, there you have it — ten reasons I, as a Catholic, loyal to the teaching Magisterium of the Church, family counselor and father, believe corporal punishment and Catholicism to not mix. I ask you to consider these reasons with an openness to the fullness of life as seen and taught by the Church, and with a real desire to seek the truth.

To renounce corporal punishment is a "conversion"; it is to begin the difficult journey which consists in "putting new wine in new skins." You will not be alone. The wisdom, grace, and love of the Holy Trinity will guide you.

However, should you decide to continue spanking, you ought to prepare a defense to Christ's pronouncement of love: "What you do to the least of these, you do to Me."

Index

About the Authors

Gregory K. Popcak, MSW, LCSW is a family counselor in private practice in Ohio. His first book, **For Better ... FOREVER!**, a guide to creating lasting marriages, has been widely acclaimed in Catholic circles. His articles on marriage and family life have appeared in numerous magazines.

Lisa Popcak was an elementary-school teacher in the Pittsburgh Catholic-school system before becoming a homeschooling mother and a trained lactation educator. The Popcaks live in Steubenville, Ohio, with their children.

Our Sunday Visitor

*Your Source for Discovering
the Riches of the Catholic Faith*

Our Sunday Visitor has an extensive line of materials for young children, teens, and adults. Our books, Bibles, booklets, CD-ROMs, audiocassettes, and videos are available in bookstores worldwide.

To receive a FREE full-line catalog, or for more information, call **Our Sunday Visitor** at **1-800-348-2440**. Or write: **Our Sunday Visitor**, 200 Noll Plaza, Huntington, IN 46750.

❑ Please send me a catalog.

Please send me material on:

❑ Apologetics/Catechetics   ❑ Reference works
❑ Prayer books   ❑ Heritage and the saints
❑ The family   ❑ The parish

Name _____

Address _____

City _____ ST _____ Zip_____

Telephone (_____)_____

                                                   AO3BBABP

❑ Please send a friend a catalog.

Please send a friend material on:

❑ Apologetics/Catechetics   ❑ Reference works
❑ Prayer books   ❑ Heritage and the saints
❑ The family   ❑ The parish

Name _____

Address _____

City _____ ST _____ Zip_____

Telephone (_____)_____

                                                   AO3BBABP

Our Sunday Visitor
200 Noll Plaza
Huntington, IN 46750
1-800-348-2440
E-mail us at: osvbooks@osv.com
Visit us on the Web: http://www.osv.com

Your source for discovering the riches of the Catholic Faith